THE FRENCH CUISINE OF YOUR CHOICE

The French Cuisine of Your Choice

Isabelle Marique and Albert Jorant

1817

HARPER & ROW, PUBLISHERS, New York
Cambridge, Philadelphia, San Francisco,
London, Mexico City, São Paulo, Sydney

ACKNOWLEDGMENTS

Isabelle Marique would like to thank the following persons for their help and support: Jerry Dunlevy, Patrick Filley, Alice and Jack Finley, Kate and Michael Flynn, Alice and Harry Frieland, Martin Grossman, Jerry Huven, Peter Holmes, Ormonde de Kay, Irene Krone, Kathleen McLoughlin, Suzanne Leve, Françoise and Raoul Nolte, Isabelle Peetermans, Mary Powers, Michael and Jane Roos, Regina Ryan, Jacqueline Springwater, Penny Wartels, Anne and Alfred Lauwers Willemart, and *les familles*: Leempoel, Marique, Brees, and Harden

FIRST EDITION

Designer: Abigail Moseley

Library of Congress Cataloging in Publication Data

Marique, Isabelle.
    The French cuisine of your choice.

    Includes index.
    1. Cookery, French.   I. Jorant, Albert.   II. Title.
TX719.M3416   1981   641.5944   81–47359
    ISBN 0–06–038007–1   AACR2

81 82 83 84 85 10 9 8 7 6 5 4 3 2 1

To my son Gregory Ross Harden
—*Isabelle Marique*

To my students
—*Albert Jorant*

CONTENTS

PREFACE

Most Americans we know agree that French food is beyond praise, but many say it takes too long to prepare, is fattening, and can, with its high cholesterol content, endanger a person's health. They are not alone: Of late the French themselves have increasingly shunned the richer dishes that delighted their forebears. Concerned restaurateurs and chefs have strived to make these dishes lighter and in doing so have effected a reformation of French cuisine billed variously as the new cuisine, the slimming cuisine, and diet cuisine.

American friends tell us, however, that the new recipes aren't always satisfactory. They were written for French cooks and must therefore be adapted for use by others. And since their authors are professional cooks, the recipes reflect the premises of restaurant cooking, with its staffs of helpers and batteries of special equipment. Typically they call for a complete assortment of stocks, which are indispensable to running a restaurant but largely unnecessary in home cooking.

Having grown up in the context of traditional French cooking and later, through teaching it to Americans, having come to know the latters' particular needs and wishes, we found ourselves in a position to do something that had never really been done, namely, adapt French cuisine to the demands of busy weight- and health-conscious Americans for good food, low in calories and cholesterol, that can be prepared quickly. And in this book we have done just that. Our 225 recipes are all you need to eat in the French manner every day, without having to put in long hours in the kitchen, let out your clothes, or consult a physician. Nearly all are pared down from the extravagant formulas of yesteryear. And many—as in no other cookbook—are accompanied by "light versions," alternate recipes that further reduce calories (and, often, preparation time) without sacrificing flavor.

How have we accomplished this? By calling on skills, techniques, and tricks of the trade we've developed or picked up in decades of cooking and experimenting. To promote speed, our shortcuts include, among others, Chef Albert Jorant's formidable *tours de main* (sleights of hand is the best translation we can come up with) in readying pastries and other foods for the oven and Isabelle Marique's use of the pressure cooker for making stocks (one of them in ten minutes instead of four hours), stews and soups, and for numerous other purposes. To promote lightness, we eliminate or reduce the lavish amounts of butter, cream, egg yolks, sugar, and other fattening elements called for in classic recipes, substituting wholesome, subtly-flavored, low-calorie ricotta cheese. (Such substitutions can't successfully be made ad lib, however, as balance is all-important; and it's a lot easier, of course, to make food more palatable by adding butter, egg yolks, cream, oil, sugar, or some other enricher than by subtracting same.) To promote health, we reduce, sometimes drastically, the cholesterol-rich ingredients like egg yolks in certain dishes, without altering the dishes' delicious taste and distinctive texture.

In addition to speed, lightness, and health, we have pursued a fourth goal: simplification. We have, for example, cut the number of sauces called for (eighty-five in one first-rate cookbook we have seen) down to about a dozen, and the number of stocks from a dozen to just three. So we have, we think, made a pretty good start in this direction.

ABOUT THIS BOOK

Our book is grounded, firstly, on a knowledge of French cuisine that in Chef Jorant's case can reasonably be termed encyclopedic. But it is also based, in equal measure, on Isabelle Marique's day-to-day experience as a Manhattan housewife and mother, in circumstances not greatly different from those confronting millions of other American homemakers and home cooks, men included. People who know us, both Americans and Europeans, can attest that each of us can be very stubborn and that neither yields easily on points of principle—so our book is not a compromise between French cookery and prevailing American ideas and preferences but a blend of the two in which each ingredient retains its character and plays its part. A cook who puts our recipes to the test will find in the resulting dishes the same delectable flavor and characteristic texture or consistency one would expect from the same dishes served in France, whether at the dinner table of French friends or in a first-class restaurant, but without having to lose so much time preparing them or gain so much weight eating them. (Note: exceptions to this last statement are a few offerings, clearly indicated as such, taken straight from the grand and glorious repertoire of *haute cuisine*; after all, you have to splurge *sometimes*, don't you?)

Some of our light version recipes are positively dietetic, but where the reduction of fat amounts to, say, less than half the fat content of the regular recipe, we must point out that there are limits to how far one can go in this direction. As a rule, cutting down too drastically on fats would mean robbing a dish of certain vital properties, particularly smoothness.

In planning our book, we decided to forego the usual chapter on appetizers on the ground that they are, in reality, full-fledged dishes, and might just as well be classified as such. And because our new approach to French cuisine entails a number of departures from standard culinary practice we have prefaced each of our chapters with an explanatory text of some length, both to expound our philosophy of cooking as it applies to the food in question and to help you understand the reasoning behind the new techniques and different ingredients and proportions we call for in place of the traditional ones.

If you love French food as we do, you are in for a thoroughly agreeable experience. Many authors of French cookbooks in English close their introductory remarks with a hearty *Bon appétit!*. Naturally, we wish you the same, and with it *beaucoup de légèreté*—light work, light food, and light spirits. Let there be lightness!

1
UTENSILS

To the non-French the term *batterie de cuisine* may conjure up a picture of cooks bashing each other with pots and pans, but in fact it means kitchen equipment, the paraphernalia a cook uses on the job. The items listed on the following pages add up to a very complete *batterie*. Unless you happen to be exceptionally well endowed with both cash and storage space, however, you probably won't want such an extensive collection, and you can certainly manage with less. Use your judgment.

For convenience, we have grouped the dozens of cooking tools making up our *batterie de cuisine* in six categories in line with their respective functions.

COOKING VESSELS

First, a few general pointers:

• Skillets, saucepans, casseroles, baking dishes, and other cooking vessels should be of a size and shape to accommodate food snugly. That way, if a liquid is involved in cooking, there won't be too much of it around the food, draining off cooking juices and washing out flavor. When food is cooked without a liquid, a comfortable fit minimizes the possibility of fat burning.

• The metals and other materials of which cooking vessels are made help determine how well they perform. Enameled cast-iron ware promotes even cooking, but it is heavy and can chip. Stainless steel with a heavy, sandwiched-copper bottom and heavy sides of stainless steel won't scorch food. Copper vessels lined with tin and nickel alloy are fine, too, copper being an excellent conductor of heat, but they cost a lot more than the alternatives and are harder to clean. Pots and pans with sandwiched bottoms (quick-heating aluminum between layers of easy-to-maintain stainless steel) perform very well too. The sides of a pan should be as thick as its bottom; otherwise, heat may cause food in it to burn.

• Cooking vessels should never react with food they contain. Those mentioned above and some of the treated aluminum don't do this, but ordinary aluminum pots and pans often discolor food.

Skillets. Whatever you cook you are going to need either an 8- or 10-inch skillet or an 8- or 10-inch *sautoir* or sauté pan. These measurements, as with those of all the round-bottomed utensils mentioned in this chapter, represent their diameter on the bottom. A *sautoir*'s sides rise straight up some 2 to 3 inches, higher than a skillet's. It is ovenproof and can therefore double as a casserole: Food can be browned in it on top of the stove and other ingredients added; then, covered with a lid, it can go into the oven for a final stage of cooking.

You will probably make more use of your *sautoir* than of any other cooking vessel. Many *sautoirs* have a small handle opposite the regular one; when filled, a *sautoir* can be heavy, and the extra handle makes lifting it easier.

Omelet pan. A 7-inch nonstick omelet pan is the ideal vessel in which to make a four-egg omelet for two. Its size and its curving sides, rising and flaring out from its flat bottom, facilitate stirring the eggs and unmolding the omelet; in a much larger pan the eggs could cook too fast and dry out, resulting in a tough omelet. The new nonstick pans, surfaced with an alloy that eliminates all the need for curing, are great for making not only omelets but lots of other dishes.

Five-inch steel crêpe pan. With its flat bottom and shallow, flared sides, this pan browns crêpes the best. Its shape makes it easy to handle. Cure it well, and to preserve its coating use it only for making crêpes. (Note: You should have two crêpe pans, so that you can make two crêpes at a time.)

To cure a pan, follow the manufacturer's instructions, or wash off the manufacturing oil which is used to coat new pans, then heat 2 teaspoons of oil with ½ teaspoon of salt in it, swirling it to coat the surface thoroughly, until the oil begins to smoke. Let it cool and wipe the surface with paper towels until a fresh paper towel, rubbed across the pan, comes away clean.

Never wash a crêpe pan with soap; just rinse it thoroughly in hot water and dry it at once so that it doesn't rust. The same curing and cleaning instructions apply to all uncoated cast-iron or steel pans.

When cooking, preheat the pan over moderate heat before you add the oil or butter; the pan's heat will help to assure that the food cooks evenly.

Saucepans. Look for a saucepan whose sides descend in a gradual curve to its bottom. If the curve is sufficiently gradual a whisk or spatula will be able to reach every point on the pan's interior. When the sides rise straight up from the bottoms, bits of sauce or custard stick in the angle where bottom and sides meet, and, not being stirred with the rest, can overcook and spoil the texture of the mixture. We suggest that you keep three saucepans on hand in the following sizes: ¾ quart to 1 quart, 1½ quarts, and 2½ quarts.

Casseroles. These come with two handles and a tight lid. They should be good conductors of heat to allow for slow cooking and braising. If possible, you should own two, one 4 quart and one 6 quart.

Roasting/baking pans. A rectangle is plainly the most convenient shape for roasting or baking food. The pan should have handles at either end to facilitate lifting and carrying. It will also serve as a *bain-marie*, a vessel containing boiling or hot water in which a smaller pan or pot rests, its contents slowly cooking or keeping warm. You should have two, one 18 by 10 by 3 inches and the other 13 by 9½ by 3 inches.

Kettle. This commodious, thin-walled pot, which the French call a *fait-tout* (makes everything), can be used for blanching vegetables and large amounts of food and for cooking sizable amounts of pasta and the like. We recommend the kind made of thin steel coated with enamel, like the old-fashioned pots of speckled blue and white. It should hold 10 quarts.

Terrine. Oval or rectangular, a terrine should be of earthenware or porcelain to permit the slow, even cooking a pâté requires. It must have a tight-fitting lid to keep its contents moist and hold 1½ to 2 quarts. .

Soufflé dishes. A straight-sided porcelain dish about three inches deep is best for soufflés. When there are several people to be fed we prefer to make two small soufflés rather than one large one; in our experience, larger soufflés don't work out as well, tending to dry out at the edges while the center is still too soft. Anyway, two small soufflé dishes are more practical than one large one. If you use a soufflé dish that holds enough to serve eight, for example, you have more than you need for four, whereas with two small soufflé dishes you can make the right amount to serve either four, six, or eight.

Fish poacher. A practical-sized fish poacher is 20 inches long, 5½ inches wide, and 4½ inches deep; it will accommodate either one fish of up to seven pounds or between half a dozen and a dozen smaller fish such as trout. If you are poaching a chunk of fish you should use a regular pot that holds it snugly.

BAKEWARE

In the old days baking pans were handed down from one generation to the next, as it was only after a pan had been blackened and cured by long use that it began to do more than simply contain the matter baking in it and instead imparted a fine, crisp crust to it. Black retains heat rather than reflecting it, so whatever bakes in a black pan cooks thoroughly and in less time. Even delicate cakes like génoise cook better in black pans which give them a light crust that seals in moisture.

Isabelle Marique is so enthused by black bakeware that she actually designs her own line and has it manufactured for her in Belgium. Her black bakeware is distributed in the United States under her own name. It is no longer necessary to blacken and cure pans now that the readymade black ones are on the market.
You will need:

Cookie or baking sheets. You should have two and they should be of good size—at least 14 by 17 by ⅜ inches.

Round molds. You will need round cake molds (1½ inches deep and 7, 8, and 9 inches in diameter, containing 5, 6, and 7 cups respectively), and other round molds, like charlotte molds and brioche molds, in 1¼ and 1½ quart sizes. These are handy for all sorts of desserts.

Bread loaf pans. These are deeper than the standard cake molds and can be used for deep cakes and breads. They are available in both round and rectangular (9 inches in diameter or 9½ by 5½ inches). Both hold 8 cups and both are 2½ inches high.

Deep tart or quiche pans. These come round and rectangular (up to 13 inches in diameter and 12 inches long by 7½ inches wide by 1⅓ inches high). The best are made of black steel with removable bottoms which make the removal of tarts and quiches foolproof. A 9-inch round serves six and an 11-inch between eight and ten.

Timbale molds. Timbales—filled pastry shells topped with a pastry lid—are easy to construct with the help of timbale molds. The mold consists of a deep tart pan base and a conical lid, both 9 inches in diameter.

Bûche de Noël cake pan. This is a special pan which simplifies the making of a bûche, though it can be used for other types of cakes as well. It is a long narrow mold, curved on the bottom, about 18 inches by 3½ inches by 2 inches. The curved bottom becomes the top of the bûche and the short sides, which are cut obliquely, simulate the cross-section of a log.

APPLIANCES

Chances are that you already have some of these devices. The first three are the most important; if you're missing any we urge you to make up the deficiency as they can save you any amount of time.

Electric blender. We believe that a large selection of speeds makes little difference to a blender's performance and that the alleged advantages of a timer and/or solid-state circuitry are much exaggerated. Some styles feature a control that turns the blender continuously off and on to agitate the materials in it. Pulsing is certainly a useful technique, but we feel that you can achieve the same results with an ordinary blender simply by flipping the on/off switch rapidly back and forth a few times. A blender produces a smoother, fluffier purée than a food processor does and can process food in amounts too small for the bigger machine to handle. Warning: you sometimes have to add liquid to a mixture in order not to put too great a strain on the blender's motor.

Food processor. The least cumbersome food processors have direct-drive motors, and the bowl sits atop the drive shaft. Features to identify before using a machine are the on/off switch and the pulse switch (which starts and stops the blades rapidly). The blade most often called upon is the standard steel cutting blade; disks for slicing, for grating and/or shredding, and French fries are likewise very useful. Most parts of most processors can be put in a dishwasher, but before you do you should check the manufacturer's instructions.

A food processor is like a flesh-and-blood helper who has mastered a number of techniques that he executes very well and with dazzling speed. A processor grates cheese in seconds, grinds and chops nuts, and slices and shreds vegetables in a twinkling. It can purée, blend, and mix; and it makes pie dough and breads a dream.

Pressure cooker. We can't proclaim too loudly the virtues of this simple and wondrously efficacious device, which, with fuel costs soaring, is today a bigger value than ever as an economizer of money as well as time. It cooks food in half or even a third of the time required by ordinary methods, while conserving its natural flavors and nutrients and imparting a fine texture to it. A cook who uses a pressure cooker regularly soon comes to think of it as indispensable, particularly for making stews, stocks, and soups. Choose one of stainless steel, a metal that never reacts with food and is easy to maintain. Since the food you cook in the cooker will never fill the chamber (the rule is, two-thirds full at most), select a model with a more capacious chamber or pot than you might think necessary. If you are cooking for a family of three or four persons, for example, you will need a cooker with a capacity of about two gallons.

As pressure builds in a cooker, it drives up the temperature of the boiling water, with the result that you are soon cooking at heats you could never achieve in an ordinary pot. Since the chamber is tightly enclosed hardly any evaporation occurs, so relatively little liquid is needed; this, together with the speed of the operation, conserves the food's nutrients and flavors.

A pressure cooker is essential for making the stocks and glazes in this book, which it does with astonishing speed. It produces a superb chicken stock in about ten minutes and a fish stock in seven, while our all-purpose meat stock requires—instead of hours—just 35 minutes. These stocks come out, moreover, thick and flavored. Pressure cooking transforms tough, stringy meat into meat that melts in your mouth, whereas ordinary cooking could only tenderize it at the expense of your time and its flavor. So pressure cooking saves you money twice: by allowing you to buy cheaper cuts of meat and by reducing in half or more the amount of fuel—gas, electricity, or, for that matter, coal or wood—you need to cook them.

Electric mixer. A hand model is the only kind you need; it is obviously more versatile than the fixed, stand-bowl model as it can be used in any bowl or pan. Find one with beaters of thin wires, like whisks, and a good, heavy-duty motor.

A stand-bowl mixer with a whisk that rotates in a bowl as it revolves is certainly not necessary, but it is a great help in making génoise and other batters that require prolonged beating, such as a meringue or ganache (chocolate cream filling). You might want to acquire one if you make a lot of pastry and bread.

Electric deep fryer. Electric deep fryers are equipped with a thermostat that performs the crucial function of keeping the oil from overheating or becoming too cool. If the oil gets hotter than 375°, its critical point, the fatty acids in it separate from the glycerine. Dehydration of the latter causes a bad smell and the acids recombine into compounds that can cause indigestion. On the other hand, if the oil temperature drops too low, the food in it becomes soggy. So long as it is functioning properly the thermostat keeps the oil temperature at around 350°. Oil should be strained through a cheesecloth between uses and kept in a glass container in the refrigerator. If the oil appears to be flowing more slowly and/or if it darkens in color it should be discarded.

Although you fill the fryer with oil to a depth of no more than one third, the oil should cover the food—sliced potatoes or whatever—by about half an inch. Always lower the basket into the hot oil gradually: some foods release quantities of steam on coming into contact with the hot oil, causing the latter to foam for a minute or two, and the agitated oil can easily shoot up in a geyser and catch fire if you have filled the pot too high. To stir, use a fork with a long handle as you can easily get burned if you approach too close.

Only deep fry food a little at a time so that the oil temperature stays as close to constant as possible. Food cooked in oil at the right temperature is instantly sealed by the heat and does not absorb oil, resulting in a crisp, light fried food.

Electric ice cream mixer. Those with a 3-quart or 5-quart capacity are the most useful. The counter models that take plain salt and ice cubes are remarkably fast and efficient. For the best balance, use one pound of salt for every five pounds of ice.

SERVICE UTENSILS

Each utensil in this category performs a specific function at a particular stage in the preparation of a given dish while containing or supporting the food being prepared. Thus, passively, these service utensils complement the active work of cutting knives, stirring spatulas, whirring blades, flying cleavers, and pounding mallets.

Cutting boards. Good quality plastic boards do not dull knives or retain odors, are easy to clean, and can go into a dishwasher. They can be moved around as needed or, alternatively, hinged to a vertical surface.

Mixing bowls. The most practical kind are of stainless steel; they do not react with foods, stand up well under the assault of electric mixers, and can be heated or cooled very fast. We suggest that you stock three: 1½ quarts, 3 quarts, and 5 quarts.

The bowls should have flat bottoms and curving sides flaring outward so that they are very wide at the top in comparison to their depth. This conformation makes it easier for a cook to beat food in them, either with an electric mixer or by hand. It also encourages food to collect at the bottom.

Racks. A baked cake or cookies should rest on 11-inch round racks with wires about ¼ inch apart. If the wires are more widely separated by, say, ½ inch or more, a cake may sag or twist out of shape. The racks should have feet to allow air to circulate under the food. You should have two of them.

Steamer. The round stainless steel steamer should lodge in the pot that contains it two inches above the surface of the water; the pot itself should have a capacity of at least a gallon, and you will need a quart of water to provide enough pressure for steaming. A tight lid is essential; if it isn't tight enough, insert foil between the lid and the pot. Food should be placed in the steamer when water boils.

Strainer. Strainers should be of stainless steel so that they don't react with foods and discolor them. You really need two: an 8-

inch hemispheric sieve with a coarse mesh for use as an all-purpose strainer and sifter and for making small amounts of vegetable sauce or passing foods which require a rough consistency; and a 6-inch fine sieve, not hemispheric but slightly conical, for fine sauces.

Colander. Buy a large one, with feet, capable of containing four quarts of food.

Serving platters. These stainless steel receptacles (you need two) should be about 17 inches long and hexagonal or rectangular, shapes that are, in general, more convenient for arranging food on them than the old-fashioned oval shape.

HAND TOOLS

The numerous utensils in this category, some simple and versatile, others slightly more sophisticated and specialized, perform so many essential functions that cooking would be impossible without them.

Knives. Because we both happen to prefer the look and feel of wood, the handles of the knives in our respective kitchens are wooden, but home cooks should follow their own inclinations in this. As for blades, everyone seems to agree that high-carbon stainless steel is the best material, as it can be sharpened to a very keen edge, won't rust, and never discolors foods. A cook should have at least five basic knives:

• A 3½-inch paring knife (the measurement, as with those cited below, denotes the length of the blade). This is an all-purpose utensil for small jobs.

• A 12-inch knife with a serrated blade. The shallow facets along the cutting edge make for smooth slicing of bread and cake, brioches, puffs, and the like.

• One 10-inch cook's or chef's knife with a wide blade for chopping and slicing. The arched shape of the blade helps the knife rock and chop with ease.

• A carving knife with a sharp and smooth cutting edge and facets along its side for slicing ham, veal scallops, and other meats as well as salmon, and certain other fish. This knife greatly facilitates carving, particularly when you want to slice very thin.

• A 10-inch palette knife with a thin and flexible blade for spreading icings and for other similar uses.

Large two-pronged fork. In addition to serving as a carving fork this utensil can perform a multitude of useful tasks in preparing food for cooking and in cooking itself.

Poultry shears. These shears, with curved 4-inch blades, one with a serrated edge, are employed for cutting poultry, as well as for cutting fish fins and heads and lobster.

Turkey lacing skewers. These shafts (you need at least six) not only help you close up stuffed birds but can also be used to test cakes and vegetables for doneness without breaking them.

Mallet. Fashioned of wood, with a short handle and a cylindrical head, a kitchen mallet weighs about a pound. Its flat end is used for general pounding and flattening, and its other end, faced with metal raised in bumps and ridges like a waffle iron, is employed to break down the fibers in tough cuts of meat.

Graters. A small stainless steel box grater is the most versatile, with a thin rasping surface for lemon and orange zest and small teeth for bits of cheese. A nutmeg grater has a little chamber in which the nutmeg is stored before it is ground fine by the grater's small rasping surface.

Peppermill. This simple device, about 4 inches high, has a knob at the top to adjust the tension—loose to obtain coarsely crushed pepper for a dish like *steak au poivre,* and tight to get finely ground pepper for sauces and the like.

Food mill. Choose a sturdy mill of about 5 to 6 quarts capacity in stainless steel that will hook onto the tops of bowls and pans by its feet and that has several interchangeable disks for coarse and fine purées.

Zester. This peeler makes thin julienne zests from the outer skins of lemons and oranges and from carrots and other hard vegetables.

Vegetable peelers. There are two kinds, one straight, the other shaped like a letter U closed at the top. Use the one that feels more comfortable. Note: the stainless steel peeling blade should not be fixed but should swivel.

Salad spinner. This device is very effective for drying lettuce leaves, mushrooms, and even strawberries. The food sits in a slotted basket that fits into a plastic bowl. The basket is spun by turning a crank or pulling a cord, and the water is forced out of the slots in the basket, coming to rest in the base of the bowl.

Whisks. Whisks should be light in weight. When you are beating a mixture, even a couple of ounces makes a difference in how tired your arm gets. Ideally, you should have three:

• A 14-inch whipping whisk or balloon whisk with fifteen or more thin wires converging at the center. There should be no central wire as it prevents the whisk from reaching the bottom of the bowl.

• A 12-inch folding whisk or mixing whisk with eight slightly thicker wires crossing at the center for folding mixtures like mousses and soufflés.

• An 8-inch all-purpose whisk, useful in particular with small amounts of sauce, mousses, and the like.

Spatula. Wooden spatulas are better than wooden spoons for stirring. Flat on both sides, they don't collect food. Because they are thin at the larger end—the business end—they are easier to move and turn in a mixture to reach into the corners and recesses of saucepans.

Rolling pin. A good rolling pin should be about 20 inches long, straight (i.e., not tapered), and in a hard wood such as maple, with a smooth finish. We both much prefer the kind without handles, because it has a longer working surface. Moreover, you are in closer contact with the dough and have better control for even rolling.

Pastry scraper. This flat piece of plastic, about 5 x 4 inches, tapering to thin edges, has a straight edge for cleaning off boards and other flat surfaces and a curved edge for scraping out bowls and saucepans. You may want to keep more than one handy.

Pastry bags and tips. Nylon bags are the easiest to wash. You should have two: one 12 inches long for small garnishing jobs and another 14 inches long for potatoes, *pâte à choux*, cookies, and meringue. To tip them you will need four round tips (nos. 3, 5, 7, and 9) and four star tips (nos. 3, 5, 9, and 11).

Pastry brush. Look for a brush about an inch wide with natural bristles that taper about two inches to a thin brushing edge. It should not be used for basting roasts in the oven or for buttering hot pans as the bristles will singe.

Metal pancake flipper. Choose a stainless steel one with a slotted rectangular head broad enough to pick up fragile food like fish without the latter coming apart. The holes in the utensil's head allow food to drain. A good size for the flat scooping surface is 4½ x 3 inches.

Degreaser. There are several varieties of this instant fat separator on the market. We like the heat-resistant Pyrex one. It is a kind of measuring cup with a spout that branches off from its bottom, enabling you to pour off fat-free liquid (cooking juices or whatever) while the fat floats on top.

CONTROLLERS

In a final category are utensils and devices that measure and/or regulate weights, volumes, and amounts of food in preparation and temperatures and time during cooking.

Measuring Instruments (four sets). These should indicate metric weights on their sides as well as the standard U.S. measures. All will most likely be (though they need not be) stainless steel.

- 1 set solid measuring cups for scooping up flour, sugar, and the like
- 2 sets measuring spoons (easier to use if you separate them)
- 1 set liquid measuring cups (1 cup, 2 cups, 4 cups)

Scale. The most practical scale is one that weighs up to 500 grams, or slightly more than 1 pound, with weights indicated in both grams and ounces. The accuracy is important for pastry, and weighing ingredients takes half the time of measuring.

Thermometers. For cooking and storing food you will need four types of temperature gauges:

- An instant-reading thermometer for meats, sauces, and liquids
- An oven thermometer, especially useful for letting you know whether your oven is preheated to the right temperature
- Freezer and refrigerator thermometers. (Frozen food spoils at over 0° F. and refrigerated food at over 38° F.)
- A candy thermometer to test for the soft ball stage of sugar syrups

Timer. The ring or buzz this device emits should be sufficiently loud, clear, and insistent that you will hear it.

Flame Tamer. The Flame Tamer is a device that controls the heat of a gas burner, distributing it evenly across the bottom of a pan or pot.

2
STOCKS AND SOUPS

Not so long ago, most people planning a meal or a menu devoted comparatively little thought to soup and were content as a rule to serve the canned or dried variety, perhaps adding herbs or spices for extra flavor and sprinkling parsley or some colorful condiment like paprika on top for visual appeal. Since then, however, the extraordinary upsurge of popular interest in cooking has raised the soup-consciousness of uncounted home cooks by several notches. These cooks have discovered that making soup is easy, quickly accomplished, and fun, and that the payoff in flavor can be fantastic. Long regarded as worthy but not very exciting meal-openers, soups have acquired a definite glamour of late and making them has become, for many, an adventure.

Soup—liquid food—has been around as long as humanity, in fact a lot longer: According to scientists, all life on this planet originated in and emerged from a kind of soup, the watery, global environment known as "primordial soup." Today, by contrast, it seems as if practically every form of life goes *into* soups: meat, fowl, fish and shellfish; vegetables, cereals, and a host of other plants; eggs and dairy products; fruit and wine. Soups range in clarity from transparent to opaque, in color from white to black, in flavor from mild to spicy, and in consistency from thin broths or consommés to thicker creams and vegetable purées, to mixtures of solid chunks of fish or fowl such as a bouillabaisse, and chicken waterzooi, that are virtually stews. With this variety goes versatility. Served hot or cold according to the season, soups can, as desired, whet appetites, help appease them, or, as meals in themselves, with bread, gratify them completely.

Until a generation or so ago, many a French wife kept a pot on her stove in which she regularly deposited edible kitchen refuse: bones from roasts, the skins, peelings, stems, and other unwanted parts of vegetables, and assorted other scraps. Left simmering for hours on end, this heterogeneous mixture could be tapped at will for bowls of hearty, life-sustaining soup. But while sentimental souls still wax nostalgic over this homemade concoction we feel that its disappearance from the scene is hardly a cause for regret. Some of its ingredients, notably overcooked bones, yielded a distinctly stale taste, but what was worse, the protracted cooking obliterated the flavor of the fresh ingredients along with a goodly portion of their nutrients. Nowadays, most home cooks would surely agree that, as the great gastronome Curnonsky said of all food, a good soup should taste of the things it is made of. It follows that these ingredients must themselves be fresh and of good quality and that they must not be cooked too long.

Many of the very best soups have a stock base, but thanks to the pressure cooker making stock is no longer a tedious operation. In some soups, however, water does just as well as stock.

When preparing to make a soup containing vegetables in a standard pot, you should chop these vegetables finely or slice them thinly. The smaller the bits, the less time it will take to cook them, and the more of their fresh flavors and nutritive values will remain in the soup. If, by contrast, you use a pressure cooker for this purpose, only a rough chopping is needed, so fast do the vegetables cook.

There is no better use to which you can put your pressure cooker than soup-making. The superheated steam breaks down the vegetable fibers swiftly and uniformly to draw forth their full flavor. The entire process takes no more than minutes.

One day a week most French families of all classes partake of a meal consisting solely of soup. Once you start making your own soups and discover how delicious they can be you will need no urging from us, we suspect, to follow their excellent example.

TAKING STOCK

Even if you eliminate all but the most important stocks in the French culinary canon you still end up with half a dozen. From a home cook's standpoint that is far too many. Even restaurants, which must be ready at all hours to meet their clients' unpredictable demands, almost never keep six different stocks on hand. All stocks are either brown, for use in dark sauces, or white, for use in light, clear ones. We have adapted one of the first type and two of the second; these three stocks can, among them, serve as base or strengthener-extender in any sauce. We discourage the use of canned broths or consommés or bouillon cubes as a base for a sauce because of their bland, commercial taste.

SUPERB STOCKS IN MINUTES

Our method for making stocks will cause eyebrows to shoot upward in some quarters, for it represents a sharp break with customary practice. Yet we offer it in perfect confidence, having employed it ourselves, with excellent results, for years. It couldn't be simpler. Instead of bones and meat, we begin with a ready-to-cook chicken or chicken parts, a cut of beef or veal with bone in it, or unboned fish. And, instead of cooking these viands for hours in a pot of water, we commit them, with just the minimum amount of water necessary, to . . . a pressure cooker.

A pressure cooker? "But that isn't *cuisine* any more!" we can hear the chefs protest. Their consternation is understandable. Unable to observe, smell, or taste the food cooking inside the closed device, they are no longer in charge. The clock is. And instead of taking hours the procedure takes minutes: 30 to 35 for our light brown "all-purpose" stock as against three to five hours by the regular method, 10 to 12 minutes for white or chicken stock compared to 1½ to 3 hours, and a mere seven minutes, as opposed to 20, for the fish stock. When the meat is fork-tender, the bones in it have released their minerals and gelatin and the stock has consequently achieved its delicate flavor. Some cuts of meat and some birds and parts thereof are, of course, tougher than others; if they aren't fork-tender by the prescribed pressure-cooking time you simply cook them a few minutes longer. All in all, pressure cooking (which we also recommend for making soups and stews) is much more rational than the usual method for making stocks.*

But time isn't all you gain with a pressure cooker. It also gives top quality. Because cooking takes place rapidly within a sealed chamber, little evaporation can occur and you can use as little liquid as you want. In consequence, nutrients aren't washed out or cooked away, and the resulting stock is full-bodied, well-flavored, and rich in nutrients.

Along with these superb stocks you end up, by our method, with perfectly cooked meat, fowl, or fish. So you may opt to combine stock-making with preparing a meal. If not, you can use the cooking viands in a great variety of dishes to be consumed later on: chicken salad or chicken aspic, meat salad, ground beef au gratin, hash, cold fish, or croquettes, to cite just a few.

Regarding stocks, the strength and body of your sauce will depend on the stock you use and on its strength. A cup of concentrated stock of the kind you obtain by our method needs less reduction, or boiling down, than a cup of less concentrated stock—from, for example, a can you might buy in your supermarket—and it therefore yields more glaze and more sauce of greater strength.

The stock you have made so effortlessly in a pressure cooker exudes a glorious aroma, and if it lacks the deep color of a standard stock it has plenty of body to strengthen a sauce and a freshness and clarity of flavor seldom found in stocks prepared the usual way. Still, the most impressive thing about it remains the speed with which it is made. A quart and a half of broth or two to three cups of concentrated stock in just ten minutes! To cooks long accustomed to a method of stock-making unchanged for centuries, such results must seem awesome, a singularly potent magic.

---

*On most pressure cookers a regulator that fits over the steam vent automatically maintains pressure at a given level, usually 15 pounds, but on some models the pressure can be set at either 15, 10, or 5 pounds. To implement a small number of recipes involving delicate ingredients lower pressure is preferable as it produces a better texture, but for almost all usual purposes 15 pounds of pressure will suffice.

ALL-PURPOSE STOCK
Fond Brun

Yield: 3 qts. stock
1½ qts. concentrated stock

3 lbs. stewing beef with bones (such as meaty short ribs or
shank), cut into 1½- to 2-inch pieces
3 lbs. veal breast or shank, cut into 1½- to 2-inch pieces
Oil
2 leeks (white part only), washed and sliced
1 medium onion stuck with 3 cloves
2 carrots, peeled and chopped
5 to 6 parsley sprigs
2 bay leaves
¼ teaspoon thyme
1 medium-size stalk celery
5½ qts. cold water
12 peppercorns
2 teaspoons salt

Preheat oven to 500°.

Put beef and veal in a large lightly oiled roasting pan. Add
the leeks, onion, and carrot. Roast for 15 to 20 minutes, turning the
pieces several times as they brown. Remove the carrot and onion
before they burn and put them into a large kettle. When the meat
has browned, transfer it to the kettle and add the remaining ingredients. The water should cover all the ingredients. Bring to a boil
and cook gently, uncovered, for 3 hours, skimming periodically.
Strain the stock through a fine sieve and discard the solids. Degrease the stock thoroughly.

To make a more concentrated stock, boil the strained stock
gently until it is reduced to 1½ quarts, skimming often. Let cool,
cover, and refrigerate or freeze. The stock will keep in the refrigerator for 2 days.

QUICK ALL-PURPOSE STOCK
Fond Brun Rapide

Yield: 6–8 cups
2–3 cups concentrated stock

1 lb. stewing beef with bones (such as meaty short ribs or shank), cut into 1-inch pieces
2 lbs. veal breast, shoulder, or shank, cut into 1-inch pieces
Oil
1 carrot, roughly chopped
1 medium-size onion, roughly chopped
1 shallot, peeled and halved
1 stalk celery, roughly chopped
2 medium-size tomatoes, peeled, seeded, and cut into chunks
4 sprigs parsley
Dried thyme
1 or 2 bay leaves
Freshly ground black pepper
2 or 3 mushrooms, quartered (optional)
1 small clove garlic, peeled and crushed (optional)
6 to 8 cups cold water

Preheat oven to 500°.

Put beef and veal in a large lightly oiled roasting pan. Add the onion and carrot. Roast for 15 to 20 minutes, turning the pieces several times as they brown. Remove the carrot and onion before they burn and put them into a pressure cooker. When the meat has browned, transfer it to the pressure cooker and add the shallot, celery, tomatoes, parsley, pinch of thyme, bay leaves, pepper to taste, mushrooms, garlic, and water. Cover and bring to a boil, but do not seal the lid. Lower the heat and simmer for 5 minutes, skimming off the scum which rises to the surface. Secure the lid and cook for 35 minutes. Strain the stock through a fine-mesh sieve, reserve the meats, but discard the vegetables, and degrease the stock thoroughly.

Notes

Cool the stock uncovered, cover, and refrigerate or freeze. The stock will keep in the refrigerator for 1 to 2 days, or it can be frozen.

To make a concentrated stock for use in sauces, add only 2 to 3 cups of water.

When the meats are cool enough to handle, trim them of bones and fat and, when completely cooled, mix them with Dill and Mustard Mayonnaise (see p. 41). Arrange on lettuce leaves for a main course salad.

CHICKEN STOCK
Fond de Volaille

Yield: 3 qts. stock
        1 to 1½ qts. concentrated stock

  6 lbs. chicken wings, or a large stewing hen
  2 carrots, peeled and sliced
  2 leeks (white part only), sliced
  1 medium-size onion stuck with 3 cloves
  5 to 6 parsley sprigs
  2 bay leaves
  ¼ teaspoon thyme
  1 medium-size stalk celery
5½ qts. cold water
12 whole black peppercorns
  2 teaspoons salt

Put all ingredients in a large kettle. Bring to a boil and boil gently, uncovered, for 3 hours, periodically skimming the scum and fat that rise to the surface. Strain the stock through a fine sieve and discard the solids. Degrease the stock thoroughly.

For concentrated stock, boil the degreased stock gently until reduced by about half. Skim often. Let the stock cool, cover, and refrigerate or freeze. The stock will keep in the refrigerator for 2 days.

QUICK CHICKEN STOCK
Fond de Volaille Rapide

Yield: 6–8 cups stock
           2–3 cups concentrated stock

3 lbs. chicken wings
1 shallot, peeled and coarsely chopped
1 medium-size stalk celery, coarsely chopped
4 sprigs parsley
1 medium-size carrot, coarsely chopped
1 bay leaf
1 medium-size onion, coarsely chopped
⅛ teaspoon dried thyme
6 whole black peppercorns
  Salt
6 to 8 cups water

Put all ingredients in a pressure cooker, salting very lightly. Secure the lid and cook for 12 minutes. Strain the stock through a fine-mesh sieve and degrease. Let stock cool uncovered and then store covered.

Notes

Stock made with 6 to 8 cups water is good for soups. For use in sauces, add only 2 to 3 cups water.

Stock will keep for 2 days in the refrigerator. It can also be frozen in ice cube trays. One cube will equal about 2 tablespoons.

The concentrated stock can be used to make a delicious Quick Chicken Aspic (Poulet en Gelée Rapide) to serve 2 or 3:

Strain and degrease the concentrated stock and let it cool to room temperature. Remove skin and bones from wings and reserve the meat. Slice the carrot from the stock and arrange it in a pattern in the bottom of a bowl or deep dish. Combine the chicken meat with 1 tablespoon minced parsley, 1 very small garlic clove squeezed through a press, and salt and freshly ground black pepper to taste. Mash the ingredients together with a fork. Pour ¼ cup of the stock over the carrots. Then lay the chicken mixture on top. Cover the chicken barely with about 1 cup of stock. Refrigerate the dish until jelled. Unmold on a chilled platter and garnish with lettuce.

FISH STOCK AND FISH FUMET
Fond de Poisson

Yield: 4–6 cups stock
           2–3 cups fumet

  3 lbs. fish bones with heads (if available), with gills removed,
    cut up (Use lean, non-oily fish, such as sole or flounder.)
  1 medium onion, thinly sliced (cut roughly for pressure
    cooker)
  1 shallot, minced (cut roughly for pressure cooker)
  2 small celery stalks, coarsely chopped (cut roughly for
    pressure cooker)
  1 medium carrot, coarsely chopped (cut roughly for pressure
    cooker)
  5 to 6 sprigs parsley
  ½ cup dry white wine
  ¼ teaspoon dried thyme, or 1 sprig fresh
  1 bay leaf
  6 whole black peppercorns
    Salt
  4 to 6 cups water

Rinse bones under cold running water. Combine all ingredients in
a kettle, salting very lightly. Bring to a boil and simmer, partially
covered, for 20 minutes, periodically skimming the scum that rises
to the surface. Strain the stock through a fine-mesh sieve and discard the solids.

To cook in a pressure cooker, put all ingredients into the
cooker, bring to a boil, and simmer, uncovered, for 5 minutes,
skimming the scum that rises to the surface. Secure the lid and cook
for 7 to 8 minutes. Strain the stock through a fine-mesh sieve and
discard the solids.

Fumet

Simmer strained stock over low heat and reduce to 2 to 3
cups, periodically skimming the scum that rises to the top.

To make fumet in the pressure cooker, use only 2 to 3 cups of
water in the basic recipe.

(continued)

Notes

Cool stock uncovered and store covered. The stock will keep in the refrigerator for 1 day. It can also be frozen in ice cube trays.

COURT BOUILLON
Vegetable-flavored Broth

Yield: 5 quarts

      5 qts. water
  1½ cups dry white wine
      2 leeks (white and pale green parts), finely chopped
      2 medium carrots, finely chopped
      2 stalks celery, finely chopped
      1 medium onion, finely chopped
         Salt
   20 whole black peppercorns
      1 teaspoon dried thyme
      3 bay leaves
      8 parsley sprigs

Combine all the ingredients in a kettle and bring to a boil covered. Uncover and boil slowly for 10 minutes. Let broth cool before using.

Notes

Leave part of the vegetables whole if needed for decoration of the final dish. Court bouillon, after being used to poach a fish, may be used immediately in a fish soup. Otherwise it should be discarded as it does not keep well.

GREEN SOUP
Potage Vert

Serves: 6

2½ tablespoons butter
2 or 3 leeks (white and pale-green parts only), sliced
1 medium onion, chopped
1 bunch watercress
2 medium-large potatoes, peeled and sliced
3 cups chicken stock (see pp. 19–20) or water
2½ cups milk
   Salt
   Freshly ground black pepper
2 egg yolks
½ cup heavy cream

✩Melt butter in a kettle and add leeks and onion. Cover and cook slowly, stirring occasionally, for 8 minutes, or until tender. Do not brown. Set aside the leaves of half the watercress. Add potatoes, stock, milk, remaining watercress, and salt and pepper to taste. Cover, bring to a boil, and simmer for 30 to 35 minutes (10 to 12 minutes in pressure cooker), or until vegetables are very soft.

Purée mixture through a food mill or in a food processor or blender and return to the pot. Blend reserved watercress with ⅓ cup purée until smooth and reserve.

Just before serving, bring soup to a simmer and remove from heat. Whisk egg yolks and cream together in a bowl. Whisk in 1 cup hot soup. Stir this mixture into remaining soup. Reheat gently, stirring, to just below a simmer. Add a little stock if soup is too thick. Remove from the heat and stir in the watercress purée.

Light variation

✩In place of 2½ tablespoons butter, use 1 tablespoon butter and 3 tablespoons water to cook the leeks and onion.

Omit egg yolks and cream. Heat the puréed soup to just below a simmer. Remove from the heat and stir in the watercress purée.

(continued)

Notes

If the soup is to be served hot, it can be prepared 1 day in advance up to the point of adding the egg yolks and cream. If it is to be served cold, finish completely, cool uncovered, then cover and refrigerate.

The watercress purée can be made several hours in advance and refrigerated covered. If you want a stronger watercress taste, blend all the watercress leaves instead of half.

TOMATO SOUP WITH THIN NOODLES
Soupe aux Tomates avec Nouilles

Serves: 6

    3 tablespoons butter
    1 medium onion, finely chopped
    2 lbs. fresh ripe tomatoes, peeled, seeded, and cut into
        chunks, or 1 35-oz. can Italian plum tomatoes, drained
    2 7-inch stalks celery, finely chopped
    1 bay leaf
    ½ teaspoon dried thyme
    ½ teaspoon sugar
      Salt
      Freshly ground black pepper
    5½ cups water
    ¼ lb. thin noodles, broken into 2-inch pieces, if necessary
    ½ cup heavy cream
    1 tablespoon finely chopped parsley

Melt 1 tablespoon butter in a large pot. Add the onions, cover, and cook over medium-low heat for 5 to 7 minutes, stirring occasionally. Add tomatoes, celery, bay leaf, thyme, sugar, and salt and pepper to taste. Cook over medium-low heat for 30 minutes, stirring occasionally.

Bring water to a boil in a saucepan and add salt and noodles. Boil slowly for 2 to 3 minutes, or until noodles are barely tender. Remove from the heat and set aside undrained.

Remove bay leaf and put stewed vegetables through the fine disk of a food mill, or purée until smooth in a blender or food processor. (Strain if using canned tomatoes.) Add to noodles and bring to a boil. Correct seasoning, if necessary.

☆Pour cream into a warm tureen. Stir in soup and 2 tablespoons butter and garnish with parsley.

Light variation

☆Omit cream and 2 tablespoons butter. Garnish hot soup with parsley and serve.

Notes

This soup can be prepared 1 day in advance up to the addition of the cream and butter.

To peel large quantities of tomatoes, put them into a pot of boiling water all at once. Count slowly to 30 and then drain. Core and peel.

CREAM OF ASPARAGUS SOUP
Potage aux Asperges

Serves: 6

2 lbs. asparagus
3 qts. water
1½ tablespoons salt
3 egg yolks
½ cup heavy cream
6 cups quick chicken stock (see p. 20)
    Freshly ground black pepper
2 tablespoons butter
1 tablespoon finely chopped parsley

Wash asparagus and cut off about 1 inch of the tough bottom of each stalk. Peel the stems beginning halfway down the stalk from the tip. Peel a second layer off the bottom 2 inches to make the asparagus evenly tender. Cut the tips to 1¼-inch lengths and re-serve the stalks.

Bring the water to a boil in a kettle. Add the salt and boil the asparagus tips for 3 to 4 minutes, or until they are just tender and crisp. Remove the tips with a slotted spoon and set aside.

Boil the stalks in the same water for 8 to 10 minutes, or until quite tender. Drain and purée through the fine disk of a food mill, or force through a sieve, or purée in a blender or food processor, pushing the purée through a sieve to remove any fibers. Add a little stock, to help blending or sieving.

☆Beat the egg yolks slightly and blend in the cream. Combine the egg yolk mixture, ▢stock, and asparagus purée in a saucepan. Heat slowly to just below a simmer, stirring constantly with a wooden spatula, making figure eights to reach all over the bottom and sides of the saucepan. Season with salt and pepper to taste.

Pour into a heated soup tureen, ✦add butter and asparagus tips, and sprinkle with parsley.

Light variation

☆In place of egg yolks and heavy cream, use 2 medium pota-toes (½ lb.), thinly sliced. Boil the asparagus stalks and the thinly sliced potatoes in the same water as the asparagus tips for 8 to 10 minutes. Drain and purée through the fine disk of a food mill, or force through a sieve, or purée in a blender or food processor, push-ing the purée through a sieve to remove any fibers. Add a little stock to help blending or sieving.

▢In place of the chicken stock, use 3 cups stock plus 2½ cups milk. Combine the stock and milk and asparagus-potato purée in a saucepan. Heat slowly to a simmer, stirring occasionally with a wooden spatula, making figure eights to reach all over the bottom and sides of the saucepan. Season with salt and pepper to taste.

✦Omit the butter. Pour the soup into a heated soup tureen. Add the asparagus tips and sprinkle with parsley.

Notes

This soup may be served hot or cold. It will keep for 2 days in the refrigerator.

The potatoes can also be added to the original version. They will give it more texture.

GREEN PEA SOUP
Potage St. Germain

Serves: 6

1 qt. water
¼ lb. lean bacon (3 or 4 thin slices)
3 tablespoons butter
2 leeks, thinly sliced (Slice roughly if using pressure cooker.)
1 large onion, thinly sliced (Slice roughly if using pressure cooker.)
3 lbs. fresh green peas, shelled, or two 10–oz. boxes frozen peas
Salt
Freshly ground black pepper
7 cups chicken stock (see pp. 19–20) or water
Croutons (see p. 63), cut into triangles
6 parsley sprigs

Bring 1 qt. water to boil in a saucepan. Add bacon and boil slowly for 10 minutes. Drain.

☆Melt butter in a large pot and add leeks, onion, and bacon. Cover tightly and cook slowly over medium-low heat for 10 minutes without browning.

Add peas and 6 cups stock or water and salt and pepper to taste and bring to a boil. Simmer for 30 to 35 minutes, or until peas are very tender (10 to 12 minutes in pressure cooker).

Remove bacon and discard it. Purée mixture in a blender or food processor and strain it through a fine-mesh sieve or the fine disk of a food mill. Return to the pot and bring to a boil. Thin with more stock if it is too thick. Pour soup into a hot tureen or individual soup plates. □Float a crouton and a sprig of parsley on each serving.

Light variation

☆In place of 3 tablespoons butter, use 1½ tablespoons butter and 3 tablespoons water to cook leeks, onion, and bacon.

□Omit croutons. Garnish each serving with a parsley sprig.

Notes

Soup can be prepared 1 to 2 days in advance. Refrigerate covered.

LEEK SOUP
Potage aux Poireaux

Serves: 6

    2½ lbs. leeks
    3½ tablespoons butter
    ¾ lb. baking potatoes, washed, peeled, and thinly sliced
    1½ qts. chicken stock (see p. 19), or water
        Salt
        Freshly ground black pepper
    ½ cup heavy cream (optional)
    1 tablespoon finely chopped parsley

Cut off the very green part of the leeks, trim, and wash well under cold running water to remove all sand. Reserve white part of 2 leeks. Cut remainder into ⅜-inch slices.

☆Melt 2½ tablespoons butter in a large pot or pressure cooker. Stir in sliced leeks, cover (do not secure lid of pressure cooker), and cook over medium heat for 10 minutes without browning. Add potatoes, stock, and salt and pepper to taste. Cover and bring to a boil. Simmer, covered, for 20 to 25 minutes (7 to 10 minutes in the pressure cooker).

Cut reserved white parts of leeks into ½-inch slices. Melt 1 tablespoon butter in a small saucepan. Stir in the sliced leeks, cover, and cook over moderate heat without browning for 10 minutes, or until tender.

Purée the potato mixture through the fine disk of a food mill or in a blender or food processor. Strain purée through a fine sieve to remove fibers. Return purée to a saucepan and add leek whites. Bring to a boil and correct seasoning, if necessary.

Pour a spoonful of ▢cream into individual warm soup plates or bowls, ladle in soup, and sprinkle with parsley. If serving the soup from a tureen, pour the cream into the tureen, ladle in the soup, and sprinkle with parsley.

Light variation

☆Do not sauté the leeks in butter. Put the sliced leeks, potatoes, stock, and salt and pepper to taste in a large pot or pressure cooker. Bring to a boil and simmer, uncovered, for 20 to 25 minutes. (To cook in a pressure cooker, cook for 7 to 10 minutes under pressure.)

□Omit the cream. Pour the soup into individual warm soup plates or bowls, or a tureen, and sprinkle with parsley.

Notes

Always trim the very green part from leeks as it is very bitter.

CREAM OF CELERY ROOT SOUP
Velouté de Célerie-Rave

Serves: 8

- 1 qt. water
- 2 tablespoons vinegar
- 3 to 3½ lbs. celery roots (about 2 lbs. peeled), or 1½ lbs. broc- .coli, trimmed, cut into flowerets and blanched for 2 minutes
- 2 qts. chicken stock (see pp. 19–20)
- 6½ tablespoons butter
- 4½ tablespoons flour
  - Salt
  - Freshly ground black pepper
- ½ cup heavy cream
- 1½ teaspoons lemon juice (optional)
- 2 tablespoons finely chopped parsley

Mix the water and vinegar together in a large bowl. Wash the celery roots, quarter them one at a time, and peel well. Drop immediately into acidulated water. Rinse and cut into 1-inch cubes.

☆Bring stock to a boil and add celery root. Return to boiling and boil slowly, covered, for 10 minutes, or until tender. Drain and reserve cooking liquid.

Heat 3 tablespoons butter in a saucepan. Add drained celery roots and cook over moderate heat, stirring, for 2 to 3 minutes without browning. Remove from heat.

Melt remaining butter in saucepan, whisk in flour, and cook

over medium-low heat, stirring, for 2 to 3 minutes, or until it thickens and bubbles all over without browning. Remove from heat and pour in reserved cooking liquid all at once, whisking constantly. Return to a boil, add celery roots, and boil slowly, stirring occasionally, for 20 to 25 minutes.

Purée mixture through a food mill or in a blender or food processor. Return to saucepan. Season with salt and pepper to taste. Stir in cream and return to simmer. Add lemon juice, if desired. Keep warm in a larger saucepan of hot water until ready to serve. Transfer to a warm tureen or individual bowls and sprinkle with parsley.

Light variation

Prepare celery root for cooking as directed.

☆Use water in place of stock. Add 2 large potatoes (¾ lb.), thinly sliced, to the boiling water with the celery root. Boil slowly, covered, for 20 to 25 minutes (10 minutes in pressure cooker). Purée through a food mill or in a blender or food processor.

Return to pan and stir in ½ cup half and half. Bring back to a simmer. Season with salt and pepper to taste. Add lemon juice, if desired. Keep warm in a larger saucepan of hot water until ready to serve. Transfer to a warm tureen or individual bowls and sprinkle with parsley.

Notes

Soup can be prepared 1 day in advance. It is delicious served cold as well as hot. Thin with a little cold milk if too thick.

CREAM OF MUSHROOM SOUP
Potage aux Champignons

Serves: 6

2½ tablespoons butter
1 medium onion, thinly sliced (cut roughly for pressure cooker)
2 medium potatoes, sliced (cut roughly for pressure cooker)
2½ cups milk
1 or 2 bay leaves

3 cups chicken stock (see pp. 19–20) or water
Salt
Freshly ground black pepper
Freshly grated nutmeg (optional)
½ lb. mushrooms, sliced
⅓ cup cream
3 egg yolks
1 tablespoon finely chopped parsley
6 croutons (see p. 63)

☆Melt the butter in a saucepan. Add onion and cover tightly. Cook over medium heat for 8 minutes without browning. (If using a pressure cooker, do not seal.) Add potatoes and cook covered for 2 to 3 minutes without browning.

Bring milk and bay leaves slowly to a boil. Add to the saucepan with the stock. Season with salt, pepper, and nutmeg to taste. Simmer, covered, for 20 to 30 minutes. Add mushrooms and simmer for 3 minutes longer. (If using the pressure cooker, add milk, stock, and mushrooms at the same time, bring to a boil, and cook for 7 minutes under pressure.)

Purée soup in batches in a blender or food processor, or force it through a sieve or food mill. Return to saucepan and bring to a boil. Remove from heat.

□Blend cream and egg yolks in a bowl and gradually whisk in 1 cup of the hot soup. Add this mixture to the rest of the soup quickly. (Add a little more broth if the soup is too thick.) Season with salt and pepper, if necessary. Heat to just under the simmer point.

Pour soup into a hot tureen or individual bowls. To serve, center a ✧crouton in each plate and ladle in the soup.

Light variation

☆In place of butter, use 1 tablespoon butter and 3 tablespoons of water to cook the onion.

□Omit the cream and egg yolks.

✧Omit the croutons.

Notes

Soup can be made 1 day in advance up to the addition of the cream and egg yolks.

ONION SOUP WITH TOAST AND CHEESE
Soupe à l'Oignon Gratinée

Serves: 6

    4 tablespoons butter
    2 lbs. yellow onions (about 8 medium), very thinly sliced
    1 tablespoon sugar
    ½ lb. potatoes (2 medium), very thinly sliced
    1 bay leaf
    ¼ teaspoon dried thyme
    ½ cup dry white wine
    7 cups quick chicken stock (see p. 19), or all-purpose stock
      (see p. 12), or water
      Salt
      Freshly ground black pepper
    12 ¼-inch-thick slices French bread (about half a loaf)
    1½ cups (about 4½ oz.) grated Jarlsberg, imported Swiss, or Par-
      mesan cheese

✫Melt the butter in a large pot or pressure cooker. Add onions, cover (do not tighten lid on pressure cooker), and cook over medium-low heat, stirring occasionally, for 6 to 8 minutes, or until onions are soft. Sprinkle sugar over onions and cook, uncovered, over moderate heat, stirring frequently until onions are a nice golden color.

Bring the stock to a boil.

Add potatoes, bay leaf, thyme, and wine to onions and cook, stirring, for 1 to 2 minutes. Stir in boiling stock, season with salt and pepper to taste, and simmer, covered, for 20 to 30 minutes (5 to 7 minutes in the pressure cooker).

□Arrange bread slices on a cookie sheet and bake in a 450° oven until lightly browned on one side. Turn and bake until the other side is also lightly browned. Slices must be dried-out to have the proper flavor.

Set individual ovenproof soup tureens or bowls on a baking sheet. Put 2 slices of toast in each tureen.✫Sprinkle half the cheese over the toast. Pour soup over the bread and sprinkle remaining cheese on top. Bake in a 400° oven for 20 minutes, then run under the broiler until the cheese is bubbling and golden brown.

Light variation

☆Use 1½ teaspoons butter plus ⅓ cup water in place of the 4 tablespoons of butter when cooking the onions initially.

□Use only six slices of bread.

✧Use only Jarlsberg cheese.

Notes

The soup itself can be prepared 1 day in advance. Cool uncovered, cover, and refrigerate. Toast can also be made in advance and stored in a tightly closed container. Reheat and assemble soup just before serving.

This makes a lovely lunch or light supper served with a salad. Prepare the soup without bread and cheese for a light first course.

MUSSEL SOUP
Soupe aux Moules

Serves: 4

- 2 tablespoons butter
- 1 large onion, thinly sliced
- 2 cloves garlic, crushed
- 2 stalks celery, thinly sliced
- 2 medium potatoes, thinly sliced
- 1 bay leaf
- ¼ teaspoon dried thyme
- ½ teaspoon saffron shreds, soaked in 2 teaspoons water
- 1 qt. fish stock (see p. 21), or 1 qt. water plus 2 lbs. fish bones
  Freshly ground black pepper
- 2 lbs. mussels, scrubbed and bearded
- ½ cup dry white wine
  Salt
- 2 tablespoons lemon juice
- 2 egg yolks
- ½ cup heavy cream
- 1 tablespoon finely chopped parsley

Melt butter in a kettle. Add onion, cover, and cook slowly for 5 to 7 minutes, or until wilted. Add garlic, celery, and potatoes and cook, stirring, for 3 minutes.

(continued)

Add bay leaf, thyme, saffron and water, stock or water and fish bones, and a few grinds of pepper to onion mixture. Cover and boil slowly for 20 minutes.

Put mussels in a kettle with wine, cover, and cook over medium-high heat, shaking pan from time to time. After 5 minutes the mussels should be open. Remove with a slotted spoon. Steam any unopened mussels a few minutes longer. Any mussels still closed after this should be discarded. Remove mussels from shells, and set aside.

Strain mussel juice and cooking liquid through a fine-mesh sieve lined with a coffee filter or dampened napkin that has been squeezed out and add to boiling soup. Taste and season with salt and pepper, if necessary. Remove fish bones if used. Put soup through the fine disk of food mill or processor and through a fine mesh sieve to make sure all bones are removed.

Bring back to a boil, stirring. Add lemon juice. Remove from heat.

☆Whisk egg yolks in a bowl with the cream. Whisk in 1 cup of the hot soup in a thin, steady stream, then stir this mixture into the remaining soup. Reheat gently, stirring, to just below a simmer. Add reserved mussels and garnish with chopped parsley.

Light variation

☆Omit egg yolks and cream. After adding lemon juice, add mussels and garnish with chopped parsley.

Notes

If soup is to be served hot, it can be prepared 1 day in advance up to the point of adding the egg yolks liaison. Cool, cover, and refrigerate. If it is to be served cold, finish completely, cool uncovered, then cover and refrigerate for 1 day.

2 lbs. small cherrystone clams can be substituted for the mussels.

Be careful with the salt. Mussel and clam juice is very salty because it is mostly sea water. Sea water contains 25 grams of salt per liter, or about 4 teaspoons per quart.

3
SAUCES

"*Travaillez bien votre sauce,*" the great Escoffier advised, and French cooks do in fact devote much care and attention to their sauces. But while many of these traditional sauces triumphantly enhance the taste of the foods they accompany, not all are satisfactory in other ways. Many take too long to prepare. Many more, with their lavish quantities of butter, flour, and cream, repeatedly boiled down to concentrate, are very fattening. And some, made with cholesterol-rich egg yolks, represent, in the long run, a threat to health.

What we have done, then, is to

• speed up the preparation of the stocks that strengthen and extend sauces, in some cases cutting the time from hours to minutes;

• eliminate the sauce bases known as brown sauce and white sauce, both based on the butter-and-flour thickener called *roux;*

• reduce the fat and cholesterol in sauces while preserving—and even concentrating and improving—their superb flavors.

The best sauces, which are also the quickest and most easily prepared, are those made from the caramelized juices of meat and fowl left sticking to the bottoms of skillets or roasting pans. Such a sauce is invariably delicious, but there often isn't enough of it to go around. Hence the need for stocks—concentrated broths from the bones and meat, fowl, or fish, plus vegetables—to extend and strengthen pan sauces.

French sauces divide into six categories: the hollandaises, mayonnaises, vinaigrettes, butter sauces, *roux*-based sauces, and pan sauces. We haven't banished any of these from our cuisine but, instead, have found first-rate light-version alternatives for each.

REPLACING BROWN SAUCE

Brown sauce—the *roux*-laden and fattening sauce base—is the traditional strengthener-extender of pan glazes derived from meat. To replace it in this role we call for concentrated stock that has been boiled down and reduced slightly. Reduction, long and firmly established in classical cookery, yields a sauce that is fresh, healthful, and notably faithful to the taste of the original meat or fowl. It can be done readily in a home kitchen if the stocks are available. Stock can be reduced to a slightly syrupy glaze or, alternately, a gravy.

SAUCE BRUNE REDUITÉ: REDUCED BROWN SAUCE

After meat or fowl has been sautéed, its caramelized juices, sticking to the bottom of the skillet, are dissolved over heat with wine, brandy, vinegar, or lemon, the acid in each of these dissolving agents making for a good emulsion and imparting a welcome tartness, in the process called *déglaçage*, or deglazing. Then these juices are reduced (boiled down) until they are slightly syrupy. Concentrated stock is added and reduced again. Finally, the mixture is bound with either butter, cream, ricotta or a touch of starch.

Sometimes the caramelized juices are deglazed with wine or stock and the binding agent added directly to the sauce, skipping the reduction. These so-called *déglaçage* sauces are less strong and full-bodied than the ones that have been reduced.

REPLACING WHITE SAUCE

To replace the *roux*-based white sauce in a recipe we follow the same procedure as for replacing brown sauce, except that no deglazing takes place. The cooking juices of veal, chicken, or fish, strengthened by a concentrated stock, are first reduced and then thickened with either a touch of cornstarch, a vegetable purée, cream, or ricotta. If a plain béchamel is called for, our Snow Sauce makes an excellent substitute most of the time.

DEGLAZING AND REDUCING IN AN OVEN

Some of our brown sauces are made in the roasting pan while a piece of meat or fowl is roasting; they faithfully reflect the flavor of their source and are, again, very easy to make. Deglazing and reducing are accomplished by adding wine and stock to the roasting meats, not all at once, but in small amounts, so as not to wash out the developing sauce. Basting during the roasting keeps the meat or fowl moist, but the sauce, too, benefits by the continuous accretion of succulent juices. Carrots, onions, and celery, cut in chunks, are added, together with any bones that might have been removed from the roast. Alternatively, vegetables can be strained into the sauce when the roast is done—or the sauce is used as is. About ten minutes before the end of the roasting, you may want to add herbs and spices for a truly marvelous sauce. Ultimately, the sauce resembles a concentrated gravy. You can serve it as is or thicken it with a touch of cornstarch or vegetable purée and enrich it with butter or cream.

Note: The pan must conduct heat well and be of appropriate dimensions, or the sauce will remain colorless and without sufficient body or will reduce too fast.

RICOTTA: KEY TO A SENSIBLE DIET
WITH NO LOSS OF TASTE OR TEXTURE

To counter the fattening effect of cream in sauces, you can substitute *fromage blanc* (white cheese) as the blender and binder. In our opinion, however, American-made ricotta (another low-fat white cheese, originally Italian) performs this task even better. Ricotta has a very fine texture and a mild, delicate, nutty flavor, imparting to a sauce, as cream does, a velvety-smooth consistency. What's more you need less ricotta than cream to bind a sauce. Like cream, it doesn't affect the taste of a preparation, but unlike cream it can't be reduced or it will curdle. Consequently, no reconcentration of fat can occur, as happens when cream is reduced, so the sauce remains light. And the flavor of ricotta is so subtle, elusive, and unobtrusive that the addition of a tablespoon or two of cream to the sauce before serving will convince almost anyone that the sauce was made with cream only.

BINDING SAUCES WITH RICOTTA

Some liquid is needed to thin ricotta to the right consistency. In a reduced sauce, the ricotta should be thinned with just enough of the reduction to give the sauce maximum taste and a good consistency, but not so much that the ricotta becomes runny (see recipe for this). You can always thin your sauce a little later with stock or milk, but you can only thicken it by adding more ricotta, which will make it blander and less flavorful. So it's important to start out with just enough liquid and no more. Remember that though cream binds a sauce by reduction, ricotta cannot be reduced because it will curdle.

In the case of a simple *déglaçage* sauce, ricotta should be thinned with milk before it is added to the glaze. At the end, the addition of a few tablespoons of cream gives the sauce extra smoothness without overly enriching it.

TIPS FOR COOKING WITH RICOTTA

1. Add lemon juice in a sauce bound with ricotta after the sauce has been brought just to the boil, thickened, and removed from the heat. Adding lemon juice to the deglaçage or reduction before the ricotta is added will curdle the sauce when heated. It should be added ½ teaspoon at a time, beating between additions, following the instructions in the specific recipe. The lemon juice causes a spontaneous thickening of the ricotta; you can thin it with stock or milk.

There is no curdling problem with uncooked sauces and dressings. You can add lemon juice to raw blended ricotta or blend the two together without curdling the cheese.

2. It is most important that the ricotta is fresh. It spoils rapidly when opened, even when kept refrigerated, and can give a cheesy taste to food instead of a fresh nutty one. Check the last sale date on the bottom of the container. Be sure the date is several weeks away. When opened, freeze it in convenient portions. A container weighs 425 grams or about a pound, enough for four *déglaçage* sauces. Defrost in the refrigerator and blend for 2 minutes or until it is free of granules.

3. Ricotta is at its peak of effectiveness at binding and imparting smoothness at the moment it comes to a boil.

A NOTE ON EGG-YOLK LIAISON

In classic French cooking a number of clear sauces and soups are bound by egg yolks, which, of course, enrich as they bind. We have banished this so-called egg-yolk liaison from our light variations, not so much because it enriches preparations unduly as because egg yolks, with their cholesterol, endanger health. We have long felt, too, that egg yolks contribute no particular character to the flavor. Altogether, the elimination of this practice is, we feel, long overdue, and a cause not for regret but satisfaction.

MAYONNAISE BY HAND

Yield: 1¾ cups

>   2 egg yolks
> 1½ cups salad oil, or 1 cup salad oil and ½ cup olive oil
>   Salt
>   Freshly ground black pepper
>   2 teaspoons Dijon mustard
>   1 tablespoon red wine vinegar or lemon juice
>   2 teaspoons hot water

Put egg yolks in a mixing bowl and whisk for a few seconds. Add 3 to 4 tablespoons oil, ½ teaspoon at a time, whisking rapidly. Make sure each addition is completely absorbed before adding the next. Add salt and pepper to taste, 1 teaspoon mustard, and 1 tablespoon vinegar. Mix well.

Start adding remaining oil while whisking rapidly. Add by teaspoons until mayonnaise begins to thicken, then add by table-spoons. If mayonnaise thickens too much between additions of oil, add more vinegar. Add remaining mustard and beat in the hot water.

Notes

Mayonnaise will keep 2 to 3 days covered and refrigerated.

The hot water dissolves the salt which can cause the sauce to separate. An electric beater can be used instead of a whisk and is faster. Oil can be added in larger additions after the first step. The vinegar and mustard are added gradually so as not to liquefy the mayonnaise.

One egg yolk can absorb up to ¾ cup oil.

Serve mayonnaise with cold meats, fish, cold vegetables, and salads.

PROCESSOR MAYONNAISE

Yield: 1 cup

    1 egg
    2 teaspoons Dijon mustard
      Salt
      Freshly ground black pepper
    1 tablespoon red wine vinegar or lemon juice
    1 cup salad oil, or ⅔ cup salad oil and ⅓ cup olive oil

Put egg, mustard, salt and pepper to taste in a food processor and blend for 5 to 10 seconds, or until combined.

✩Continue blending, adding oil gradually in a very thin stream. As mayonnaise thickens, oil can be added faster. Add vinegar and blend for 5 seconds.

Light variation

✩Instead of 1 cup oil, use ⅔ cup oil and ⅓ cup ricotta, blended in food processor. Add oil as directed. Blend in vinegar and add ricotta. Blend for 5 seconds.

Notes

Mayonnaise with only oil keeps for 3 days, covered and refrigerated. The light version with ricotta keeps for 1 day.

The mayonnaise can be made with 1 egg yolk only. It gives a firmer, thicker consistency.

DILL AND MUSTARD MAYONNAISE

Yield: 1 cup

6 to 8 sprigs (½ bunch) dill
¾ cup oil
4 tablespoons plain yogurt
1 egg yolk
1 teaspoon vinegar
2 tablespoons Dijon mustard

Snip dill and put in a blender with 1 tablespoon oil and 1 tablespoon yogurt. Blend until dill is liquefied, scraping down sides of container as needed. Reserve.

Make a thick mayonnaise by hand or machine: Put egg yolk in bowl and beat with a whisk for a few seconds. Add 3 to 4 tablespoons oil, ½ teaspoon at a time, while whisking rapidly. (Make sure each addition is completely absorbed before adding the next.) Add salt and pepper to taste, 2 teaspoons Dijon mustard, and 1 teaspoon vinegar. Mix well.

Start adding remaining oil while whisking rapidly. Add by teaspoons until mayonnaise begins to thicken; then add by tablespoons. Stir in remaining Dijon mustard and yogurt and the reserved puréed dill.

Notes

The mayonnaise will keep for 1 day, refrigerated and covered.

This sauce is delicious with cold steamed mussels or cold poached shrimp or fish.

GREEN MAYONNAISE
Mayonnaise Verte

Yield: 1 cup

⅓ cup fresh watercress or dill
2 tablespoons fresh parsley
½ tablespoon fresh tarragon leaves, or ½ teaspoon dried tarragon
1 tablespoon oil
1 cup mayonnaise (see pp. 39–40)

Blend watercress, parsley, and tarragon in a blender with oil until liquefied. In bowl combine well with mayonnaise.

LEMONY HOLLANDAISE

Yield: 1 to 1⅓ cups

3 egg yolks
2 tablespoons cold water (for use with fish, use cold fish stock, see p. 21, if available, or court bouillon, see p. 22)
1 tablespoon lemon juice
Salt
Freshly ground black pepper
10 to 14 tablespoons butter, at room temperature

Whisk together egg yolks, water, lemon juice, and salt and pepper to taste in a small saucepan.

Put about 1½ inches water in a large saucepan and put small saucepan in it. Bring water to a simmer over moderate heat, whisking yolks steadily. Be sure to maintain the water just at a simmer and froth constantly, touching all surfaces of pan. Cook until the sauce has thickened to the consistency of mayonnaise.

Remove from heat, leaving smaller pan in larger pan. Immediately beat in butter, 1 tablespoon at a time, making sure each piece is thoroughly incorporated before adding the next.

Notes

When preparing a Hollandaise or Béarnaise, the liquid added to the egg yolks should equal the quantity of egg yolks. One egg yolk equals 1 tablespoon, so add 1 tablespoon liquid per egg yolk.

An egg yolk will absorb and form an emulsion with 3½ to 5½ tablespoons butter.

Hollandaise and Béarnaise will keep for up to 2 hours over water at 125°. Stir occasionally. (Or cool, cover, and refrigerate the sauce. Reheat in a larger pan of warm water.) Hollandaise or Béarnaise spoils if left over water at 85° as this temperature produces poisonous bacteria.

LIGHT HOLLANDAISE SAUCE
Sauce Hollandaise Allegée

Yield: ¾ cup

    1 tablespoon cornstarch
    2 egg yolks
    1 tablespoon butter
    ½ cup hot water
    1 tablespoon lemon juice
       Salt
       Freshly ground black pepper

Put the cornstarch, egg yolks, and butter in a small saucepan. Put about 1½ inches water in large saucepan and put the small pan in it. Bring water to a simmer over moderate heat, whisking yolks steadily, touching all surfaces of pan, until well combined. Remove from large pan and quickly put in hot water in a thin, steady stream. Add lemon juice and season with salt and pepper to taste. Return to large pan, and cook, frothing over moderately high heat until sauce has a creamy light consistency. Water can now reach a slow boil, but be careful not to overcook and curdle the sauce.

Notes

The sauce will keep, in the large pan, covered, for 1 to 2 hours. If sauce cools and needs to be reheated do so in larger pan of water at 125°.

BÉARNAISE SAUCE

Yield: 1½ cups

  ½ cup white wine vinegar
  ½ cup dry white wine
  1 tablespoon minced shallots
  2½ teaspoons dried tarragon, or 4 teaspoons minced
      fresh tarragon
      Dried thyme
  ¼ bay leaf
  2 teaspoons minced parsley
  6 whole black peppercorns, crushed
      Salt
  3 egg yolks
  1 tablespoon cold water
  10 to 12 tablespoons butter, at room temperature

Put vinegar, wine, shallots, 2 teaspoons dried tarragon or 3 tea-spoons fresh, a tiny pinch of thyme, bay leaf, 1 teaspoon parsley, peppercorns, and salt to taste in a small saucepan. Bring to a boil, and boil slowly until reduced to 2 tablespoons. Strain, pressing with back of spoon to extract all liquid. Reserve liquid and discard solids.

Rinse saucepan. Add egg yolks and whisk for 30 seconds. Stir in water and reserved cold reduction. Put about 1½ inches water in a larger saucepan and put smaller pan in it. Bring water to a sim-mer over moderate heat, frothing yolks steadily, touching all sur-faces of pan. (This step lightens and increases the volume of the sauce.) Do not let water boil or mixture will curdle (if mixture does curdle, blend in food processor or blender until smooth). Cook, whisking, until sauce thickens to the consistency of light cream. Remove from heat, leaving pan in larger pan, and beat in butter 1 tablespoon at a time, making sure each piece is thoroughly incorpo-rated before adding the next. Stir in remaining tarragon and pars-ley. Season with salt and pepper, if necessary.

Notes

Béarnaise will keep, covered, in the larger pan at 125° for 1 to 2 hours. If sauce cools and needs to be reheated, do so over warm water.

One egg yolk can absorb 3½ to 5½ tablespoons butter.

LIGHT BÉARNAISE SAUCE
Sauce Béarnaise Légère

Yield: ¾ cup

    2 tablespoons white wine vinegar
    1 tablespoon minced shallots
 1½ teaspoons dried tarragon, or 1 tablespoon minced
      fresh tarragon
    2 teaspoons minced parsley
    6 whole black peppercorns, crushed
      Dried thyme
  ¼ bay leaf
      Salt
      Freshly ground pepper
    2 egg yolks
    1 tablespoon butter
    1 tablespoon cornstarch
  ½ cup hot water

Put vinegar, shallots, 1 teaspoon dried or two teaspoons fresh tarragon, 1 teaspoon parsley, peppercorns, a tiny pinch of thyme, and bay leaf in a small saucepan. Simmer slowly until reduced to 1 tablespoon. Strain, pressing with the back of a spoon to extract all liquid. Discard solids and reserve liquid.

Rinse saucepan and add egg yolks, butter, and cornstarch. Put about 1½ inches of water in a large saucepan and put the small saucepan in it. Heat the water to just below a simmer, whisking the egg yolks steadily, touching all surfaces of the pan, until well combined.

Remove small pan from large pan, pour in hot water into

beaten egg yolks in a thin, steady stream, beating, and add reserved reduction. Season with salt and pepper, if necessary. Put saucepan back into large pan and cook, frothing, over moderately high heat until sauce has a creamy light consistency. Water can now reach a slow boil, but be careful not to overcook and curdle the sauce. Remove from large pan and stir in remaining tarragon and parsley.

Notes

Sauce will keep, covered, in the large pan for 1 to 2 hours. If sauce cools and needs to be reheated, do so over large pan of water heated to 125°.

To make a Sauce Choron, omit tarragon and add 1½ teaspoons tomato extract.

ISABELLE'S VINAIGRETTE

Yield: ½ cup

    1 tablespoon red wine vinegar or lemon juice
    2 teaspoons Dijon mustard
      Salt
      Freshly ground black pepper
    1 teaspoon finely chopped fresh tarragon, or ½ teaspoon
      dried tarragon (optional)
    1 tablespoon finely chopped parsley
    1 medium shallot, or 2 scallions, minced
    4 tablespoons oil, or 2 tablespoons olive oil and 2 tablespoons
      corn oil, or 4 tablespoons heavy cream

Combine vinegar in a soup plate with mustard, salt and pepper to taste, tarragon, if desired, parsley, and shallot. Mix well with a fork. Add oil all at once and beat with fork, keeping the tines flat against the bottom of the dish and making a horizontal circular motion. The dressing will emulsify.

To make dressing in a food processor, cut shallot or scallions roughly. Do not chop tarragon or parsley. Put ingredients in food processor and turn on/off 3 or 4 times until well blended.

Notes

Dressing made with vinegar and oil only keeps in refrigerator for 2 to 3 days. Remove from refrigerator 15 minutes before use and beat a little before tossing with salad.

If using lemon juice, do not make dressing more than 2 hours beforehand. Lemon tends to lose its fresh taste while standing.

Dressing made with cream should be prepared shortly before using.

Variations

The proportions of 1 tablespoon vinegar or lemon juice to 4 tablespoons oil make a mild dressing perfect for tender lettuce such as Boston, leaf, or Bibb. For a stronger dressing, use 1½ tablespoons vinegar or lemon to 4 tablespoons oil which is good for green beans, tomatoes, and cucumbers.

Add 1 hard-cooked egg for cold vegetable salads like broccoli, asparagus, or leeks. Add it chopped to the handmade dressing, or quartered for the last on/off burst of the processor.

LIGHT SHALLOT SAUCE
Sauce aux Eschalotes Légère

Yield: 2 cups

6 tablespoons minced shallots
2 tablespoons white wine vinegar
½ cup dry white wine
½ cup water
2 tablespoons heavy cream
5 tablespoons cold butter, cut in pieces
1⅓ cups ricotta, blended in food processor
    Salt
    Freshly ground black pepper

Put shallots, vinegar, wine, and water in a small saucepan and reduce over moderate heat to 1 tablespoon. Put about 1½ inches of water in a large saucepan and put small pan in it. Bring water to a simmer. Add cream. Beat in the butter, 1 tablespoon at a time, making sure each piece is thoroughly incorporated before adding the next. Whisk constantly. Add ricotta and salt and pepper to taste, beating until sauce is well combined and lukewarm.

Strain sauce through a fine mesh sieve, if desired.

Notes

This sauce is especially delicious with poached fish. Sauce will keep, covered, over water at 125°.

UNCOOKED TOMATO SAUCE
Sauce aux Tomates Crues

Yield: 4 cups

   1½ lbs. vine-ripened egg or regular tomatoes, peeled, seeded, and diced, or a 35-oz. can Italian plum tomatoes, drained
   2 cloves garlic, minced
   Juice of ½ lemon
   1 tablespoon fresh chopped basil, or ½ teaspoon dried
   1 tablespoon fresh chopped parsley
   Salt
   Freshly ground black pepper
   1 cup ricotta, blended in food processor
   2 tablespoons heavy cream

Put tomatoes, garlic, lemon juice, basil, and parsley in a stainless steel bowl. Add salt and pepper to taste. Mix well and let stand at room temperature to blend flavors for at least ½ hour. Adjust seasoning, if necessary.

Just before serving, add ricotta, combine well, and add cream.

Notes

Tomatoes can be puréed instead of diced.

Toss immediately with hot, drained pasta, or serve with poached eggs, broiled chicken, or poached fish.

VEGETABLE SAUCE
Sauce aux Légumes

Yield: 2¼ cups

- ½ cup vegetables used in poaching meat, poultry, or fish, or 6 tablespoons vegetables and 2 tablespoons mushrooms if they were used
- 1 cup stock
- 2 to 3 tablespoons heavy cream
- ½ cup ricotta, blended in food processor
  Salt
  Freshly ground black pepper

In food processor or blender blend vegetables and stock until smooth. Pour into a saucepan and stir in cream and ricotta. Season with salt and pepper to taste. Bring to boil over moderate heat, stirring. Remove from heat immediately. Keep warm in a larger saucepan of water.

LIGHT MUSHROOM SAUCE
Sauce Légère aux Champignons

Serves: 6

- ¾ lb. Braised Mushrooms, prepared without butter or lemon juice (see p. 244)
- ¾ cup ricotta, blended in the food processor with ½ cup mushroom juice from Braised Mushrooms
- 2 tablespoons heavy cream
  Salt
  Freshly ground black pepper
- 1 tablespoon finely chopped parsley

In a saucepan combine the drained mushrooms with the ricotta mixture and the cream. Bring to a boil slowly, stirring with a wooden spatula. Remove from the heat immediately and add salt and pepper to taste. Stir in parsley. (If necessary, thin the sauce with more mushroom juice or milk.)

TOMATO FONDUE
Fondue de Tomates

Yield: 2½ cups

2 tablespoons butter
1 large onion, thinly sliced
2 lbs. tomatoes, ripe but still firm, peeled, seeded, and chopped, or a 35-oz. can Italian plum tomatoes, drained
1 teaspoon finely chopped garlic
¼ teaspoon dried thyme
1 bay leaf
  Salt
  Freshly ground black pepper
1 tablespoon finely chopped fresh basil, or ½ teaspoon ground dried

☆Melt the butter in a skillet. Add onion and cook slowly, stirring occasionally, for 5 minutes, or until it is soft but not brown.

Stir in tomatoes, garlic, thyme, bay leaf, and salt and pepper to taste and cook over moderate heat, covered, for 3 minutes, or until tomatoes have released their juice. Boil briskly, uncovered, stirring often, for 7 to 10 minutes, or until juice has evaporated. Tomatoes should remain fairly chunky. Remove from heat, stir in basil, and season with salt and pepper, if necessary.

Light variation

☆Omit butter. Put onions and 3 tablespoons water in a skillet and steam over low heat, covered, until soft but not brown.

Notes

Cool sauce, and refrigerate, covered. Sauce keeps, refrigerated, for 1 to 2 days, or freeze.

To peel a lot of tomatoes, drop in a pot of boiling water and count to 30, then drain and peel.

Use this sauce with poached eggs, pasta, fish, chicken, or as a filling for omelets (see p. 58).

RICH VELOUTÉ SAUCE
Sauce Suprême

Yield: 3 cups

4 tablespoons butter
3 tablespoons flour
2 cups stock, heated to boiling
½ cup heavy cream
2 egg yolks
Salt
Freshly ground black pepper
1 to 2 tablespoons lemon juice

Melt 3 tablespoons butter in a heavy saucepan, blend in flour, and cook over low heat, stirring, until *roux* thickens and bubbles. Do not let it color. Remove from heat and let it stop bubbling. Add boiling stock all at once, whisking vigorously.

Bring sauce to a boil and boil, whisking, for 2 minutes. Be sure to reach the bottom and sides of pan with the whisk to avoid scorching and lumping. Gradually stir in cream and bring to boil slowly, stirring occasionally.

Combine egg yolks and remaining butter in a large bowl. Pour in ⅓ cup of the hot sauce in a thin, steady stream, stirring constantly. Add remaining sauce all at once, stir, and return to saucepan. Season with salt, pepper, and lemon juice to taste.

Notes

Use chicken or fish stock (see p. 19–22), depending on what is to be sauced.

If sauce is to be used immediately, keep warm, covered, in a larger saucepan of simmering water.

If sauce is not to be used immediately, film it with 2 to 3 tablespoons stock, or rub surface with a piece of chilled butter held on a knife tip to prevent a skin from forming. Let it cool, cover, and refrigerate. It will keep 1 to 2 days. Reheat over warm water.

SNOW SAUCE
Sauce Neige

Yield: 1¼ cups

> ¾ cup ricotta
> ⅓ cup milk
> 2 tablespoons heavy cream
> ½ cup grated Jarlsberg cheese
>   Salt
>   Freshly ground black pepper
>   Freshly grated nutmeg

Blend ricotta and milk in food processor until smooth. Combine with cream in a saucepan and bring slowly just to a boil, stirring. Remove from heat immediately, add cheese, and season with salt, pepper, and nutmeg. Keep sauce warm in a larger saucepan of warm water.

Notes

Use sauce on boiled vegetables, such as asparagus, broccoli, cauliflower, or artichoke hearts.

LEMON BUTTER SAUCE
Sauce au Beurre au Citron

Yield: 1 cup

> ¼ cup fish stock (see p. 21) or water
> ¼ cup lemon juice
> 1½ sticks chilled butter, softened with a rolling pin
>   Salt
>   Freshly ground black pepper

Combine stock and lemon juice in a heavy saucepan and boil slowly until reduced to 2½ tablespoons. Let cool for 30 seconds.

Beat in butter all at once, beating for 4 to 5 minutes, or until sauce is creamy. Season with salt and pepper to taste.

Notes

Sauce can be reheated in a larger saucepan of lukewarm water for 1 to 2 seconds. If water is hotter than lukewarm, sauce will separate.

Beating in the cold butter all at once produces a smooth, creamy emulsion.

GREEN PEPPERCORN BUTTER
Beurre au Poivre Vert

Yield: 1 cup

  2 sticks (½ lb.) butter
    Salt
  2 tablespoons finely chopped parsley
  1 tablespoon green peppercorns, drained and roughly chopped
  2 tablespoons lemon juice
  1½ tablespoons Dijon mustard

☆Blend all ingredients in a food processor until smooth and thick.

Sprinkle water on a sheet of wax paper 10 inches long. Spread the butter mixture on the paper and roll it into a sausage 1½ inches thick. Twist ends closed and store in the freezer. Cut a slice whenever needed and return the roll to the freezer.

Light variation

☆In place of the butter use 8 tablespoons butter and ½ cup ricotta. The light variation may separate a bit because of the lemon juice, but continue to blend and it will regain a creamy consistency.

Notes

Butter will keep for a month in the freezer.

Dampening the wax paper keeps the butter from sticking.

If the butter is to be used on beef brochettes or broiled meat or chicken, add additional mustard to taste.

SHRIMP BUTTER
Beurre de Crevettes

Yield: 1½ cups

> 2 sticks (½ lb.) butter
> ¼ lb. medium shrimp, shelled and deveined
> 1 large shallot, minced
> 2 tablespoons lemon juice
>   Salt
>   Freshly ground black pepper
> 2 tablespoons finely chopped parsley

Heat 1 tablespoon butter in a skillet until hot but not brown. Add shrimp and shallot and sauté, stirring and tossing, for 5 minutes, or until the shrimp turn pink and are cooked through. Let cool.

Blend the mixture in a food processor until smooth. Transfer to a bowl. ☆Blend remaining butter, lemon juice, and salt and pepper to taste in a food processor until smooth and creamy. Add shrimp mixture and parsley and blend with a few on/off turns.

Sprinkle water on a sheet of wax paper 12 inches long. Spread the shrimp mixture on it and roll into a sausage shape 1½ inches thick. Twist the ends of the roll closed and store in the freezer.

Light variation

☆In place of ½ lb. butter, use 1 stick (8 tablespoons) butter and ½ cup ricotta. Blend the 8 tablespoons butter with the ricotta, lemon juice, and salt and pepper to taste. This variation may separate a bit because of the lemon juice, but continue to blend and it will reach a creamy consistency.

Notes

Dampening the wax paper keeps the butter from sticking.

This butter will keep for a month in the freezer. Cut off slices as they are needed.

Use the butter for poached fish or as a sauce for broiled fish.

4
EGGS

The eggs you buy by the dozen in your supermarket have a re-markable range of potential uses. Coming in its own container (which may double as a serving cup), an egg can be cooked in minutes and emerge in any of several appetizing forms. And even as it adds flavor to a developing dish it can work actively in it, as a thickener, a binder, an emulsifier, a leavener, or a glaze. No wonder the American Egg Board calls it

THE INCREDIBLE, EDIBLE EGG

Being so versatile, eggs turn up in recipes throughout this book. Below, we show you techniques for making four basic egg dishes: omelets, hard-cooked eggs, scrambled eggs, and poached eggs. (Here, as throughout these pages, the term egg signifies an extra large one, weighing about 2¼ ounces or 65 grams.)

Eggs are low in calories and high in protein: Two provide as much high-quality protein—about 15 grams—as a serving of meat, poultry, or fish, but only 190 calories. They do, however, contain some fat. The fat in the yolk of an egg is saturated and, therefore, very high in cholesterol (350 milligrams per egg); for this reason the American Heart Association recommends that you consume only three or four eggs a week. For a family of four that works out to three or four cakes or two omelets weekly, which hardly consti-tutes deprivation and in any case makes for a good dietary balance between eggs and other basic foods used in French cuisine. (Remember that the A.H.A.'s caution about cholesterol doesn't apply to dishes made with the *whites* of eggs.)

TIPS

Buy only eggs bearing the USDA Grades AA or A, as they are the freshest. (Eggs lose weight as they age.)

Cook eggs over low heat, or if over high heat, as with an omelet, cook them quickly. Too high a temperature or too prolonged cooking makes eggs tough.

Remove eggs from the heat a few seconds before they seem done as they will continue to cook in the skillet.

Eggs separate most readily when they are cold.

Old egg whites are better for beating than fresh whites. Refrigerated in an uncovered jar, whites will keep for as much as a month.

To freeze whites for future use drop them in an ice tray, the white of one egg to each compartment, and freeze; when they are frozen transfer the solid egg-white cubes to a plastic bag and store in the freezer.

When you add eggs to a hot mixture, stir a little of the mixture into the eggs first to warm them and keep them from curdling.

A handy rule of thumb is: one egg yolk equals about 1 tablespoon; the white of one egg equals about 2 tablespoons.

HARD-COOKED EGGS
Oeufs Durs

Prick each egg twice with egg pricker or pin at broad end of egg (there is an air pocket). Put in saucepan and cover with cold water by ¼ inch. Bring just to a boil and lower heat to very low. Water should not move. Keep eggs in hot water for 14 to 15 minutes. Remove eggs one at a time. Knock egg on a hard surface all over to crack the shell and peel gently under cold running water. (Do not cool them in cold water or it will be difficult to peel them.)

Notes

Piercing eggs keeps them from cracking and thus prevents whites from leaking.

If eggs are cooked at low heat, not boiled, the outside of the yolks will not discolor, which can spoil its taste. The egg will be more tender, too.

It is very important not to cool the eggs. If they are cooled, the inner skin sticks to the egg and it is difficult to peel it well. Kept hot, steam stays between eggs and skin and the shell comes off easily.

Cold hard-cooked eggs are delicious on a leaf of lettuce with wedges of tomatoes topped with vinaigrette or mayonnaise. They can be served warm, topped with Sauce Neige and put under the broiler (see p. 52).

Hard-cooked eggs are sublime in *Asparagus à la Flamande:*

- 6 warm stalks of boiled asparagus per person
- 2 warm hard-cooked eggs per person, halved
  Chopped parsley
- 3 tablespoons melted butter per person
  Salt
  Freshly ground black pepper

Arrange asparagus on each plate with the hard-cooked eggs and sprinkle with parsley. Let each guest make a sauce by crushing egg on plate and blending in the butter along with salt and pepper to taste. Each guest dips his asparagus in the sauce.

PLAIN OMELET
Omelette Nature

Serves: 2

> 4 eggs
> Salt
> Freshly ground black pepper
> 1 tablespoon butter

Special equipment

6-inch (bottom diameter) omelet pan with curved sides (A stoneware non-stick surface is excellent.)

Beat eggs in a bowl with a fork or whisk until well blended, about 30 strokes. Season with salt and pepper.

Heat omelet pan over moderate heat for 1 to 2 minutes. Add butter and tilt the pan so the butter swirls and films the bottom and sides of the pan. When the butter has just started to turn light brown, add the eggs all at once. Let set for 3 seconds. Then stir rapidly with a fork, holding the tines flat against the bottom of the pan. Begin making a few small circles counterclockwise in the center of the pan. Then move to the outer edge and stir all around the outer edge, making small counterclockwise circles (in effect, a curli-cued circle). The eggs will form creamy layers. When almost set, lift edges and let any uncooked egg run underneath. Lift edges all round to make sure omelet is loose. Tilt the pan and use the fork to help fold omelet over in thirds.

Tilt the pan so that the omelet slides onto the curved edge of the pan. Grasp the handle from underneath and hold the pan at a 45° angle. Hold a warm plate on an angle up to the pan and turn the omelet out onto the plate by turning the pan almost upside down over the plate.

Notes

Some good fillings are: sprigs of crisp watercress arranged on top before folding (use about a quarter of a bunch); ¼ lb. green beans blanched and sautéed in a little butter with 2 slices of pros-ciutto; ¼ lb. Sautéed Mushrooms (see p. 245); ¼ cup Tomato Fondue (see p. 50); ¼ cup Country-style Vegetables (see pp. 254–255).

SCRAMBLED EGGS WITH HERBS
Oeufs Brouillés aux Herbes

Serves: 4

> 3½ tablespoons butter, at room temperature
> 6 eggs
> Salt
> Freshly ground black pepper
> ¼ cup heavy cream
> 2 tablespoons finely chopped parsley
> 2 tablespoons finely chopped chives
> 1 teaspoon finely chopped fresh tarragon, or ½ teaspoon dried tarragon, ground
> 4 toast shells (see p. 63)

☆Spread butter all over the bottom and sides of a saucepan.

Fill a soup plate or cake pan larger than the cooking saucepan with cold water and set aside. This will be used to cool and stop the cooking of the eggs.

In a bowl combine the eggs, salt and pepper to taste, cream, half the parsley and chives, and the tarragon, and beat just to break and blend the eggs, about 20 strokes.

Set the prepared saucepan over very low heat. Pour in the egg mixture and whisk constantly, reaching all over the bottom and sides of the pan, making figure eights so the mixture moves and cooks evenly.

As soon as the eggs just begin to set (it will only take them a few seconds to become the smooth, creamy consistency desired), remove the pan from the heat and put it immediately into the bowl of cold water for about 10 seconds to stop the cooking.

Spoon the eggs into toast shells, sprinkle with the remaining parsley and chives, and top with the toast lids. Or spoon into a warm dish (not too hot or the eggs will continue to cook), and serve immediately.

Light Variation

☆Use only 2 tablespoons of butter to coat the saucepan.

(continued)

Notes

If the eggs become overcooked, remove the pan from the heat immediately and vigorously whisk in 1 beaten egg.

To prepare the eggs in advance, put the egg mixture in the buttered pan with the seasonings 2 to 3 hours before cooking and refrigerate. The eggs will take on the flavor of the herbs even more.

POACHED EGGS
Oeufs Pochés

Serves: 2

    5 cups water
    ¼ cup white vinegar
    4 eggs
       Salt

Special equipment
    2½-quart saucepan

Bring water and vinegar to a full boil in a large saucepan. Break each egg into an individual cup and sprinkle a small pinch of salt on each yolk. With the water at a full boil, slip 2 eggs at a time into the water with a quick motion. Let boil for 5 to 7 seconds to help eggs to re-form so whites do not spread out. Lower heat and simmer for 3 minutes, or until whites are firm to the touch but yolk is still soft. Remove eggs from water with a slotted spoon and transfer to a bowl of cold water if they are to be used cold, or to a bowl of warm water (140°) if they are to be used warm.

When ready to serve, remove with a slotted spoon, dry on a towel, and trim edges, if necessary.

Notes

The bubbling of the water helps the whites to close up and set around the yolks, and it is essential that the water does not stop boiling when the eggs are slipped in.

Poached eggs are superb served with Creamed Spinach (see p. 247), Country-style Vegetables (see pp. 254–255), or a vegetable purée, nestled in a toast shell, and topped with Hollandaise Sauce (see pp. 42–43) or Béarnaise Sauce (see p. 45). Or put eggs in a puff pastry shell with asparagus tips and Hollandaise.

It is essential to have very fresh eggs. Eggs from a reliable health food store work very well. To determine how fresh an egg is, put it in cold water to cover completely. If the egg lies horizontally, it is 1 to 5 days old. If it lies obliquely, the egg is 5 to 10 days old; if the egg stands straight up, it is 15 to 21 days old. If the egg floats, throw it away. An egg loses weight as it gets older.

CHEESE PUFFS
Délicieux au Fromage

Serves: 6

    1 cup water
    6 tablespoons butter, cut into pieces if chilled
    ½ teaspoon salt
    1 cup all-purpose flour, sifted
    4 eggs
      Freshly ground black pepper
    1 cup grated Swiss cheese, or ½ cup each grated Swiss and
      Parmesan
    1 bunch parsley, washed and thoroughly dried, with part of
      the stems left on

Special equipment
    Deep fryer with basket

Bring water to a boil in a saucepan with the butter and salt. The butter should melt before the water begins to steam and evaporate. Remove from the heat and add the flour all at once, beating rapidly with a whisk or spatula. Put the pan back on medium-high heat and continue beating with a wooden spoon for 5 to 7 seconds to dry the dough.

Beat 2 eggs lightly together and add to the dough, beating vigorously with a whisk or spatula until well incorporated. The dough should be of a smooth, creamy consistency. Beat the third egg lightly and add to the dough, beating vigorously until totally incorporated and the dough is smooth and creamy. Beat the fourth egg lightly. Beat half of it into the dough. Check the consistency of the dough; when lifted, it should fall off a spatula in 4 to 5 seconds. If it does not, add the remaining egg (and perhaps an extra teaspoon of water) to get the correct consistency.

Use two spoons to shape the dough into balls about the size of walnuts: Scoop up a portion of dough with a spoon, shaping it by scraping it against the side of the bowl. (The dough will be quite sticky and the balls will not be perfectly shaped.) Use the second spoon to push the ball of dough into the hot oil. Stir in the grated cheese and taste for seasoning.

Make only a few balls at a time (depending on the size of the deep fryer), and cook in hot oil for 5 minutes, or until puffs are golden brown, triple in volume, and crisp. Do not overload the fryer or the puffs won't have room to expand properly or cook evenly. Remove at once and shake in the fry basket to drain. Turn out onto a warm platter lined with paper towels and keep warm in a low oven with the door open.

When all the dough is cooked, put the parsley sprigs into the deep fryer basket and lower into the hot oil. Fry for 1 to 2 seconds and lift out immediately. Shake well to drain. Mound the cheese puffs on a platter and garnish with fried parsley.

Notes

These delicious puffs are a perfect first course for a light dinner. If the oil is the proper temperature, it cooks the outside of the food immediately, sealing it, so that the food does not absorb the oil, which would make it heavy and greasy.

Smaller puffs, about the size of olives, can be made to serve with drinks.

CROUTONS AND TOAST SHELLS

Yield: 6

6 regular slices good-quality white bread, crusts removed (Try to find a semi-soft, unsweetened bread, not the spongy, cottony kind.)
2 tablespoons butter, softened

Preheat oven and baking sheet to 450°.

For soups and decoration, cut slices diagonally into 2 triangles. Butter both sides and put on the heated baking sheet. Bake for 1 to 2 minutes on each side, or until golden. Watch carefully because they brown quickly.

To make toast shells, cut the corners off the trimmed slices to make octagons. Butter both sides and put on the heated baking sheet. Bake for 1 to 2 minutes on each side, or until golden. Starting ½ inch from the edge of the bread, cut a shallow circle, holding the knife almost parallel to the bread and going about halfway through the bread. Carefully lift and pry out this circle. Cut the lid in half diagonally. Fill the center of the toast shell, top with a sauce, if desired, sprinkle with parsley, and arrange lid halves on top attractively.

Notes

When croutons are baked, they use less butter than when they are sautéed in butter in a skillet, which is the classic method of preparation.

Croutons and toast shells can be made in advance, but they should be crisped in a 350° oven just before serving.

To make a pretty garnish to surround a dish, dip one tip of a crouton into the sauce of a dish, then dip the same tip into chopped parsley.

Centers of toast shells can be filled with a poached egg and topped with Hollandaise Sauce (see pp. 42–43), Scrambled Eggs (see p. 59), or with Sautéed Mushrooms (see p. 245).

SPINACH QUICHE
Quiche aux Épinards

Serves: 6

6 qts. water
Salt
1½ lbs. fresh spinach, washed and coarse stems removed, or 2
10-oz. boxes frozen leaf spinach
1 tablespoon butter
1 shallot, minced
Freshly ground black pepper
Freshly grated nutmeg
1 lb. Short Pastry, made with whole egg and no sugar (see
p. 333)

Basic quiche mixture
4 eggs
2 cups heavy cream
Salt
Freshly ground black pepper
Freshly grated nutmeg

Special equipment
9-inch quiche pan, 1⅜ inches deep, with fluted sides and removable bottom

Bring water to a boil. Add 2½ tablespoons salt and the spinach. If
cooking fresh spinach, drain as soon as the leaves wilt. If using
frozen spinach, drain as soon as the frozen block separates into
leaves. Refresh by running under cold water.

Squeeze the spinach dry with the hands to remove the last
drop of water. This prevents the quiche from becoming soggy.
There should be about 1 cup of squeezed-out spinach. Chop the
spinach finely with a knife, or process briefly in a food processor.

Melt the butter in a skillet and add the shallot. Cook, stirring,
for 1 minute. Add the spinach and salt, pepper, and nutmeg to
taste. Cook over moderate heat, stirring, for 2 minutes, or until any
remaining moisture evaporates. Transfer to a bowl and let cool
slightly.

Preheat oven to 425°.

Sprinkle a pastry board lightly with flour and roll the pastry into a 13-inch circle about ⅛ inch thick. Roll the pastry carefully over the rolling pin and transfer it to the quiche pan. Put the dough in the pan and press lightly with the fingers so the dough conforms to the shape of the pan. Press a ¼-inch collar of dough to the inside of the rim and roll the rolling pin over the pan to cut off any excess dough. Push the dough collar above the rim of the pan and flute a decorative edge.

Line the pastry shell with foil and fill it with raw rice or beans to hold the dough against the pan during baking. Bake for 15 minutes, remove foil and rice or beans, and bake for 5 minutes, or until inside bottom is lightly colored.

Lower oven temperature to 375°.

Using a whisk, beat together the eggs, ☆cream, and salt, pepper, and nutmeg to taste. Stir in the cooled spinach mixture. Pour the filling into the precooked shell. Bake in the middle of the oven for 35 minutes, or until the top is puffy and the tip of a knife inserted in the center comes out clean.

Light variation

☆Substitute 1 cup milk for one of the cups of heavy cream.

BROCCOLI QUICHE
Quiche au Brocoli

Serves: 6

> 5 qts. water
> Salt
> 1 bunch broccoli
> Basic Quiche Mixture (see p. 64)
> Freshly ground black pepper
> Freshly grated nutmeg
> Prebaked pastry shell (see p. 64)

Bring 5 qts. water to a boil in a large pot. Add 2 tablespoons salt.

Cut off the tough bottom 1½ inches of the stem of each stalk of broccoli. Halve or quarter the stalks lengthwise, depending on thickness. Peel the stem of each piece down to the pale green inner flesh. Rinse under cold running water.

Plunge broccoli into the boiling water. Cover and bring back to a boil, then uncover and boil for 4 minutes. Drain and spread on a cloth or paper towels to dry completely.

Purée enough of the broccoli through a food mill or in a food processor to make ¾ cup smooth purée.

Preheat oven to 375°.

Stir purée into basic quiche mixture. Season with salt and pepper, if necessary, and nutmeg. Pour into prebaked pastry shell and bake for 35 to 40 minutes, or until top is golden brown and puffy and the tip of a knife inserted in the center comes out clean.

CRABMEAT QUICHE
Quiche au Crabe

Serves: 6

> 2 tablespoons butter
> 1 shallot, finely chopped
> ¾ cup cooked crabmeat (fresh, frozen, or canned)
> 2 teaspoons tomato paste
> 2 tablespoons Cognac
>   Salt
>   Freshly ground black pepper
>   Basic Quiche Mixture (see p. 64)
>   Prebaked pastry shell (see p. 64)
> 3 to 4 tablespoons freshly grated Jarlsberg or imported Swiss cheese

Melt 1 tablespoon butter in a skillet, add shallot, and cook for 1 to 2 minutes, or until soft. Add crabmeat, tomato paste, Cognac, and salt and pepper to taste. Stir well and cook for 1 to 2 minutes, or until Cognac has evaporated. Spread mixture in bottom of prebaked pastry shell.

Pour basic quiche mixture over crabmeat. Sprinkle top with cheese and dot with remaining butter. Bake 35–40 minutes in the middle of a preheated 375° oven, or until top is golden brown and puffy and the tip of a knife inserted in the center comes out clean.

STUFFED GREEN CRÊPES
Crêpes Vertes Fourrées

Yield: Stuffing for 40 crêpes
Serve 2 per person as first course
Serve 3 to 4 per person as main course

  1 cup loosely packed fresh dill
  ¼ cup milk
  Plain crêpe batter (using only 1 cup plus 1½ tablespoons of milk in the batter)
  ½ lb. mozzarella cheese, coarsely chopped or shredded to yield about 1 cup
  ½ lb. prosciutto, very finely chopped to yield about 1 cup
  2½ oz. salami, very finely chopped
  2½ cups ricotta cheese
  Salt
  Freshly ground black pepper
  ¼ cup freshly grated Parmesan cheese
  3½ tablespoons butter, melted

Put dill in the container of a blender and chop, periodically scraping down the sides of the container. (Because of the small amount involved, the food processor will not chop the dill well.) Add the milk and blend for 1 minute, or until the dill is completely liquefied.

Make the crêpe batter, adding the dill mixture with the milk. Cook the crêpes, following the instructions on p. 301.

Put the mozzarella, prosciutto, and salami in a bowl with the ricotta. Season lightly with salt and liberally with pepper and mix well.

(continued)

Preheat the oven to 350°.

Lightly butter a baking dish with some of the melted butter.

Put each crêpe, better-looking side down, on a flat surface and spoon 1 heaping tablespoon of the filling in the center. Fold opposite sides into the center and overlap to enclose the filling and make a square package. Arrange filled crêpes, seam side down, in the prepared baking dish. Sprinkle Parmesan over the crêpes and pour the remaining melted butter over all. Cover the dish with foil and bake for 20 minutes, or until the crêpes are completely heated through and the cheese is melted.

Notes

The recipe may be prepared 1 to 2 days in advance up to the point of baking. If the dish has been refrigerated up to cooking time, add 10 to 15 minutes to the baking time.

Stuffing recipe can be halved. However, the crêpes freeze beautifully when they are stuffed, so it is worthwhile making a double batch of crêpes and stuffing them to have them on hand. Remember, if the crêpe batter is doubled, double the amount of dill used.

5

FISH AND SHELLFISH

Today people are eating much more fish and shellfish than they once did. Why so? The explanation can't be economic; years ago most types of fish *were* cheap, but as demand for them grew their prices climbed to equal or exceed those of all but the costliest meats. No doubt pleasing tastes and textures have turned many people into habitual consumers of fish. No doubt other attributes have reinforced their appeal to cooks, notably the relative simplicity of preparing most types of fish. But there is another factor that certainly helps to account for this new popularity: the public's increased sophistication in matters nutritional and dietetic.

In terms of nutrition and diet, fish has a great deal going for it. Pound for pound, it provides about the same amount of high-quality protein as meat and poultry, plus phosphorus and, in the case of saltwater fish, iodine. Compared to almost all farm animals and fowl, fish is lower in fat, calories, and cholesterol. And its fat, unlike that in meat, is unsaturated. A particularly lean fish (see the table on page 76) may be less than 1 percent fat by weight, and even a fish containing lots of oil—up to 14 percent by weight in some species—will, if cooked by the methods we describe below, release enough oil to convert it into a non-fattening dish. Incidentally, the oil in the fatter fish—generally speaking the tastier ones, with firmer flesh—is distributed throughout its body, whereas the oil in leaner fish is concentrated in its liver. (A familiar example is cod liver oil, the cod being the leanest of all fish regularly consumed by humans.)

Because it contains so little fat, fish requires less time to cook than either meat or poultry. Thus it meets all three of the busy home cook's major requirements—being nutritious, non-fattening, and quickly prepared.

In part because the demand for them has made supplies scarcer, long-established favorites like salmon, striped bass, and sole have become expensive. As a result all sorts of less-familiar fish are showing up in fish stores and supermarkets like sea trout (weakfish), tile fish, blackfish, butterfish, monkfish, porgie, and whiting. This enables you to be adventurous and arrive at happy discoveries. To find out which you like, buy whatever is freshest and reasonably priced and take it home to cook by any of the four basic methods: poaching, steaming, broiling, or braising. But remember that fish spoils easily, so easily that just 1 hour in an overheated kitchen or car can do it in; fish should be refrigerated at once, and if you don't eat it that day you certainly should the next.

COOKING WHOLE VERSUS
COOKING IN PARTS

Fish sold in supermarkets or even fish stores are, as a rule, already filleted or cut into steaks or chunks, so there is no need for us to go into a lengthy discussion about how to dress them. We might say in passing, however, that, having been raised in the French school of cooking, we both used to take it for granted that there was only one proper way to cook a fish: i.e., whole, with the insides removed but not the head, tail, or bones. (On a practical plane this procedure permits you to retain the gelatinous juices of the bones, but you can do this just as well by placing the bones and the severed head around the fish as it cooks.) Now, however, we have come to accept the American view on the matter. "After ten years of showing my students how to cook a fish whole and watching them shrink away in horror at the end product," Isabelle Marique relates, "I realized that even though their squeamishness seemed a little excessive, they still had a point. As they told me, you don't eat the head or tail or bones, so why keep them? Besides, a headless, tailless, boneless fish is easier to serve and in the end just as appealing to look at." A useful fact to keep in mind when you *do* buy a whole fish is that its viscera, bones, head, and tail add up to about 60 percent of its weight.

When we call for a whole fish to be braised or broiled, we mean a boned fish and just that portion between the head and tail, consisting of two large fillets, one lying on top of the other, skin left on to keep the flesh from breaking. When a whole fish or a chunk is poached in a *court bouillon*, however, the bones stay in to hold it together.

AN EASILY AVOIDABLE PROBLEM: OVERCOOKING

An old French saying, coined before the advent of refrigeration, asserts that *C'est la sauce qui fait passer le poisson*—it's the sauce that makes fish edible. Its original meaning is obvious, but the saying can still apply. Today, a sauce isn't needed to cover up deterioration but the effects of overcooking. Says Isabelle Marique: "I will always remember Fridays at school when the entire building stank of fish and I had to face the awful prospect of eating it for lunch. In my opinion a fish should *never* be cooked to a point where its temperature goes above 150° F.; above that heat it loses its juices and dries out, and the flavor is completely lost. Then you have to hunt around for a sauce that will add some moisture to the poor dried-up thing and give it a little taste, so as to make it, like the fish in the old saying, at least edible."

Timing the cooking of fish. Nowadays there is no longer any excuse for overcooking fish, even if you have no thermometer. All you need is a clock, a flat object (book, postcard, cigarette box), and a ruler.

Of the several formulas we have seen for timing the cooking of fish, the most reliable, we find, is one developed by the Canadian Department of Fisheries. It is both simple and easy to remember. Whether you are poaching, steaming, broiling, baking, or roasting your fish, at whatever temperature the recipe specifies, you allow ten minutes for each inch of the fish's thickness—plus additional minutes corresponding to additional fractions of an inch.

To determine a fish's thickness, place it on its side on a counter and lay your flat object on its thickest part so it extends beyond the fish. With your rule measure the distance between the object and the counter. The same formula applies to thick fillets. However, we don't use the formula for poaching thin fillets such as flounder or sole. The timetable for these is described in the body of the individual recipe.

The Canadian formula works perfectly because, as we have learned by experimenting, the alloted time is just sufficient to allow the heat to penetrate to the center of the fish.

BUYING FISH AND SHELLFISH

Like fish, most shellfish (crustaceans and mollusks) are low in fat and calories; they also lend themselves readily to our light-version treatment. On the other hand, they are comparatively high in cholesterol. It is more on account of their out-of-sight prices, however, than their cholesterol content that we say nothing in this book about lobsters, crayfish, crabs, or oysters.

When shopping for fish, depend on your sense of smell. What you are after is a sweet-salty fragrance lacking any suggestion of fishiness. If you suspect that a fish may be contaminated, open its gills and sniff; a whiff of gasoline will tell you if it came from polluted waters.

Whole fish. Any fish you buy must be, before anything else, fresh. Look for bright red gills and a clear unveiled eye bulging up at you. Sniff for that slightly salty, non-fishy scent. And prod the fish with a finger. If it is fresh the flesh will spring back.

If it *is* fresh, a fish will display a good color; the flesh of a fresh salmon, for example, will show a fine pink. And any fresh fish will present a glossy appearance.

Remember, too, in calculating what you are paying for, that even with its viscera removed 40 percent of the weight of any whole fish represents sheer waste.

Fish fillets and scallops. These should be firm, glossy, and full-looking. In a fish store sole and flounder fillets are usually displayed on a tray in a bed of ice. If there is a considerable amount of liquid in the tray, assume that the fillets have lost some of their juice and have probably been there too long to warrant your taking them home.

Shrimp. If you live in a port with a shrimp fleet or if you have good reason to repose full confidence in your fish store, the "fresh shrimp" you are offered will probably be just that. But be warned: Most shrimp are, on being taken from the water, frozen at once on the shrimp boats, and a good deal of the rest is frozen on shore soon after the boat has landed. Much of what passes for fresh shrimp has in fact been frozen and then thawed. The best advice we can give you is to buy all shrimp raw. Above all, don't buy cooked shrimp, a horrid, rubbery mess wholly devoid of flavor.

Look for shrimp with the fresh smell of the ocean that appear firm and tight in their shells. If they look dull and opaque rather than shiny and/or if their juice shows at the bottom of their tray or bin, forget about them. Incidentally, in working out our recipes we have assumed shrimp of medium size, about twenty to the pound. Their shells, which will be discarded, amount to twenty percent of their weight without even counting another waste element: the head.

Mussels and clams. Make sure they are alive. The test for this is whether or not they resist your attempts to open them. Be careful to check all of them for a single bad one could cause you at best some discomfort.

Frozen fish and shellfish. Thaw frozen fish and shellfish completely in the refrigerator over the course of 24 hours to retain their juices except shrimp which should be cooked frozen. Do not freeze more than 2 months.

PREPARING FISH AND SHELLFISH
FOR COOKING: A FEW TIPS

Folding fillets. The skin side of a fish fillet—that is, the side to which the skin had previously clung—is covered by a thin membrane that contracts on exposure to heat. When folding a fillet before cooking it, be sure that the skin side is on the inner side of the fold so that the membrane in contracting keeps the fillet's shape intact. If the fillet is folded with the skin side out, the membrane will shrink and pull the fillet out of shape. To keep this from happening you can also prick the membrane through with a fork as you would a pie crust.

Preparing a whole fish for cooking. In preparing to poach a whole fish make sure all of its scales are removed. If the head is left on, remove the gills. Being an organ (the fish's lungs), they spoil quickly. Then wash the fish under cold running water.

Before baking or broiling a whole fish (bones left in and head and tail on), dry the fish thoroughly and sprinkle the cavity with salt and pepper. Then, taking a knife and inserting its blade at the backbone, cut several deep diagonal slashes across the thickest part of the fish down to the ribs but no further. The slashes should correspond to the number of anticipated servings. Repeat on the other side of the fish. While the fish is being basted these deep cuts will enable the juices to penetrate it evenly, making for more even cooking, and when the fish is done they will facilitate its division into servings.

Shelling and deveining shrimp. Grasp the little fan at the end of the tail between thumb and forefinger and twist it, being careful not to break it off. Next, holding the tail at the narrow part, unwind the shell slowly, starting at the wide part, and, finally, tug gently at the tail to extract the shell. If it refuses to come out don't worry. The next shrimp will be more cooperative.

The shrimp is now exposed. With a sharp paring knife slit it to a depth of ⅛ inch along the ridge of its back, starting at the wide end about two thirds of the way up. Then scrape out the black vein.

Cleaning mussels. Pull off the black "beards," then place mussels in a bucket and run cold water over them. Wash them vigorously, as you would dirty laundry, rubbing them against each other for ten minutes. Next, check them out, one by one, for signs of life. Pinch any open mussels at the thin end. If the mussle is alive it will pull its shell closed. Test closed mussels by rubbing the top and bottom shell between thumb and forefinger in opposite directions. A live mussel will resist your attempt to separate the two halves. Discard any mussels that fail to pass these tests. Finally, transfer the mussels to a bowl and refrigerate. Don't add water or they will open up and void their essential juices. Mussels will keep this way for twenty-four hours.

THE FOUR CLASSIC METHODS
OF COOKING FISH

Like the traditional methods for cooking meat and poultry, those for cooking fish have evolved over the ages and possess the great virtue of simplicity.

Poaching. In poaching fillets bear in mind that these small, flat strips of flesh are fragile and will break apart if they are cooked unevenly or overcooked. Place the fillets in a baking dish into which they fit snugly, then add cold broth. One cup wine to 2 cups water makes a good broth. Cover the dish and put it in a 400° F. oven for fifteen or twenty minutes. Check the fillets frequently. They are done before the liquid reaches a simmer. Larger fillets may require a few more minutes to cook.

Poaching a large whole fish or several smaller ones is done in a *courtbouillon* in a fish poacher. Lay the fish (singular or plural) on the poacher rack and lower the rack into the poacher, then submerge fish and rack in a cold or lukewarm *courtbouillon.* (Boiling liquid tightens and distorts the shape of the fish.) Cover and bring to a boil, then uncover and let simmer for ten minutes per inch of thickness. Let the fish cool for fifteen minutes in the broth.

A poacher is too big for poaching smaller pieces of fish, and it requires too much *courtbouillon,* which washes out the flavorful juices of the fish. Instead, use a pot just large enough to contain the piece.

Steaming. Because pressure builds under steam, fish cooked in this manner cook rapidly. The water should boil continuously so that the fish is surrounded by steam. To assure that no steam escapes, a tight-fitting lid is a prerequisite. Whole fish, steaks, and fillets can all be steamed. (See recipe, page 82.)

Broiling. It's not a good idea to broil large fish, fish that are more than two inches thick, because the surface will overcook before the flesh cooks through. But broiling is fine for smaller fish (up to two pounds if whole or three pounds boned), as well as steaks and fillets. When broiling whole fish, cut diagonal slashes on each side (see *Preparing a Whole Fish for Cooking,* p. 74). The temperature in the broiler and the distance from the source of heat are factors to consider, in addition to thickness, when determining how long to broil fish.

Braising. We call this method "white braising" because the fish is not browned first. It is used for large whole fish (three pounds and up) and for large pieces of fish, both of which need time to absorb the aromatic cooking liquid. The fish is placed on a bed of thinly sliced or julienne vegetables that have been sautéed in butter, then wine or stock or a mixture of the two is added to a depth of two-thirds of its thickness. The fish should fit snugly in the baking dish. The liquid is brought to a boil on top of the stove, after which the fish bakes uncovered in a moderately hot oven, being basted frequently in the process.

Monkfish and swordfish are an exception. They are braised like veal—that is, covered—but for a shorter time. Monkfish, swordfish, and tuna, by the way, do very well in a pressure cooker.

SUGGESTED AMOUNTS FOR SERVINGS

When you buy a fish or a portion of a fish the following table, showing how much you will need per recommended serving, will help you determine how much to get to feed all your guests.

Fillets	5-6 oz. (150 grams)
Steaks	½ lb. (225 grams)
Whole fish with bones, head, and tail	¾ lb. (350 grams)

LEAN FISH AND FATTER FISH

The figures in parentheses following the names of the fish listed below indicate the percentage of the total weight made up of fat.

Less Than 5 Percent Fat	*More Than 5 Percent Fat*
Cod (0.3)	Weakfish (5.6)
Sea Bass (0.5)	Whitefish (8.2)
Flounder (0.8)	Tuna (8.2)
Red Snapper (0.9)	Lake Trout (10.0)
Halibut (1.2)	Herring (11.3)
Striped Bass (2.7)	Mackerel (12.2)
Whiting (3.0)	Salmon (13.4)
Bluefish (3.3)	Eel (18.3)

POACHED WHOLE FISH
Poisson Poché Entier

Serves: 6 to 8

> 1 5-lb. whole fish, such as striped bass, salmon, or red snap-
> per, cleaned, preferably with head and tail left on but fins
> and gills removed
> Court Bouillon (see p. 22)
> Hollandaise Sauce (see pp. 42–43), Lemon Butter Sauce (see
> p. 52), or Shallot Sauce (see p. 47) for warm fish; or Mayon-
> naise (see pp. 39–40) or Green Mayonnaise (see p. 42) for
> cold fish

Special equipment
Fish poacher with rack

Lay fish on the poacher rack and lower into the poacher. (If fish
poacher is too short, cut off the head and/or tail of the fish. They
can be cooked with the fish, then reassembled on the serving platter.)

Pour in enough court bouillon to cover the fish by ¼ inch.
Cover the poacher and bring just to a boil. Uncover and simmer
gently for 10 minutes per inch of thickness (see pp. 71–72 for timing the cooking of fish). Remove from heat and let fish rest in the
court bouillon for 15 to 20 minutes. (During the cooking and short
rest, the fish will absorb the flavor of the court bouillon and become more mellow.) Lift the fish out of the poacher and let drain
on the rack.

Make the sauce while the fish poaches.

Use a paring knife to carefully peel away the skin of the fish.
Scrape away any gray-brown coating between the skin and flesh.
(This thin coating can stay on if desired; the taste is delicious and
strong, and the texture is soft. But if a little is pulled off, it is best to
remove it all for esthetic reasons.) The fish spine will be pulled
away when the skin is removed.

To serve the fish warm, slide it onto a warm platter and serve
immediately. (The fish can also be kept warm, covered with foil, in
a 200° oven.) To serve the fish cold, let it cool completely, uncovered.

(continued)

Notes

If serving hot, garnish the fish with lemon slices and parsley sprigs. If serving cold, cucumber slices are an attractive additional garnish. If the head or tail were cut off, reassemble the fish on the platter and mask the break with parsley, lemon slices, or cucumber slices.

If there is no time to make a Court Bouillon, cut the vegetables into the thinnest possible slices, lay them in the bottom of the poacher, lower the fish on top, and add wine and tepid water to cover the fish by ¼ inch.

Court Bouillon should be cold because pouring in boiling liquid might cause the fish to bend out of shape.

If the fish is to be served cold, it can be poached and skinned 1 day in advance. Let cool, cover with plastic wrap, and refrigerate. Remove from the refrigerator 30 minutes to 1 hour before serving.

ALL FISHES CAPRICE
Caprice pour Tous Poissons

Serves: 4

1 3½- to 4-lb. whole fish, such as red snapper, sea bass, bluefish, or striped bass, head and tail left on, if desired, cleaned and fins and gills removed; or the fillets from a 3½- to 4-lb. fish; or a 2-lb fish steak, such as halibut, swordfish, or cod, 1½ inches thick
5½ tablespoons butter
1 large onion, finely minced
1 tablespoon cornstarch dissolved in 1 tablespoon water
1½ cups fish fumet (see p. 21) or water
5 parsley sprigs
¼ teaspoon ground thyme
¼ teaspoon ground bay leaves
¼ teaspoon ground rosemary
Salt
Freshly ground black pepper
Juice of ½ lemon

Lemon slices
Parsley sprigs
1 tablespoon finely chopped parsley

Preheat oven to 500°.

Rinse fish inside and out under cold running water.

☆Heat butter in a baking pan, add onion, and cook over moderate heat, stirring, for 5 to 7 minutes, or until soft but not brown. Add parsley, thyme, bay leaves, rosemary, and salt and pepper to taste. Heat stock in a saucepan and add to onions. Remove from heat and stir in cornstarch mixture. Bring to a boil, stirring, and remove from heat.

Lower oven temperature to 400°. Lay fish over mixture, baste, and bake for 35 minutes, basting 1 or 2 times (see pp. 71–72 for timing the cooking of fish).

Transfer fish carefully with spatulas to a platter, cover loosely with foil, and keep warm in a 200° oven with the door ajar.

Strain sauce through fine sieve into a small saucepan, pressing with the back of a spoon on the onions to extract all the juices. Season with salt and pepper, if necessary. Bring to a simmer slowly, stirring. Sauce should be creamy and coat a spoon. Thin with stock or water if necessary, or reduce if too thin. Remove from heat and add lemon juice to taste. Garnish fish with lemon slices and parsley sprigs and coat with a little sauce. Sprinkle with chopped parsley and serve remaining sauce in a warm sauceboat.

Light variation

☆Use 2½ tablespoons butter and 2 to 3 tablespoons water in place of 4½ tablespoons butter.

Notes

Boiled potatoes are a good accompaniment for this fish.
Fish will keep for 20 minutes in a 200° oven.

STRIPED BASS OR SEA BASS WITH SORREL
Bar ou Loup de Mer à l'Oseille

Serves: 6

      Unskinned fillets from a 5-lb. striped bass or sea bass
      Salt
      Freshly ground black pepper
1½ cups dry white wine
1¾ lbs. sorrel
  6 tablespoons flour
  ⅔ cup heavy cream
  7 tablespoons butter
     Freshly grated nutmeg
  1 hard-cooked egg
     Parsley sprigs

Preheat oven to 425°.

Melt 3½ tablespoons butter in a baking pan and remove from heat. Arrange fillets on top of one another in the pan, sprinkle with salt and pepper, and bake for 10 minutes.

Scald the wine and pour half around the fish. Bake for 10 minutes, baste, and pour remaining wine around fish. Bake for 10 minutes, baste, and bake for 10 minutes, or until there is no trace of blood between fillets. Transfer to heated platter, skin, and keep warm, covered with foil.

Wash sorrel carefully, dry, and remove stems and coarse inner ribs.

☆Put flour in a small bowl and gradually add cream, beating with a whisk until smooth.

▢Melt remaining butter in a saucepan, add sorrel, and cook over moderate heat, stirring carefully, for 1 to 2 minutes, or until sorrel wilts and changes color. Remove from heat, stir in flour mixture, and season with salt, pepper, and nutmeg. Bring to a simmer over moderate heat and simmer, stirring, for 1 to 2 minutes.

Strain fish cooking liquid and reduce over high heat until slightly syrupy. Glaze fish with reduction. Arrange sorrel mixture in a ribbon along both sides of fish. Scatter hard-cooked egg on top and garnish with parsley sprigs.

Light variation

☆Use milk instead of cream.

□Omit butter when cooking sorrel. Cook sorrel in saucepan over very low heat with 2 to 3 tablespoons water, stirring constantly for 1 to 2 minutes, or until leaves wilt and change color.

Notes

Fish can be kept warm on platter in a 200° oven, covered with foil but not sauced, for 20 minutes.

BROILED STRIPED BASS WITH CHAMPAGNE
Bar Grillé au Champagne

Serves: 4

1 3- to 3½-lb. striped bass or red snapper, preferably with head and tail left on (have lateral bones removed at fish market, but leave spine bone in so fish holds together) or the unskinned fillets from a 3- to 3½-lb. fish
Salt
Freshly ground black pepper
8 tablespoons butter
1 cup dry Champagne or white wine
1 tablespoon finely chopped parsley
8 lemon slices
Parsley sprigs

Preheat broiler.

Rinse fish inside and out under cold running water. Dry thoroughly and sprinkle cavity or individual fillets with salt and pepper.

Butter a baking pan with 1½ tablespoons butter and put fish in it. (If fillets are used, lay one on top of the other.) ☆Dot with remaining butter. Put under broiler about 5 inches from the heat, and broil for 10 minutes, basting occasionally.

Heat Champagne or wine, pour over fish, and return fish to broiler. Broil for 10 minutes, basting, or until no trace of blood shows in the cavity. (For more specific directions, see pp. 71–72.)

Carefully transfer fish to a platter using 2 long spatulas. Keep warm in a turned-off oven with the door ajar.

Strain pan juices through a fine sieve into a saucepan and bring to a simmer. Add salt and pepper, if necessary, and simmer for 1 to 2 minutes. Remove from heat, stir in chopped parsley, and pour into a warm sauceboat. Surround fish with lemon slices and parsley sprigs and serve with sauce.

Light variation

✦Dot fish with only 2½ tablespoons butter.

Notes

Sautéed Cherry Tomatoes (see p. 248) and Parsleyed Potatoes (see p. 210) are good accompaniments for this fish.

Instead of Champagne or white wine, use ⅔ cup dry white wine and ⅓ cup dry vermouth. Add vermouth during the last 5 minutes of broiling.

STEAMED FILLETS OF SOLE
Filets de Sole à la Vapeur

Serves: 6

    4½ tablespoons butter
    6 medium carrots, cut into julienne strips or finely diced
    6 leeks (white part only), cut into julienne strips or finely
        sliced
    1 celery heart, cut into julienne strips or finely diced (If celery
        heart is not available, use 7 or 8 stalks celery about 8 inches
        long and peel tough stalks.)
    ½ teaspoon dried thyme
    1 or 2 bay leaves
        Salt
        Freshly ground black pepper
    6 fillets of sole or flounder, about 5 oz. each
        Fish stock (see p. 21) or water
        Light Shallot Sauce (see p. 47)
    1 lemon, thinly sliced
    2 tablespoons finely chopped parsley

Special equipment

Perforated rack and casserole or steamer, with tight lid wide enough to hold fillets flat. Steam fish in two batches, if necessary.

☆Heat the butter in skillet. Stir in carrots, leeks, celery, thyme, bay leaves, and salt and pepper to taste, and cook over medium-low heat, covered tightly, stirring occasionally, for 6 to 8 minutes, or until cooked but still crunchy.

Rinse fillets under cold running water, pat dry, and, on a cutting board, cut fillets in half lengthwise with a sharp knife, running it through the middle of the backbone. Bone each half fillet, holding the knife against the edge of the bone and slicing down the length of it.

Butterfly each piece, cutting horizontally with a sharp, thin knife in from the thin edge toward the thick part of the fillet to within ¼ inch of where the backbone was cut out. Open the fillets like a book, spread 2 tablespoons of the julienne vegetables over one side of each fillet, then close them. Reserve remaining vegetables.

Lay fillets on the perforated rack. Pour stock or water into the casserole or steamer. (Stock should be about 1 inch below the rack.) Put the fillets on the rack into the steamer. Bring to a boil, cover, and steam for 4 to 6 minutes.

Transfer fillets carefully with long metal spatulas to a warm serving platter. Keep warm, covered with foil, in a low oven. Heat reserved vegetables, covered, over low heat, stirring occasionally.

Arrange the vegetables on platter on both sides of fillets. Garnish with lemon slices and chopped parsley. Serve with Hollandaise (see p. 42), Light Shallot Sauce (see p. 47), or Lemon Butter (see p. 52) in warm sauceboat.

Light variation

☆Instead of 4½ tablespoons butter use 2½ tablespoons butter and ¼ cup water.

Notes

Fillets can also be cut all the way through and the two pieces filled with vegetables like a sandwich.

Fillets can be assembled in the morning and refrigerated. Steam just before serving.

MACERATED FISH FILLETS BAKED IN FOIL
Poisson Macéré en Papillotes

Serves: 6

6 fish fillets, such as flounder or sole, about 5 oz. each

For the maceration
    3 shallots, finely chopped
    3 tablespoons finely chopped parsley
    2 tablespoons Dijon mustard
    ½ cup heavy cream
      Juice of 1 lemon
    ½ teaspoon ground fennel seed
      Salt to taste
      Freshly ground black pepper to taste

    1 egg, lightly beaten

Special equipment
    6 pieces heavy-duty aluminum foil about 15 x 12 inches, or
about 2½ inches bigger than fish all around.

Combine well all the ingredients for maceration. Pour half into a
non-aluminum dish large enough to hold fillets in a single layer.
Put fillets in dish and spread remaining maceration on top. Refrigerate covered for at least 1 hour.
    Preheat oven to 425°.
    Fold pieces of foil in half lengthwise. Cut into ovals with scis-
sors, without cutting through fold, open, and turn up edge 1 inch
all the way around one half to form a "boat." Put a fillet in each
"boat" with some of the maceration.
    Brush a 1-inch border around foil "lid" with egg. Close packet
by folding over the edges and crimping them together securely so
that maceration and air do not come out. There should be a space of
about 1½ inches between fish and border.
    Put packets on baking sheet and bake for 15 minutes. Packets
will puff. Serve on heated plates and let each guest open his own
packet.

Notes

Parsleyed Potatoes (see p. 210) are the best accompaniment.

Packets may be prepared in advance and refrigerated for several hours.

SOLE FILLETS STUFFED WITH FISH MOUSSE
Filets de Sole Farcis de Mousse de Poissons

Serves: 6

3 fillets of sole or flounder, weighing at least 5 oz., cut in half lengthwise
Baked Fish Quenelles (see pp. 88–89)
2 tablespoons finely chopped parsley

Special equipment

6 pieces parchment paper about 8½ by 11 inches each.

Preheat oven to 450°.

Butterfly each piece of fish carefully, cutting horizontally toward the center but not through it. Open the fillet like a book, spread equal portions of mousse over the whole surface, and roll up.

Bring 2 qts. water to a boil in a baking pan. Butter parchment paper and wrap the fish tightly in them, folding the ends like a package and tucking under. Put packages in pan, cover with boiling water, and bake for 20 minutes.

Unwrap rolls, drain off cooking liquid in each package, and reserve. Arrange rolls on a warm platter, spoon reserved juices over them, and sprinkle with parsley.

Notes

The fish can be assembled, wrapped in parchment, then refrigerated several hours before cooking.

Serve the fish with Buttered Rice (see p. 203).

Serve with Hollandaise (see pp. 42–43), Shallot (see p. 47), or Uncooked Tomato Sauce (see p. 48), if desired.

SOLE FILLETS WITH SEAFOOD
Filets de Sole aux Fruits de Mer

Serves: 6

> Braised Mushrooms, made with ½ lb. mushrooms (see p. 244)
> 1½ tablespoons butter, at room temperature
> 2 tablespoons minced shallots
> 6 fillets of sole (about 2 lbs.), halved and boned
> ½ lb. bay scallops
> ½ lb. shrimp, shelled and deveined
> Salt
> Freshly ground black pepper
> 1 cup dry white wine
> Rich Velouté Sauce, made with reserved cooking liquids (see p. 51), or Sauce Aux Legumes see p. 49)
> 2 tablespoons finely chopped parsley

Preheat oven to 400°.

Drain mushroom cooking liquid through a sieve into a measuring cup and reserve.

Butter a gratin dish and sprinkle shallots over the bottom.

Rinse the fillets under cold running water. Fold fillets in half, skin side inside. Put them close together in the baking dish, overlapping slightly at narrow ends. Scatter scallops and shrimp on top. Sprinkle lightly with salt and pepper. Add the wine and water to cover. Bake, covered with parchment paper or foil, in the middle of the oven, for 15 to 20 minutes, or until fish just starts to flake.

Drain cooking liquid through a sieve into measuring cup with mushroom juice.

Add mushrooms to fish, and keep warm, covered, in a low oven. Do not let the fish overheat while preparing the sauce.

Make Rich Velouté Sauce (see p. 51) or Sauce Aux Legumes (see p. 49) with the reserved liquids. Drain off any liquid which may have accumulated in the baking dish, spoon sauce over fish, and sprinkle with parsley.

Notes

A delicious accompaniment is Riz Créole (see p. 203). Or serve the fillets and seafood in a timbale (see pp. 342–343).

MONKFISH THE AMERICAN WAY
Lotte à l'Américaine

Serves: 6

2½ lbs. monkfish fillets (reserve bones, if possible)
Salt
Freshly ground black pepper
Flour
2 tablespoons butter
2 tablespoons oil
¼ cup Cognac
¼ lb. crabmeat, fresh, frozen, or canned, picked over to remove bits of shell
3 shallots, finely chopped
2 cloves garlic, crushed
1 7-inch stalk celery, halved
1½ cups dry white wine
2 tablespoons raw rice
2 cups chicken stock (see pp. 19–20)
1½ lbs. tomatoes, peeled, seeded, and chopped
1 tablespoon tomato paste
2 tablespoons finely chopped fresh tarragon, or 2 teaspoons dried tarragon
3 tablespoons finely chopped parsley
2 teaspoons dried chervil

Season fillets on both sides with salt and pepper and dredge in flour.

Heat butter and oil in a skillet until very hot and just beginning to color. Add fillets and cook over moderate heat for 4 minutes per side. Pour in Cognac and ignite. When flame dies, transfer fish carefully to a heated platter.

Add crabmeat to skillet and toss over moderate heat for 1 to 2 minutes. Add fish bones, if possible, shallots, garlic, and celery and sauté, stirring, for 2 minutes.

Add wine and reduce by half over high heat. Add rice, stock, tomatoes, tomato paste, half the tarragon, half the parsley, and half the chervil, and salt and pepper to taste. Simmer covered for 18 minutes, stirring occasionally. Discard bones.

(continued)

Purée mixture in blender or food processor until smooth and strain through a fine sieve. Put sauce and fillets back into skillet and simmer for 10 minutes, or until cooked through.

Transfer fillets to a cutting board and cut them into ½-inch-thick pieces. Transfer to a heated platter and keep warm.

Season sauce with salt and pepper, if necessary. If sauce is too thin, boil it rapidly until it has a light creamy consistency. Stir in remaining parsley, tarragon, and chervil and spoon over fillets.

Notes

Fish may be prepared several hours in advance and reheated in a double boiler.

BAKED FISH QUENELLES
Mousselines de Poisson Gratinées

Serves: 4

For the fish mousse

    1 lb. skinned whiting, halibut, flounder, or sole fillets, well chilled
    Salt
    Freshly ground black pepper
    Freshly grated nutmeg
    1 egg
    1 cup heavy cream, well chilled

To cook and gratiné the quenelles

    3 tablespoons butter
    ½ cup freshly grated Swiss or Parmesan cheese, or a mixture of both

Special equipment

    Pastry bag with wide plain tip

Preheat oven to 350°.

Cut fillets into 1-inch pieces. Combine with salt, pepper, and nutmeg to taste in a food processor. Blend until very smooth. Add egg and blend well.

☆With machine running, slowly add cream in a thin stream. Blend just until completely absorbed. Do not overmix.

Butter sides and bottom of a skillet. Transfer fish mousse to pastry bag and squeeze mousse into ovals (about 2½ x 1½ inches) close to each other in the skillet. Or shape mousse with 2 table-spoons, dipping them repeatedly into cold water.

Bring 2 qts. water to boil in a kettle and ladle enough boiling water into skillet to cover quenelles. Bring to a simmer and poach for 8 to 10 minutes.

Using a slotted spoon, carefully transfer the quenelles to paper towels to drain.

Butter gratin dish. Arrange quenelles close together in dish. Dot with butter and sprinkle with ▫cheese. Heat in oven for 5 to 7 minutes. Then put under broiler for 1 to 2 minutes, or until top is golden brown.

Light variation

☆Use 1 cup well-chilled ricotta in place of cream. Add to fish mixture ½ cup at a time. Blend just until completely absorbed. Do not overmix.

▫Use ½ cup freshly grated Jarlsberg cheese in place of Swiss or Parmesan cheese.

Notes

Bone and skin fish thoroughly as food processor will not purée them.

Although the quenelles made with ricotta are not as smooth and light as those made with cream, they have an interesting texture and are delicious.

Dish can be prepared 1 day in advance, covered and refrigerated. Heat in oven and under broiler as directed.

FISH CUSTARD
Flan de Poisson

Serves: 4 as an appetizer
2 as a main course

4½ tablespoons butter
1 medium carrot, finely chopped
1 leek (white part only), finely chopped
1 shallot, finely chopped
½ lb. bones and trimmings of lean fish, such as whiting, flounder, halibut, or red snapper, cut in small pieces
1 cup dry white wine
4 eggs
½ cup heavy cream
Salt
Freshly ground black pepper
Freshly grated nutmeg

Special equipment
Four ½-cup soufflé molds, or a 1-pint soufflé dish

Preheat oven to 350°.

☆Heat 3½ tablespoons butter gently in a saucepan. Add carrot, leek, shallot, and fish trimmings. Cover and cook over low heat for 5 to 7 minutes without coloring. Add wine and bring to a simmer.

Simmer very, very slowly for 35 to 40 minutes, or until liquid is reduced to 5 tablespoons. Strain through a fine sieve and let cool.

Butter molds generously with remaining butter.

▫Whisk together eggs, cream, cooled reduction, and salt, pepper, and nutmeg to taste until just blended. Pour into prepared molds. (If using individual molds, they should be three quarters full.) Put molds in a large pan and pour 1 inch of boiling water into the pan. Bake in the middle of the oven for 30 minutes, or until a thin skewer plunged into the center of the custards comes out clean. Do not let the water boil during the cooking or the custard will curdle. Serve warm or cold.

Light variation

☆Use butter only for molds. Cook carrot, leek, shallot, fish trimmings, and wine together very, very slowly for 35 to 40 minutes, or until liquid is reduced to 5 tablespoons. Strain through a fine sieve and let cool.

▢In place of heavy cream use ½ cup milk.

Notes

The pressure cooker works beautifully for this very simple recipe and cuts down to almost no time the preliminary long reduction. Another advantage is that instead of trimmings, a piece of fish can be cooked under pressure and used for another meal.

If cooking in a pressure cooker, use only ½ cup wine. Cook under pressure for 6 to 7 minutes. No reduction is necessary; simply use 5 tablespoons of the liquid.

SALMON TERRINE
Terrine de Saumon

Serves: 8 to 10 as a first course

- 1 lb. boned and skinned fresh salmon, or two 7¾-oz. cans of salmon picked over, with juice reserved
- 1 qt. court bouillon (see p. 22)
- 1 envelope unflavored gelatin
- ¼ cup cold water
- ⅔ lb. (2¾ sticks) butter, at room temperature
- ⅔ lb. smoked Nova Scotia or smoked salmon
- 2 to 3 teaspoons chopped green peppercorns, or freshly ground black pepper to taste
  Salt
- ¼ teaspoon ground allspice (optional)
- 12 pistachio nuts (optional)

Special equipment
  5-cup terrine

If using fresh salmon, put it in a pot just large enough to hold it, pour in court bouillon to cover by ¼ inch, and simmer for 20 minutes (see pp. 71–72 for timing the cooking of fish). Drain immediately and let cool, uncovered.

Sprinkle gelatin over cold water and let soften.

Strain court bouillon and reduce in saucepan over high heat to ½ cup. Or bring reserved salmon juice to a boil, adding a little water to make ½ cup. Remove from heat, add gelatin, and stir until completely dissolved. Let cool, stirring occasionally. Butter terrine generously.

☆Put remaining butter in bowl and beat with a whisk for 2 minutes, or until creamy and smooth.

Reserve 3 slices smoked salmon for garnish. Crush remaining smoked fish and salmon with a fork. It is better to do this by hand rather than in a food processor since a coarse texture is desired. Put fish into another bowl and beat in gelatin mixture with a wooden spoon. Add salt to taste, peppercorns, a pinch of allspice, if desired, and butter. Mix well, but don't overbeat. Pack mixture into terrine and refrigerate for at least 2 hours.

Cut reserved smoked salmon into ⅓-inch strips and top terrine with a lattice of strips. ▫Insert pistachio nuts in spaces, if desired.

Light variation

☆In place of ⅔ lb. butter, use ⅓ lb. butter and add to it ⅔ cup ricotta, blended in a food processor.

▫Omit pistachio nuts

Notes

The terrine will keep for 1 day, refrigerated.

Other fish, such as whiting, sole, flounder, and halibut can be substituted for the fresh salmon. These fish could be combined with cooked lobster or crabmeat as a substitute for the smoked salmon. Choose an appealing combination and prepare, using the same proportions.

LIGHT SALMON MOUSSE

Serves: 8

    1 envelope unflavored gelatin
¼ cup cold water
    1 8-oz. container plain yogurt
½ cup (scant) ricotta
    1 lb. fresh poached salmon (see p. 77), or two 7¾-oz. cans salmon
1½ teaspoons butter
    1 large shallot, minced
    1 tablespoon lemon juice
    1 tablespoon finely chopped dill (optional)
    Salt
    Freshly ground black pepper
    2 egg whites

Special equipment
    6-cup mold

Put gelatin in a small saucepan with water and let soften.

Blend yogurt and ricotta in a food processor until smooth and creamy and transfer to a bowl. Blend salmon until smooth and add to ricotta and yogurt.

Heat butter in a small skillet until hot but not brown. Add shallot and sauté, stirring and tossing the shallot, for 1 minute, or until soft. Add to salmon mixture with lemon juice, dill, and salt and pepper to taste. Blend thoroughly.

Put gelatin over very low heat and stir until dissolved. Add to salmon and blend well. Chill mixture over bowl of ice, stirring occasionally, until it begins to thicken.

Beat egg whites with a pinch of salt and a few drops of lemon juice until stiff (see p. 271) and immediately fold into the salmon mixture with a whisk. Rinse mold with cold water, pour in the salmon mixture, and refrigerate.

Unmold onto a chilled platter and garnish with Cucumber Salad (see p. 257) or Asparagus Vinaigrette (see p. 224), if desired.

(continued)

Notes

Mousse can be made up to 1 day in advance. Unmold when set and cover with plastic wrap.

Canned salmon is excellent in this recipe, but, of course, fresh poached salmon is delicious.

If fresh dill is not available, use ½ teaspoon ground dried dill.

A pretty presentation is to use a savarin (ring) mold. Circle the outside of the mold with cucumber and stand asparagus tips in the center.

BAKED WHOLE RED SNAPPER WITH JULIENNE VEGETABLES
Poisson Braisé aux Légumes

Serves: 6

> 1 4- to 4½-lb. red snapper, striped bass, or sea trout, cleaned, with fins and gills removed, head and tail left on, if desired, or use unskinned fillets from a 4- to 4½-lb. fish, one on top of the other.
> Salt
> Freshly ground black pepper
> 3 tablespoons butter
> 3 to 4 carrots, cut into julienne strips or thinly sliced
> 1 whole celery heart, or 8 8-inch stalks without leaves (peel any tough ones), cut into julienne strips or thinly sliced
> 1 large onion, cut into julienne strips or thinly sliced
> 2 bay leaves
> ¼ teaspoon dried thyme
> 4 sprigs fresh parsley
> 1½ cups dry white wine
> ¾ cup fish stock (see p. 21) or water
> ⅓ cup heavy cream
> 2 teaspoons cornstarch dissolved in 4 teaspoons white wine
> 1 to 2 tablespoons lemon juice
> 2 tablespoons finely chopped parsley

Preheat oven to 425°.

Rinse fish inside and out, dry, and sprinkle cavity with salt and pepper. Cut 4 to 5 diagonal slashes about 2½ inches long down to the backbone into the thick part of the fish. Be careful not to cut through the bone or into the belly of the fish. The cuts help the fish cook evenly.

Melt the butter in a skillet, add carrot, celery, and onion, season with salt and pepper, and cook over moderate heat, stirring occasionally, until vegetables are just softened. Arrange vegetables in the bottom of a baking pan and put fish on top. (If using fillets, overlap them.) Add bay leaves, thyme, parsley, wine, and stock, and bring to a boil. Bake, basting occasionally, for 35 to 45 minutes, or until no trace of blood shows inside the cavity of the fish.

Transfer fish carefully to a warm platter using 2 long spatulas. Transfer vegetables with a slotted spoon, holding them over the baking pan and pressing on them lightly with the back of a wooden spoon to extract some of their juice. Arrange the vegetables attractively around the fish. Cover with foil and keep warm.

Strain the pan juices through a fine sieve into a saucepan. Bring to a boil and cook for 1 to 2 minutes. ☆Add cream and boil for 1 to 2 minutes.

Remove from heat and blend in enough cornstarch mixture to get a light, creamy consistency. Season with salt and pepper and add any juices that have accumulated on the platter. Remove from the heat and stir in lemon juice to taste.

Ladle a little sauce over the fish and serve the remainder in a warm sauceboat. Sprinkle the parsley over the fish, vegetables, and sauce.

Notes

Another equally good version is to substitute 3 leeks and ¾ pound mushrooms, thinly sliced, for the carrots and onion. Or lay fish over Duxelles (see p. 243).

RED SNAPPER STUFFED WITH SHRIMP
Dorade Farcie

Serves: 4

½ lb. medium or small shrimp, shelled and deveined
Salt
Freshly ground black pepper
Freshly grated nutmeg
¼ cup heavy cream
2 medium shallots, finely chopped
2 tablespoons chopped parsley
1 3½-lb. red snapper, or striped bass, sea trout, blue fish, or
   pompano, cleaned and gills removed. (If head and tail are
   left on, have the ribs and lateral bones removed at the fish
   market, but leave the spine bone in so fillets hold together.)
3 tablespoons butter
2 medium tomatoes, peeled, seeded, and thinly sliced
1 bay leaf
1 bunch parsley
1 lemon, thinly sliced

Preheat oven to 400°.

Blend shrimp with salt, pepper, and nutmeg to taste in a food processor until mixture is smooth. Add enough cream to just bind mixture. Add shallots and parsley just to combine.

Stuff cavity of fish with shrimp mixture. Butter a baking dish with 1 tablespoon of butter and arrange sliced tomatoes in the bottom. Lay fish on top. Add bay leaf and dot fish with remaining butter.

Bake for 30 tc 35 minutes, basting three times. (If fish becomes dry, add water, 1 tablespoon at a time.) Using two long spatulas, carefully transfer fish to a warm platter. Cover loosely with foil, and keep warm in a 200° oven.

Simmer cooking juices over moderate heat for 1 to 2 minutes. Season with salt and pepper to taste. Serve sauce as is, or strain through a fine sieve, pressing down with the back of a spoon to push the tomato pulp through.

Arrange a few sprigs of parsley and some lemon slices around the fish. Serve the sauce in a warm sauceboat.

Notes

Fish can be stuffed in the morning for serving at night. Cover, refrigerate, and cook just before serving.

Another good stuffing is Duxelles (see p. 243), made with ½ lb. mushrooms.

Substitute scallops for the shrimp.

TROUT WITH ALMONDS AND GRAPEFRUIT
Truites aux Amandes avec Pamplemousse

Serves: 4

> 2 tablespoons oil
> 4 brook trout, about 1 lb. each, cleaned, with head and tail removed, if desired
> 3 to 4 tablespoons butter
> Salt
> Freshly ground black pepper
> ¼ lb. blanched almonds, chopped
> 2 grapefruit, peeled and segmented
> Parsley sprigs

Heat oil in a heavy skillet large enough to hold the trout in one layer. When hot, add the trout and cook over moderate heat for 4 minutes per side.

Transfer fish to a dish and peel away skin, which will come off easily. Discard oil in the skillet and wipe the skillet out with paper towels.

Melt the butter in the skillet (if the heads and tails of the fish have been removed, only 3 tablespoons of butter will be necessary). Add the trout and cook over moderate heat for 5 minutes per side, or until cooked and nicely golden. Season with salt and pepper to taste. Carefully transfer to a heated platter, cover with foil, and keep warm.

Toss the almonds in the butter remaining in the skillet over moderate heat until golden. Scatter them over the trout. Garnish with grapefruit segments and parsley sprigs.

FISH STEAK HOME-STYLE
Steak de Poisson Ménagère

Serves: 4

> 2 tablespoons oil
> 3 tablespoons butter
> 1 lb. onions, thinly sliced
> 1 lb. tomatoes, peeled, seeded, and chopped
> 2 cloves garlic, minced
> 2 tablespoons finely chopped parsley
> 1 teaspoon dried basil, or 1 tablespoon finely chopped fresh
>   basil leaves
>   Salt
>   Freshly ground black pepper
> 2 lbs. halibut, swordfish, blue fish, or cod steaks, about 1 inch
>   thick

Preheat oven to 400°.

☆Heat oil and 1 tablespoon butter in a skillet until hot but not brown, add onion, cover, and cook slowly, stirring occasionally, for 5 minutes, or until onion is soft. Stir in tomatoes, garlic, 1 tablespoon parsley, basil, and salt and pepper to taste. Cover and cook over moderate heat for 2 to 3 minutes, or until tomatoes have released their juice. Uncover and boil over moderate heat, stirring occasionally, for 5 to 7 minutes, or until juices have evaporated and fondue has thickened. Tomatoes should remain fairly chunky. Reserve 3 tablespoons fondue.

Rinse fish steaks under cold running water, pat dry, and season with salt and pepper. Lay steaks on top of fondue in baking dish. Top with reserved fondue. ▫Melt remaining butter and pour over top.

Bake for 20 minutes, or until fish is still firm and just starting to flake. Transfer fish carefully to a warm platter, cover with fondue, and sprinkle with remaining parsley.

Light variation

> ☆Use 2 to 3 tablespoons water instead of 2 tablespoons oil.
> ▫Omit melted butter.

MARINATED AND BRAISED SWORDFISH
Thon en Fricandeau

Serves: 6

1 2½- to 3-lb. piece swordfish

For the marinade

1 tablespoon oil
2 medium onions, finely sliced
2 medium carrots, thinly sliced
1 7-inch stalk celery, thinly sliced
6 cloves garlic, crushed
¼ teaspoon dried thyme
½ teaspoon ground rosemary
¼ teaspoon freshly ground black pepper
½ teaspoon salt
1 cup red wine
1 cup chicken stock (see pp. 19–20)

To cook the swordfish

Salt
Freshly ground black pepper
Flour
1 tablespoon butter
3 tablespoons oil
4 medium tomatoes, peeled, seeded, and coarsely chopped
2 tablespoons finely chopped parsley

Put all the ingredients for marinade in a saucepan. Cover and bring to a boil. Simmer for 15 minutes and let cool.

Put swordfish steak in a non-aluminum dish just large enough to hold it snugly. Pour in marinade and marinate in the refrigerator for at least 2 hours, turning fish occasionally.

Remove fish from marinade and dry on paper towels. Strain marinade through a fine-mesh sieve into a bowl, reserving vegetables. Season fish with salt and pepper and dredge it lightly with flour.

Preheat oven to 375°.

(continued)

Heat butter and oil in an ovenproof pan until hot but not browned. Brown fish and transfer to a platter. Add reserved vegetables to pan and cook over moderate heat, stirring, for 3 minutes, or until they begin to color. Add tomatoes and swordfish and pour in marinade. Liquid should come almost two thirds of the way up fish. If not, add a little more stock. Season with salt and pepper, if necessary, and bring to a boil on top of the stove. Bake in the middle of the oven for 30 minutes. Transfer fish to a heated platter, cover loosely with foil, and keep warm in a low oven.

Remove bay leaf and blend juices and vegetables in a food processor until smoothly puréed. Strain through a sieve and heat in a saucepan over moderate heat, stirring. Boil rapidly for 1 to 2 minutes if sauce is too thin. It should have a nice creamy consistency. Season with salt and pepper, if necessary.

Cut fish into portions, spoon sauce over, and sprinkle with parsley.

Notes

Marinade can be prepared 1 day in advance.

Leftover swordfish is delicious served cold in a Salade Niçoise.

FISH STEW
Marmite de Poisson

Serves: 4

6 tablespoons butter
1 tablespoon finely chopped shallots
¼ cup dry white wine
1½ lbs. mussels, scrubbed and bearded (see p. 74)
1 medium onion, chopped
1 leek (white and pale green parts), washed and chopped
1 stalk celery, chopped
1 medium sweet green or red pepper, chopped
2 medium tomatoes, peeled, seeded, and chopped, or 1 cup drained canned Italian plum tomatoes

1½ qts. fish stock (see p. 21) or water
Salt
Freshly ground black pepper
 1 lb. halibut, skin and bones removed, cut into 1-inch-thick by 2-inch-long pieces
1½ lbs. monkfish, skin and bones removed, cut into 1-inch-thick by 2-inch-long pieces
 ½ lb. medium shrimp, shelled and deveined
 1 fillet (about 4 oz.) sole or flounder (Remove bone in center of fillet and cut each half into pieces crosswise.)
 3 tablespoons flour
 ½ cup heavy cream
 ½ teaspoon curry powder
 ¼ teaspoon ground fennel seed
 3 tablespoons finely chopped parsley
16 croutons (see p. 63), optional

*Heat 1 tablespoon butter in a 4-qt. pot until hot but not brown. Add shallots and cook over moderate heat, stirring, for 1 minute. Add white wine and mussels.

Cover and cook, shaking the pot occasionally to toss mussels, for 5 minutes, or until they open. Steam any unopened mussels a few minutes longer. Discard those that still do not open. Remove mussels with a slotted spoon and shell them. Put mussels in a tureen, reserving 8 mussels and 4 double shells for decoration. Strain mussel liquid through a fine sieve lined with a linen or cotton tea towel that has been dampened and squeezed out. Reserve liquid.

In a 5-qt. pot, □heat 2 tablespoons butter until hot but not brown. Stir in onion, leek, and celery and cook, covered, over moderate heat, stirring 1 or 2 times, for about 5 minutes, or until vegetables are soft but not brown. Add green pepper, and cook, covered, for 2 to 3 minutes. Add tomatoes and cook, covered, for 5 to 7 minutes. Add fish stock and salt and pepper to taste. Cover and bring to a simmer.

Add halibut and monkfish and simmer for 8 to 10 minutes, or until fish is still firm and just starting to flake. Using a slotted spoon, transfer fish to a tureen, cover, and keep warm. Add shrimp and sole to stock and simmer for 2 to 3 minutes. Transfer shrimp to tureen as soon as they turn pink. Transfer sole to tureen. Remove stock from heat and strain, reserving vegetables.

✧Melt remaining butter in saucepan. Add flour and cook slowly, stirring, for 2 minutes, or until mixture bubbles without browning. Remove from heat and add hot stock all at once, beating vigorously with a whisk. Add reserved mussel liquid and reserved vegetables. Bring to a boil, and simmer for 5 minutes, stirring occasionally. Remove from heat and gradually stir in cream. Add curry powder and fennel seed. Bring to a simmer and season with salt and pepper to taste.

Ladle soup over fish in tureen. Put reserved mussels in reserved shells and arrange on top of soup. Sprinkle with chopped parsley and serve ○croutons on the side, if desired.

Light variation

☆Put shallots, wine, and mussels in pot without butter and cook as directed.

□Use only 1 tablespoon butter and 2 to 3 tablespoons water when cooking vegetables.

✧Omit *roux*. Bring hot soup with vegetables, mussel liquid, and ½ cup half-and-half to a boil. Stir in curry powder and fennel. Remove from heat and blend in 2 tablespoons cornstarch dissolved in 2 tablespoons water in place of cream. Boil slowly for 1 to 2 minutes. Season with salt and pepper to taste and ladle over fish in tureen.

○Omit croutons.

Notes

The stew can be made a day ahead. Let fish and soup (omitting the cream) cool separately uncovered. Cover and refrigerate. Slowly reheat soup to warm and stir in cream. Add fish and bring just to simmer to reheat fish.

MUSSELS WITH MUSTARD SAUCE
Moules à la Sauce Moutarde

Serves: 4

½ cup dry white wine
2 shallots, finely chopped, or 1 small onion, chopped
Freshly ground black pepper
3 sprigs parsley
4 lbs. mussels in their shells, scrubbed and bearded (see p. 74)
Heart of 2 Bibb or 1 Boston lettuce
Juice of 1 lemon
Dill and Mustard Mayonnaise (see p. 41)
1 carrot, finely shredded
1 tablespoon fresh finely chopped parsley

Bring wine, shallots, pepper to taste, and parsley sprigs to a boil in kettle. Add mussels, cover tightly and cook over moderate heat, shaking the kettle occasionally, for 6 to 7 minutes, or until all the shells are opened. Steam any unopened mussels a few minutes longer. If they still do not open, discard them.

Remove mussels with a slotted spoon, strain cooking broth through a fine sieve lined with a damp linen or cotton towel, and reserve for soup (see p. 33). (It can be refrigerated or frozen.)

Shell mussels, reserving 1 double shell per person for garnish.

Arrange lettuce on individual salad plates and squeeze lemon juice over lettuce. Put a shell on each plate, put a mussel in each shell, and arrange the rest on the lettuce. Spoon a little Dill and Mustard Mayonnaise over each mussel. Garnish plates with a few shreds of carrot and a light sprinkling of chopped parsley.

Notes

The mussels and the Dill and Mustard Mayonnaise can be prepared 1 day in advance. Cover separately and refrigerate.

STUFFED MUSSELS SAILOR-STYLE
Moules Marines Farcies

Serves: 4

    2 tablespoons butter
    1 small onion, chopped finely
    4 lbs. large mussels, scrubbed and bearded (see p. 74)
      Freshly ground black pepper
    ⅔ cup dry white wine
      Kosher salt

For the sauce
    1 tablespoon olive oil
    2 tablespoons vegetable oil
    ¼ lb. shallots, finely chopped
    2 medium garlic cloves, minced
    1 lb. tomatoes, peeled, seeded, and roughly chopped, or
      a 16-oz. can Italian plum tomatoes, drained and roughly
      chopped
      Salt
      Freshly ground black pepper
    ⅛ teaspoon dried thyme
    1 bay leaf
    1 3- to 4-inch piece of celery
    3 sprigs parsley
    1 tablespoon butter
    2 tablespoons finely chopped parsley
    1 cup freshly grated Parmesan or Swiss cheese, or a mixture
      of both

✭Melt butter in a kettle and add onion. Cook for 5 minutes, or until soft, and add mussels, pepper to taste, and wine.

Cover tightly and cook over medium-high heat, shaking kettle occasionally, for 6 to 8 minutes, or until the mussels are opened. Steam any unopened mussels a few minutes longer. If they still do not open, discard them.

Discard one half of each shell, reserving mussel juices, and arrange the remaining half shells with mussels in them in a large shallow baking dish lined with a layer of kosher salt to keep shells from tilting.

Strain reserved mussel juice through a fine-mesh sieve lined with cloth napkin or tea towel, dampened and squeezed out, into a small saucepan and reserve.

Preheat broiler.

□Heat the oil in a skillet, add shallots and garlic, and cook, stirring occasionally, for 2 to 3 minutes without browning. Add tomatoes, salt and pepper to taste, thyme, bay leaf, celery, and parsley sprigs. Cook over medium-high heat for 15 to 20 minutes, or until liquid has evaporated. Discard bay leaf, parsley sprigs, and celery.

Bring reserved mussel juice to a boil and reduce to 3 to 4 tablespoons. Stir into tomato sauce, add salt and pepper to taste, and bring to a simmer over moderate heat. Remove from heat and stir in butter and chopped parsley.

Spoon a little of the sauce over each mussel and sprinkle some grated cheese on top. Put mussels under broiler until browned.

Light variation

☆Omit butter and cook onion, mussels, pepper, and wine together.

□Omit vegetable oil in sauce, replacing it with 2 to 3 tablespoons of water.

Notes

The dish can be assembled 1 day in advance, covered, and refrigerated. Remove from refrigerator 30 minutes before placing under the broiler.

To make assembling the dish easier (though the presentation will not be as nice), lightly butter a shallow baking dish and spread shelled mussels over the bottom. Cover with the sauce and sprinkle with the cheese. Use this method for smaller mussels.

This is also a delicious combination to serve over spaghetti.

PAELLA THE PARISIAN WAY
Paella à la Parisienne

Serves: 8

  1 sweet green or red pepper
1½ qts. water
     Salt
  1 lb. fresh peas, shelled, or 1 10-oz. package frozen peas
  2 lbs. mussels, scrubbed and bearded (see p. 74)
  ½ cup water
2¼ cups chicken stock (see pp. 19–20) and ½ cup mussel broth
  ½ teaspoon powdered saffron, or 1 teaspoon thread saffron
  1 tablespoon tomato paste
  5 tablespoons oil
  1 2½-lb. chicken, cut into 8 pieces, or 2 whole chicken breasts
     (about 2 lbs.), split in half and quartered crosswise
  1 large onion, finely chopped
1½ cups rice
  2 or 3 cloves garlic, finely minced
     Freshly ground black pepper
  2 chorizo sausages (Spanish garlic sausages), or kielbasa, cut
     into ⅜-inch-thick slices
  1 large or 2 small fresh hot peppers, seeded and minced
1½ lbs. halibut, skin and bones removed, cut into 1- x 2-inch
     pieces
  ¾ lb. shrimp, shelled and deveined

Preheat broiler.

Put sweet pepper on a foil-lined baking pan and broil 5 inches from heat until charred almost all over. Immediately put pepper in a bowl and cover. (The trapped steam makes the pepper easier to peel.) When cool enough to handle, peel pepper, core, and cut it lengthwise into ¼-inch-wide strips. Reserve one third of the strips for garnish.

Bring 1½ qts. water to a boil and add 2 teaspoons salt. Drop peas into boiling water, cover, and bring to a boil. Boil fresh peas uncovered for 4 to 7 minutes, depending on their size. Refresh peas under cold running water and reserve 3 tablespoons for garnish.

Preheat oven to 400°.

Put mussels in a kettle with ½ cup water. Cover and steam over moderate heat, shaking kettle occasionally, for 5 minutes, or until mussels open. Using a slotted spoon, transfer mussels to a bowl. Steam any unopened mussels a few minutes longer and discard any that still do not open. Shell mussels, reserving 12 whole shells for garnish. Strain any mussel juice and the cooking liquid through a fine sieve lined with a linen or cotton towel that has been dampened and squeezed out. Reserve ½ cup.

Heat stock and reserved mussel juice in a saucepan with the saffron and tomato paste, stirring occasionally.

Heat oil in a large ovenproof casserole. Add chicken skin side down and brown lightly over moderate heat. Transfer chicken to a plate. Add onion and cook, stirring until soft. Add rice and cook, stirring, for 1 minute, or until well coated with fat. Stir in garlic, hot broth, and salt and pepper to taste. Add chicken, chorizo, sweet and hot peppers, peas, and halibut. Bring to a boil, cover tightly, and bake for 18 minutes.

Scatter shrimp over top and bake for 2 minutes. Add mussels and let paella stand, covered, for 5 to 7 minutes. (The mussels will reheat in the steam.) Stuff reserved mussel shells with reserved pepper strips and peas.

Spoon paella onto a warm platter, arranging shrimp and mussels on top, and stuffed mussel shells around the edge of the platter.

Notes

The paella may be prepared 1 day in advance. Let it cool, uncovered. Then cover and refrigerate. Remove shrimp and mussels before reheating so they will not dry out. Reheat in a 350° oven for 30 minutes, adding a little water to compensate for evaporation. Add shrimp and mussels to the paella during the last 5 minutes.

POACHED SCALLOPS
Saint Jacques Pochées

Serves: 3

    1 lb. bay scallops or sea scallops, sliced across the grain into
        ⅜-inch-thick slices
    ½ cup dry white wine
    ¼ teaspoon dried thyme
    1 small bay leaf
    1 shallot, minced
    3 or 4 parsley stems
        Salt
        Freshly ground black pepper
    1½ cups cold water

Rinse scallops under cold running water. If improperly cleaned at
the fish market, the hard hinge muscle might still be on them.
Check each scallop for this muscle and pull it off. It comes away
easily but causes a rubbery texture if left on.

Simmer wine, thyme, bay leaf, shallot, parsley, and salt and
pepper to taste in saucepan for 1 to 2 minutes. Add scallops and just
enough water to cover. Bring to a simmer, and poach for 1 to 2
minutes, or until scallops are opaque. Do not let them boil. Drain
immediately.

Notes

Cooking liquid may be used in soups such as Marmite de
Poisson (see p. 100) or Mussel Soup (see p. 33) and will keep 1 day,
covered and refrigerated, or it can be frozen.

Cooked scallops will keep 1 day covered and refrigerated. Reheat carefully in a hot sauce or soup for 1 to 2 minutes. Do not let
the mixture boil.

Scallops can be tossed with a mild vinaigrette or mayonnaise
and served on lettuce leaves.

SCALLOPS AND VEGETABLES IN CREAM SAUCE
Coquilles St. Jacques Jardinière

Serves: 4 to 6

- ¾ lb. mushrooms
- 1 lb. bay scallops or sea scallops, sliced across the grain into ⅜-inch slices
- 3 tablespoons butter
- ¾ lb. carrots, cut into julienne strips or thinly sliced
- 2 8-inch cucumbers, cut into julienne strips or thinly sliced
  Salt
  Freshly ground black pepper
- ¾ cup heavy cream
- 2 teaspoons cornstarch dissolved in 2 teaspoons water
- 2 tablespoons lemon juice
- 1 tablespoon finely chopped parsley

Trim ¼ inch off mushroom stems. Wash, pat dry, and cut into ⅜-inch slices. If mushrooms are small, quarter them.

Rinse scallops under cold running water. If improperly cleaned at the fish market, the hard hinge of muscle might still be on them. Check each scallop for this muscle and pull it off. It comes away easily but causes a rubbery texture if left on.

✩Melt butter in skillet, stir in carrots, cucumbers, and salt and pepper to taste, and cook over moderate heat for 5 to 7 minutes, stirring occasionally. Add mushrooms, cover, and cook for 2 to 3 minutes, or until they render their juice. Drain vegetables in a sieve set over a bowl, pressing gently on them with a wooden spoon to collect most of the juices. Reserve vegetables in the sieve and return juices to skillet. Add scallops and □heavy cream, bring to a simmer, and cook for 1 to 2 minutes. Do not boil. Using a slotted spoon, transfer scallops to sieve.

Bring cooking liquid to a boil and boil, stirring, for 2 minutes. Remove from heat, stir in enough of the cornstarch mixture to give a creamy consistency. Bring the sauce to a boil and boil, stirring, for 1 to 2 minutes. Add scallops and vegetables and bring to a simmer.

(continued)

Season with salt and pepper, remove from heat, and add lemon juice to taste.

Spoon into a warm gratin dish or individual shells and sprinkle with parsley.

Light variation

☆Use 1 tablespoon butter and 3 to 4 tablespoons water instead of 3 tablespoons butter.

□Use half-and-half instead of cream.

Notes

If preparing in advance, rub surface of sauce with a piece of cold butter. Let scallop mixture cool and refrigerate, covered with foil. It will keep up to 1 day. Reheat in a larger saucepan of warm water.

SCALLOPS WITH MUSHROOMS
Coquilles Saint Jacques aux Champignons

Serves: 6 as a first course
         4 as a main course

   4½ tablespoons butter
   2 lbs. bay scallops or sea scallops, sliced across the grain into ⅜-inch slices
   2 tablespoons minced shallots
   1 garlic clove, minced
   2 teaspoons lemon juice
   1 cup dry white wine
     Braised Mushrooms, made with ⅔ lb. mushrooms, juices reserved (see p. 244)
     Cayenne pepper
     Salt
   3 to 4 tablespoons dry bread crumbs
   3 tablespoons finely chopped parsley
   1½ tablespoons melted butter
   1 egg yolk
   ⅔ cup heavy cream

Preheat broiler.

Butter a gratin dish with 1 tablespoon butter. Rinse scallops under cold running water. If improperly cleaned at the fish market, the hard hinge muscle might still be on them. Check each scallop for this muscle and pull it off. It comes away easily but causes a rubbery texture if left on.

Melt remaining butter in skillet, add scallops, and toss over moderate heat for 1 minute to coat them in butter. Add shallots, garlic, lemon juice, wine, a pinch of cayenne, and salt to taste. Bring to a simmer and poach for 2 to 3 minutes. Drain immediately through a fine sieve into a bowl. Combine juice with reserved mushroom juices. Spoon scallops into gratin dish, scatter mushrooms over them, and top with 2 tablespoons parsley. Sprinkle with bread crumbs. ☆Pour melted butter on top and keep warm, loosely covered with foil, in a low oven.

In a saucepan, reduce reserved juices to ¼ cup over high heat. ▢In a bowl beat egg yolk with 1 tablespoon cream. Whisk remaining cream into reduced juices gradually and boil over moderate heat, stirring, until sauce has a light creamy consistency. Whisk sauce rapidly into egg yolk mixture in a thin steady stream.

Put gratin dish under broiler about 4 to 5 inches from heat for 1 to 2 minutes, or until top is golden brown. Serve with sauce in a warm sauceboat.

Light variation

☆Use 3, instead of 4½, tablespoons butter.

▢In place of 1 egg yolk and ⅔ cup heavy cream, use ½ cup ricotta, blended in food processor, and 1 to 2 tablespoons cream. Reduce reserved juices to ⅓ cup. Remove from heat, stir in ricotta and cream, and bring just to a boil over low heat, stirring. Remove from heat immediately and add lemon juice ½ teaspoon at a time. Thin sauce with a little more juice, if necessary.

Notes

For a delicious variation, substitute shrimp for scallops.

Dish can be prepared an hour in advance, up to the point of adding the egg yolk mixture.

POACHED SHRIMP
Crevettes Pochées

Serves: 3

¾ lb. medium shrimp, shelled and deveined
½ cup dry white wine
1½ teaspoons salt
1 bay leaf
  Pinch of dried thyme
8 whole black peppercorns, crushed
4 parsley stems
1 shallot, finely chopped
1½ cups cold water

Simmer wine, salt, bay leaf, thyme, peppercorns, parsley, and shallot in a saucepan for 1 to 2 minutes. Add shrimp and just enough water to cover. Bring just to a simmer, and poach for 1 to 2 minutes, or until shrimp turn pink. Drain immediately.

Notes
  Shrimp will keep 1 day covered and refrigerated.

AVOCADO STUFFED WITH SHRIMP
Avocats Farcis aux Crevettes

Serves: 6

For the sauce
3 to 4 tablespoons lemon juice
1 tablespoon Dijon mustard
  Salt
  Freshly ground black pepper
5 tablespoons oil
½ teaspoon dried tarragon, or 2 teaspoons fresh
2 medium shallots, minced
5 sprigs of parsley
½ teaspoon Worcestershire sauce (optional)

1 tablespoon ketchup (optional)
1 tablespoon Cognac or brandy (optional)

3 avocados
¼ lb. mushrooms, sliced
2 medium tomatoes, peeled, seeded, and cut into bite-size pieces
1 lb. shrimp, poached and halved lengthwise (see p. 112)
6 whole crisp leaves of Boston lettuce
2 hard-cooked eggs, chopped
  Chopped parsley
  Lemon wedges

☆Blend sauce ingredients in a food processor or blender for 3 to 4 seconds, or until emulsified.

Halve and pit avocados. Using a teaspoon, carefully remove avocado pulp from skin. Do not pierce the skin as the empty shells will be filled with the salad mixture later. Break pulp into bite-size pieces with spoon.

Put avocado pulp in bowl with mushrooms and fold in one half of the dressing. Do not let avocados and mushrooms stand undressed or they will discolor. Add tomatoes and shrimp and fold together with a wooden spatula. Do not overmix.

Heap avocado shells with salad and arrange each shell on a lettuce leaf on a platter or individual plates. Spoon remaining dressing over shells, sprinkle with chopped eggs and parsley, and serve with lemon wedges.

Light variation

☆Use 3 tablespoons oil and 2 tablespoons concentrated chicken stock (see p. 19) instead of 5 tablespoons oil.

Notes

The dressing can be made 1 day in advance and kept covered in the refrigerator. The salad is at its best when tossed together no longer than ½ hour before serving. A longer wait softens the ingredients so they are no longer crisp and distinct.

Arrange remaining salad mixture in mounds on the lettuce leaves beside the avocados.

COMPOSED SALAD WITH SCAMPI OR CRABMEAT
Salade Composée aux Scampis ou Crabe

Serves: 4 to 6

> Isabelle's Vinaigrette, made with lemon juice (see p. 46), strong version
> 1 grapefruit, peeled and segmented (reserve 3 tablespoons juice and a few thin strips of zest)
> ½ lb. mushrooms, sliced
> ¾ lb. poached shrimp (see p. 112), halved lengthwise, or crabmeat, fresh, frozen, or canned, picked over to remove bits of shell
> 2 medium tomatoes, peeled, seeded, and diced
> Salt
> Freshly ground black pepper
> Juice of 1 lemon
> 1 head of Boston lettuce or large Bibb lettuce, leaves separated

Prepare vinaigrette, adding reserved grapefruit juice.

Set aside a few grapefruit segments and combine the rest with the shrimp, tomatoes, and mushrooms in a bowl.

Pour dressing over and toss salad, using 2 forks. Season with salt, pepper, and lemon juice.

Arrange lettuce leaves on chilled plates or a platter and squeeze lemon juice over them. Mound portions of salad on lettuce. Cut reserved grapefruit sections into cubes and use with zest to garnish salad.

Notes

Salad can be prepared, with the exception of the mushrooms, 2 hours in advance. Slice and add mushrooms just before serving to prevent discoloration.

TOMATOES STUFFED WITH SHRIMP
Tomates Farcies aux Crevettes

Serves: 6

> 6 medium tomatoes, firm but ripe, 2½ to 3 inches in diameter
> Salt
> Juice of lemon
> 1 lb. medium shrimp, poached (see p. 112)
> ½ cup mayonnaise, made with lemon juice (see p. 39)
> 1 shallot, minced
> 2 tablespoons minced parsley
> 1 head of Boston lettuce, leaves separated
> Lemon wedges

Peel and core the tomatoes. Cut a thick slice off the bottom of each and reserve slices. Carefully hollow out tomatoes with a teaspoon, being careful not to pierce the skin. Sprinkle the insides with salt, and invert shells on a plate, and let drain for 15 minutes. Squeeze ½ teaspoon lemon juice into each shell.

Halve shrimp lengthwise and cut in thirds crosswise. In a bowl combine with mayonnaise, shallot, and 1 tablespoon parsley.

Fill tomatoes with stuffing. Line a serving dish with lettuce leaves, arrange tomatoes on top, and top shells with reserved slices as lids. Sprinkle with remaining parsley and serve with lemon wedges.

Notes

Can be prepared several hours ahead and refrigerated.

6
MEAT AND POULTRY

Being both simple and sensible, the methods of cooking meat and poultry that evolved over the ages remain virtually unchanged. They are braising, broiling, poaching, sautéing, and roasting. The introduction of modern cookware and such appliances as the pressure cooker have facilitated cooking by these methods and in some cases speeded it up.

BUYING MEAT AND POULTRY

Obviously the quality of the meat or poultry you select will determine to no small degree the quality of the dish you prepare from it. A good basic rule is never to have anything to do with ungraded meat or poultry. You should buy only top-grade cuts and fowl—for beef, lamb, and veal, prime or choice; for pork, U.S. No. 1; and for poultry, USDA Grade A. These gradings, however, will tell you nothing about the age of the foods, and in order to distinguish between what is truly fresh and what is not you should develop an eye for color, texture, and other telltale features. (Your nose needs no tutoring. If something smells bad, don't buy it.)

Following are suggestions as to what to look for, together with other information that should prove useful.

Beef. The cut should be red in color, a bright but not a flaming red, and its surface smooth and thinly grained, while the surrounding fat should be creamy white and thin rather than yellow and thick. The bones should be white too. Tender cuts should be marbled with very fine, lacelike tracings of fat. Examine the edges of the cut. If they are even faintly purplish or greenish, even in just one spot, the meat is too old.

Veal. This meat should ideally be pale salmon in color with very white fat, but since such cuts are all but impossible to find, a light, light pink will do. The grain should be exceptionally fine, almost invisible.

Lamb. The most tender, spring lamb, is sold between the end of March and the end of September; winter lamb is older and less tender and has a more pronounced flavor and smell akin to mutton. In color, lamb should fall in the range between red and brown, and as a rule the younger it is the lighter its color will be. The meat should be finely-grained, and its fat white or off-white.

Pork. The meat, showing a fine grainy texture, should be a light gray pink in color and the fat white and soft.

Chicken. Regardless of the size of the bird you choose, look for a plump breast, a tight round body, and yellow skin. A yellow skin normally indicates that a chicken was fed on corn, though unscrupulous suppliers sometimes tint the flesh yellow with artificial coloring.

Duck. Thanks to the very thick layer of fat that insulates and protects its flesh, this bird takes very well to freezing, and except in the few places where ducks are raised commercially it is invariably sold frozen. Commercial ducks are in fact ducklings; they weigh approximately five pounds and serve three to four people, whereas a chicken of the same weight serves six.

Turkeys. Although about four of every five turkeys sold in the U.S. are now sold frozen, fresh ones are obtainable in most areas the year round, ranging from delicate little spring turkeys to monsters weighing as much as forty pounds in the holiday season. We recommend those in the 9- to 12-pound range and suggest that if you want to serve one as the centerpiece of a Thanksgiving or Christmas feast, when both supplies and demand are at their peak, you order it fresh-killed in advance.

FROZEN MEAT AND POULTRY

The quick-freezing of fowl and slaughtered animals has made meat and poultry available in areas where they never were before and obtainable even out of season. These frozen products are, however, second-best to the fresh. All the same, if they have been properly frozen and if you defrost them and cook them without mishap, few if any of your guests will notice the difference.

A few tips regarding refrigeration:

• Since it is impossible to judge the quality of frozen meat and poultry, do, if possible, buy them fresh and freeze them yourself, wrapping each item in freezer paper and sealing it with freezer tape to avoid freezer burns. Keep the freezer temperature at 0° F. or lower. According to the Department of Agriculture, meat will keep in a frozen state for long periods: beef and lamb, twelve months; pork, eight months; ground beef and ground lamb, four months; pork sausage, three months.

• We recommend that you defrost meat and poultry completely in your refrigerator and then cook it without delay. Once defrosted, frozen meats don't keep as well as fresh ones and continue to lose their juices.

• Freshly ground meat should be cooked the day it is bought. Cut-up meat will keep three days in a refrigerator and a roast one week at 30° F.

Now, let's look at the five classic methods of cooking meat and poultry, oberving how each in its way makes for lightness, in a gustatory sense, by eliminating fat and/or not absorbing it.

BRAISING

The braising scenario is as follows: meat and poultry, cooked for a long time in liquid, release their fat into the cooking juices, which are then degreased (see *Tips* at the end of this section). The fat is not reabsorbed by the meat. The cooking juices can be used as a sauce, either as they are or enriched.

Meat or poultry to be braised should first be browned and then put in a pot in which it fits fairly snugly so that you don't have to add too much liquid, diluting the sauce. Pour in hot liquid—usually a rich stock or stock plus wine which supply flavor and color—to about two-thirds of the way up the food, then cover the pot tightly and place it in the oven, where the liquid will boil gently and continuously, suffusing the meat with heat and steam. Two or three times in the course of braising, the meat or poultry should be turned so that it cooks evenly and so that the exposed surfaces do not dry out. Also it insures against the meat's sticking to the bottom of the pot. Oven braising surrounds the pot with an even heat. The braising liquid reduces both through evaporation and because the meat absorbs some liquid, though not the fat.

Stewing is done the same way except that the meat is cut in pieces, fit snugly into the pot to the depth of at least one layer, and cooked covered with liquid.

Important note: the long cooking time required for braising can be shortened to a fraction, with no loss whatever of either flavor or texture, simply by letting a pressure cooker do the job.

BROILING

When you broil—cook by direct radiant heat—fat drains from the meat or bird into a receptacle, making the food lighter and more digestible.

For a broiled steak the broiler should be preheated, the rack oiled and a pan, skillet, or other receptacle placed below the rack to catch the melted fat and drippings. The steak's thickness dictates its proper distance from the flame or coil. A two-inch steak should be about two inches from the heat source and should broil four or five minutes on each side.

Beef brochettes are placed on an oiled rack and the rack placed on top of a skillet or roasting pan; they should be 2½ inches from the flame or coil. The skewer should be a foot long and flat, with each side about a quarter of an inch wide so that when you turn it, it doesn't simply rotate inside the meat.

POACHING

To poach is to cook in a boiling or simmering liquid such as stock, wine, water, or even syrup. The meat or poultry is completely submerged. Like braising, poaching makes food lighter by forcing it to release some of its fat, which drains into the surrounding liquid; if this liquid is to be used as a sauce it must first be degreased.

SAUTÉING AND BROWNING

For some dishes meat is cooked through (sautéed); for others, it is simply browned as a preliminary step. If meat or poultry is properly seared in the process, a crust forms around it that prevents it from absorbing much of the cooking fat, which can be discarded before the sauce is made. This results in a lighter and more digestible dish than you might expect using this method.

To brown or sauté, heat a small amount of fat in a skillet (use butter mixed with oil to prevent the former from burning or oil only) until hot enough to assure that the meat or poultry is instantly seared on contact with it, sealing in its juices and giving it a fine, brown (with chicken, golden brown) crispy coating. Do not turn the meat or poultry until its underside is lightly browned. Pieces of meat should be kept separated so that they don't steam but not so far apart that the fat between them burns. To discourage sticking and encourage browning lift each piece in turn and let the fat flow back under it. The temperature in the pan should be controlled so that the fat stays hot without burning or smoking; the sound should be a crisp sizzling. The pieces should be browned evenly on all sides. Sautéing or browning meat or chicken imparts to it a highly distinctive flavor, appearance, and character.

Note: When sautéing or browning cut-up chicken you should place the parts skin down in the skillet or the skin will become soggy and fail to brown properly. Pork chops present a different problem. No matter how juicy they may be when you buy them, the prolonged cooking needed to kill the organisms that cause trichinosis is certain to dry them out unless a method of moist cooking is used. Sauté the chops first to brown them on each side, then cover the pan and let them cook slowly in their own juices, cooking evenly from top to bottom, for a moist and tender result.

ROASTING

Our own preferred method of roasting is to sear and brown at high heat, then reduce the heat to continue cooking. The roast, whether a large piece of meat (e.g., a rib roast of beef or a leg of lamb) or a whole bird (chicken, duck, turkey) should fill the roasting pan comfortably. If the pan is too large the melted fat or drippings will burn or stock will evaporate too quickly. Cracked bones and various vegetables—a carrot, celery, an onion, and perhaps one or two unpeeled cloves of garlic—can be placed around the roast as it cooks, enriching the flavor of the pan gravy.

You should start checking for doneness after cooking one hour at approximately 400 to 425 degrees for a 5- to 6-pound leg of lamb, a 3½- to 4-pound chicken, or a 4- to 5-pound duck, and after 35 minutes for a 3- to 3½-inch thick filet mignon of any weight.

After roasting, meat or poultry should be left to stand before it is carved so that the juices that have contracted to its center can flow back into the tissues, enabling the meat to relax and become more tender. If allowed to rest, the juices tend to stay in the muscle and flesh when carved instead of spilling out onto the carving board.

Covered with foil, roasted meat and poultry can be kept warm in an oven for half an hour at 200° F. and for two hours at 140° F.; after that they will inevitably taste as if they had been reheated. You can, of course, cook a dish of this kind a day in advance, then let it cool and refrigerate it. To bring it back to life you wrap it in foil and reheat it for about half an hour at 400° F. (You can also keep it at the right temperature on a hotplate set at 120° F. for a while.)

OBTAINING A SAUCE:
DEGLAZING, LIAISON WITH CREAM, REDUCTION,

Deglazing (from the French verb *déglaçer*) means to release or lique-fy the degreased cooking juices that caramelize in lumps on the bottom of a skillet or pan after browning, sautéing, or roasting. While almost any liquid can be used for deglazing, the best deglaz-ing agents are wine, vinegar, and lemon juice, which, being acid, dissolve the thick, sticky residue very efficiently, making for a sauce that is concentrated and rich in color and imparting to it a brisk, tart flavor. Deglazing should be done as soon as the food is removed, for once the skillet or pan cools, achieving the necessary emulsion becomes difficult. Add the liquid to the hot skillet or pan in small amounts.

For a liaison with cream, boil the mixture until it is slightly syrupy, then add cream, reducing for a minute or so until the new mixture thickens to a light, creamy consistency. Alternately, after reducing the released cooking juices and deglazing liquid, you can add stock, allow the mixture to reduce and then add cream and reduce. (The proportions for 4 to 6 servings are ½ cup wine or ¼ cup brandy, reduced to about 3 tablespoons. Add about 1 cup of stock and reduce to ⅓ cup. Then add ⅔ cup heavy cream and re-duce to a light creamy consistency, or ½ cup ricotta and 1 to 2 tablespoons heavy cream and bring just to a boil.) The reductions give you more sauce and strengthen it. Of course, you can dispense with the acid bath reduction and cream altogether and do your deglazing with water or stock only; this will result in a delicious concentrated gravy but one lacking that certain pleasing "bite"— and, obviously, it will not produce much in the way of quantity.

TIPS

Fat around meat. Some cooks place extra pieces of fat around the meat before cooking in the belief that it enriches the meat's flavor. We disagree. The practice enriches only the butcher—and prolongs the cooking time. Prior to cooking, meat should be trimmed of most of its fat. Certain pieces of meat should be tied with string according to the directions given in the recipes to ensure that they retain their shapes.

Fat in meat. A useful fact to remember is that the fat in chicken (not counting the skin) and veal is less saturated than that in beef, lamb, and pork—another reason, besides economy, to serve chicken more often than the other foods. (As between chicken and veal, the former is not only much cheaper but also, thanks to stricter product controls, more apt to be of top quality.)

Relaxation. All meat and poultry should be left to stand for a time after they are cooked—as explained under Roasting—to allow them to relax and attain the proper texture.

Carving. Meat and poultry should always be cut against the grain so that when you bite into a slice the meat will yield readily to the teeth.

Degreasing. There are several ways to rid stocks and sauces of grease, and the choice usually depends on how soon the stock or sauce is needed. Here are three.

• The simplest method is to tilt the pan or skillet to gather juice, and then spoon off the fat floating on top.

• With larger amounts of liquid a degreaser can be of great help. This device is simply a measuring cup with a spout that rises from the bottom, enabling you to pour off juices while the fat, being lighter, stays in the degreaser. Various models are available in stores carrying kitchen equipment.

• A third method is to refrigerate the liquid, causing the fat to congeal so that it can be easily removed.

BURGUNDIAN STEAK
Bifteck Bourguignon

Serves: 4

1½ to 2 lbs. boned and trimmed shell or sirloin steaks, cut 1 inch thick

Marinade

3 shallots, minced
2 tablespoons minced parsley
⅛ teaspoon dried thyme
2 bay leaves, crushed
6 whole black peppercorns, coarsely ground
2 tablespoons lemon juice
3 tablespoons oil

Sauce

1½ tablespoons butter
1½ tablespoons oil
1 medium onion, minced
2 cloves garlic, crushed
½ lb. mushrooms, sliced ¼ inch thick
Salt
½ cup red wine
1 cup concentrated chicken stock (see p. 19)
⅔ cup heavy cream
Freshly ground black pepper
1 tablespoon finely chopped parsley
4 croutons (see p. 63)

✭Mix marinade ingredients well and spread half in a non-aluminum dish large enough to hold the steaks in one layer. Add steaks, spread in remaining marinade, and marinate in the refrigerator for at least 1 hour. When ready to cook, remove steaks from marinade scraping them well, and dry on paper towels.

Heat butter and oil in a skillet until very hot and light brown. Add steaks and cook for 4 to 5 minutes. Turn steaks and cook for 4 to 5 minutes longer. Transfer to a warm platter and cover with foil.

Add onion to skillet and cook over moderate heat, stirring, for 5 minutes. Add garlic and cook for 30 seconds. Add mushrooms, cover, and cook over moderate heat for 3 to 4 minutes. Salt lightly and transfer the mushrooms to a warm dish, using a slotted spoon. Add wine and marinade to skillet and reduce to ¼ cup. Add stock and any juices that have accumulated around the steaks and reduce to ⅓ cup.

□Add cream and boil slowly, stirring, for 1 to 2 minutes, or until the sauce has a creamy consistency.

Season the sauce with salt and pepper to taste. Strain the sauce over the steaks. Arrange the mushrooms around the meat, sprinkle with parsley, and garnish with croutons.

Light variation

☆Omit oil in marinade and use 1 tablespoon red wine vinegar in place of the 2 tablespoons lemon juice.

□In place of heavy cream, use ½ cup ricotta, blended in a food processor, and 2 tablespoons heavy cream. Remove pan juices from heat, stir in processed ricotta and 2 tablespoons cream, and bring slowly to a boil, stirring. Remove from heat immediately. (If necessary, the sauce can be thinned with stock.) Season the sauce with salt and pepper to taste. Strain the sauce over the steaks. Arrange the mushrooms around the meat, sprinkle with parsley, and garnish with croutons.

Notes

This is really a maceration, not a marinade—a short herb bath which adds a piquant fresh taste to the meat. It can be used for fish and chicken as well.

BEEF BRAISED IN BEER
Carbonnades Flamandes

Serves: 6

    3 lbs. boneless chuck in one piece
    ¼ lb. thickly sliced lean bacon, diced
    1½ tablespoons butter
    1½ tablespoons oil
    1½ lbs. (about 6 medium) yellow onions, thinly sliced
    1 teaspoon minced garlic
      Salt
      Freshly ground black pepper
    2 sprigs fresh thyme, or ½ teaspoon dried
    2 bay leaves
    1 tablespoon brown sugar
    2 cups light beer
    1 cup all-purpose stock (see pp. 17–18) or water
    3 slices white bread, crusts removed
    3 tablespoons imported mustard, such as Dijon or Düsseldorf
    2 tablespoons red wine vinegar
      Chopped parsley

Preheat oven to 325°.

Cut the meat into ¾-inch-thick slices, and cut slices into 2-inch pieces. Pat dry on paper towels and reserve.

Cook bacon in skillet until lightly brown and crisp. Transfer to a casserole or pressure cooker with a slotted spoon, leaving fat in skillet. Add butter and oil to skillet, one third of the meat, and cook over medium-high heat on one side until well browned. Do not overcrowd skillet or let pieces touch as they brown. Turn pieces so they brown on all sides. Do not let fat burn. Transfer meat to the casserole or pressure cooker and continue cooking until all meat has been browned. Two skillets can be used to speed up this process.

Add onions to remaining fat and juices in the skillet and cook over medium heat, stirring occasionally, for 5 to 7 minutes or until soft. The onions will have deglazed the pan. Add onions to beef with garlic, salt and pepper to taste, thyme, bay leaves, sugar, beer, and stock. Spread both sides of bread with mustard and lay on top of stew. Cover tightly and bring to a boil on top of the stove. Transfer to the oven and bake for 1½ to 2 hours (or cook 40 minutes in pressure cooker). Cooking time will depend on the tenderness of the meat.

Transfer meat to a bowl with a slotted spoon. Strain cooking liquid through a fine-mesh sieve into a saucepan, pressing hard on onions with the back of a ladle. Tilt saucepan and degrease liquid thoroughly. Add vinegar and bring to a boil.

Return meat and liquid to pot and bring to a simmer. Simmer for 5 minutes and season with salt and pepper to taste. Arrange meat on a warm platter, spoon sauce over it, and sprinkle with parsley.

Notes

This dish is even better when made a day or so ahead of time and refrigerated. Reheat in a preheated 325° oven for 20 to 30 minutes, depending on whether the stew is at room temperature or comes from the refrigerator. Stew also freezes well.

BEEF TENDERLOIN STUFFED WITH MUSHROOMS
Filet de Boeuf Charlemagne

Serves: 8

  1½ tablespoons butter
  1½ tablespoons oil
   3 lbs. beef tenderloin, trimmed and tied
     Salt
     Freshly ground black pepper
     Duxelles (see p. 243 and prepare 1½ times the recipe)
  ¼ cup Sercial Madeira
     Béarnaise Sauce or Hollandaise Sauce (see pp. 42–44). If using Light Version, double recipe.
     Watercress sprigs

Preheat oven to 475°.

Melt butter and oil in a roasting pan. Add meat and roll evenly to coat with fat. Season lightly with salt and pepper. Roast meat for 10 minutes, turning 2 or 3 times. Lower heat to 425° and roast in upper part of oven for 30 to 35 minutes. Transfer meat to a platter and let cool completely.

Prepare Duxelles and sauce and let cool.

Pour off fat from roasting pan, add wine, and reduce until slightly syrupy over medium high heat. Stir and scrape with wooden spoon to dissolve the brown particles of juice that stick to the bottom of the pan. Strain juices into Duxelles.

Cut meat into 16 ½-inch-thick slices. Spread each slice on one side with 1 tablespoon Duxelles. Re-form roast in buttered baking dish, keeping slices in the order they were cut. The roast will stay together more easily if it is inclined slightly. Stick a small skewer through each end piece to secure it.

Spread the entire surface with Béarnaise or Hollandaise and bake in the top of a 400° oven for 15 to 20 minutes, or until golden brown on top. Garnish with watercress.

Notes

Serve roast with French Fried Potatoes (see p. 209).

The entire roast can be made and assembled the day before up to the final baking. Refrigerate, covered loosely with foil. When beef is done, it will stay warm for an hour in an oven not warmer than 140°.

Roast can also be cooked entirely on top of the stove, which results in a better crust and more flavor (but requires more attention). Heat 1½ tablespoons oil and 1½ tablespoons butter until very hot but not brown in a pan big enough to hold the meat. Brown meat on all sides for 20 minutes, or until done to desired degree.

This is also a good way to make a fancy dish out of a leftover roast. Slice, spread slices with Duxelles, reassemble, cover with sauce, and heat.

SAUTÉED BEEF EXPRESS
Sauté de Boeuf Express

Serves: 4

- 1½ lbs. lean, tender, trimmed beef, such as tenderloin tail, cut into 2- x 2- x ¾-inch cubes
- 2 tablespoons butter
- 1 tablespoon oil
- 2 cloves garlic, minced
- 2 medium shallots, minced
- ½ cup red wine
- 1 cup concentrated all-purpose or chicken stock (see pp. 17–20)
- 1 tablespoon tomato paste
- ½ teaspoon dried rosemary
- ⅔ cup heavy cream
  Salt
  Freshly ground black pepper
- 1 tablespoon finely chopped parsley
  Watercress sprigs

Dry beef well on paper towels. Heat oil and butter in a skillet until very hot and starting to turn golden. Add meat and brown well over medium-high heat, turning. Do not let fat burn. (The total cooking time is 7 to 8 minutes. Meat should be pink inside.) Do in two batches, if necessary, and do not crowd skillet. Transfer meat to a platter and keep warm in a 200° oven. Pour off most of fat from skillet, leaving a thin film. Stir in the garlic and shallots, and cook over moderate heat for 1 minute.

Add wine and reduce over moderate heat to 2 to 3 tablespoons, scraping bottom and sides of skillet with a wooden spoon to dissolve the brown glaze. Add stock, tomato paste, and rosemary and cook sauce over moderate heat, stirring, until reduced to ⅓ cup. ☆Add cream and reduce, stirring, to a nice velvety consistency, or until sauce coats a spoon. Season with salt and pepper, if necessary. Add any juices that have accumulated in the platter. Sprinkle meat with parsley and surround with watercress. Serve sauce separately.

Light variation

☆In place of ⅔ cup heavy cream, use 1 to 2 tablespoons heavy cream and ½ cup ricotta, blended in food processor. Cook sauce, stirring, over moderate heat, until reduced to ⅓ cup. Remove from heat, stir in ricotta and cream, and bring sauce just to the first boil. Remove from heat immediately. Season with salt and pepper. Thin out with warm stock if necessary.

Notes

Serve with Buttered Rice (see p. 203).

If skillet is too small, it will be necessary to sauté the meat in two batches. Overcrowding produces steam, prevents meat from crusting, and causes a lot of juice. Do not overcook meat or it will become rubbery. Meat should stay pink inside.

STEAK WITH GREEN PEPPERCORNS
Steak aux Poivres Verts

Serves: 4

  1½ to 2 lbs. (after boning and trimming) shell or sirloin steaks, or fillet of beef, cut into 1-inch-thick slices
  3 tablespoons oil
  3 tablespoons soft green peppercorns, drained
  1 tablespoon butter
  Salt
  ¼ cup Cognac
  1 cup chicken stock (see pp. 19–20) or all-purpose stock (see pp. 17–18)
  ⅔ cup heavy cream
  Watercress sprigs

Put steaks in a non-aluminum dish big enough to hold them flat in 1 layer. ☆Add 1 tablespoon oil and turn steaks to coat them on all sides.

Press 2 tablespoons of green peppercorns onto both sides of the steaks. Let stand for 30 minutes. Chop remaining peppercorns and set aside.

Heat butter and remaining oil in a skillet until very hot and just starting to turn golden. Add steaks and cook for 4 to 5 minutes. Turn, sprinkle with salt, and cook for 4 to 5 minutes on the other side. Cook longer for well-done meat. (Green peppercorns have a tendency to jump out of the skillet while cooking, so be careful.)

Heat the Cognac in a small skillet. Ignite it and pour it over the steaks, protecting the face and hair. Let flame die and transfer steaks to a warm platter. Cover loosely with foil and keep warm in a 200° oven.

Add stock to skillet and reduce to ⅓ cup over medium-high heat, scraping up the browned cooking juices with a wooden spoon. □Add cream and chopped peppercorns and cook, stirring, over medium-high heat until cream thickens slightly. Add any juices that have accumulated around the steaks in the platter. Season the sauce with salt to taste.

Spoon sauce over the steaks and garnish with watercress.

Light variation

☆Do not coat the steaks with oil before pressing the 2 tablespoons of green peppercorns onto both sides of the steaks.

□In place of cream use ½ cup ricotta, blended in a food processor, and 2 tablespoons heavy cream. After stock has been reduced to ⅓ cup, remove pan from the heat and stir in ½ cup processed ricotta, 2 tablespoons heavy cream, and the chopped peppercorns. Blend well. Return to the heat and bring just to the first boil, stirring. Remove from heat and add any juices that have accumulated around the steaks in the platter. Season the sauce with salt to taste.

Notes

Use good lean ground beef and follow the recipe to make Hamburgers with Green Peppercorns.

The chopped green peppercorns are stirred into the sauce at the end to avoid too strong a sauce. It is always a good idea to taste the peppercorns before using them. One brand can be stronger than another, and, if so, the amount called for in the recipe can be reduced.

This recipe can also be prepared with the strongest black peppercorns. A good, but not overpowering, way to do this is to let the steaks stand in the refrigerator for 1 hour with 4 crushed black peppercorns pressed into each side. Before sautéing the steaks, scrape the peppercorns off and reserve them. Add the peppercorns to the sauce when reducing the cream. The sauce will have a much better flavor than if there is a layer of crushed peppercorns on the steaks. And the sauce will not burn the stomach.

BROCHETTES OF BEEF
Boeuf en Brochette

Serves: 6

2½ to 3 lbs. lean tender beef, such as tenderloin, trimmed and cut into 1½-inch cubes

Marinade
4 medium shallots, very finely chopped
2 cloves garlic, minced
1 7-inch stalk celery, minced
2 tablespoons chopped parsley
2 bay leaves
1 teaspoon dried rosemary
1 teaspoon dried thyme
Juice of ½ lemon
1 teaspoon coarsely ground or crushed whole black peppercorns
1 teaspoon salt
1 tablespoon oil

Sauce
2 tablespoons butter
1 large onion, minced
1 cup red wine
2 tomatoes (¾ lb.), peeled and seeded
½ teaspoon sugar
2 tablespoons Dijon mustard
1 tablespoon lemon juice
1 tablespoon chopped parsley
Salt
Freshly ground black pepper

Special equipment
6 12-inch skewers

Combine marinade ingredients in a glass or porcelain bowl large enough to hold the meat. Add meat and mix so that all pieces are coated. Cover and marinate for at least 1 hour.

Melt butter in a skillet over medium-low heat and add onion. Cook covered, stirring occasionally, for 5 to 7 minutes, or until soft without browning.

Scrape marinade off meat and add to onion with wine, tomatoes, and sugar. Cook over medium low heat for 10 to 15 minutes, or until lightly thickened. Remove bay leaves. Purée in blender or food processor until smooth. If sauce is too thin, reduce over moderate heat, stirring, until it reaches a thick, creamy consistency like mayonnaise. Let sauce cool slightly after reducing and blend in mustard, parsley, lemon juice, and salt and pepper to taste.

Dry beef well on paper towels. Thread 6 cubes on each skewer and broil about 2½ inches from very hot heat, turning, for 8 minutes. Serve with sauce in a sauceboat.

Notes

Do not marinate meat in a corrosive metallic bowl, such as aluminum—it gives a metallic flavor to food. Meat can be marinated up to 1 day in advance, and refrigerated covered.

These brochettes are excellent for an outdoor party—guests can participate and grill their own.

MARINATED FILLET OF BEEF
Tournedos Sauvages

Serves: 6

    1 2- to 2½-lb. fillet of beef, cut into 1-inch-thick slices, or boned and trimmed shell or sirloin steaks

For the marinade
- 2 tablespoons oil
- 1½ cups dry red wine
- 2 tablespoons Cognac
- 1 medium onion, minced
- 1 medium stalk celery, minced
- 2 cloves garlic, minced
- 1 shallot, minced
- 8 juniper berries
- 10 whole black peppercorns

To sauté steaks
- 1½ tablespoons butter
- 1½ tablespoons oil
- 3 tablespoons Cognac
- 1 cup chicken stock (see pp. 19–20) or all-purpose stock (see pp. 17–18)
- 2 teaspoons cornstarch dissolved in 2 teaspoons red wine
- 1 teaspoon wine vinegar
- Salt
- Freshly ground black pepper
- Watercress sprigs

☆Mix marinade ingredients well. Pour half the marinade into a non-aluminum dish big enough to hold the steaks flat in one layer. Add the steaks and pour in the remaining marinade. Marinate in the refrigerator for about 12 hours. When ready to cook, remove steaks from marinade and dry on paper towels. Reserve the marinade.

    Heat butter and oil in a skillet until very hot and just beginning to color. Add steaks and cook for 4 to 5 minutes. Turn steaks, season with salt and pepper, and cook for 4 to 5 minutes on the second side. Pour in the Cognac, ignite it, and let the flame die.

(Protect hair, face, and hands.) Transfer the steaks to a warm platter and keep warm in a low oven.

Add only half the marinade and half the vegetables to the skillet. Reduce to 4 tablespoons over moderate heat, scraping up any browned cooking juices with a wooden spatula. Add stock and reduce to ⅔ cup. Remove from the heat and stir in enough of the cornstarch mixture to give the sauce a light creamy consistency. Add vinegar and season with salt and pepper to taste. Strain sauce over the steaks, pressing the vegetables with the back of a spoon to extract all juices. Garnish with watercress sprigs.

Light variation
☆Omit oil in the marinade.

HAMBURGERS WITH HERBS AND SHALLOTS
Hamburgers aux Herbes et Echalotes

Serves: 4

  1½ tablespoons butter
    5 shallots, minced
    2 cloves garlic, minced
    3 tablespoons minced parsley
  1½ cups dry red wine
     Salt
     Freshly ground black pepper
    1 bay leaf
    ¼ teaspoon dried thyme
    1 4-inch piece celery stalk, finely chopped
    1 egg, lightly beaten
  1½ pounds very lean beef, ground
    ⅛ teaspoon nutmeg
    ½ tablespoon butter and 1 tablespoon oil
    6 croutons (see p. 63), optional
    ⅓ cup heavy cream
    1 to 2 teaspoons lemon juice

☆Melt butter in small skillet, add shallots, and cook, stirring, for 2 to 3 minutes without browning. Add garlic, half the parsley, ¾ cup wine, salt and pepper to taste, bay leaf, thyme, and celery and reduce slowly, stirring occasionally, until liquid has evaporated completely. Remove from heat and beat in egg rapidly. Let cool completely.

Put meat in a bowl, add herb mixture, and season with salt, pepper, and nutmeg. Mix thoroughly with a wooden spoon. Shape into 4 round or oval patties and flatten to ¾ inch thick.

Heat butter and oil in a skillet and, when quite hot but not brown, add hamburgers, and cook over medium-high heat for 3 minutes per side for medium rare, or to desired degree of doneness. Slip a spatula under hamburgers once or twice during cooking to let fat run underneath to prevent sticking. Transfer to a warm platter, on top of croutons, if desired.

Add remaining wine to skillet and reduce to 4 tablespoons over medium-high heat, using a wooden spoon to scrape up any cooking juices that have stuck to the bottom of the skillet. Add cream and boil, stirring, until cream thickens slightly.

Season with salt and pepper, if necessary. Remove from heat and stir in lemon juice. Mask each hamburger with a good spoonful of sauce. Sprinkle remaining parsley on top of sauce.

Light variation
❖Omit butter and cook herb mixture in wine.

Notes
Hamburgers can be assembled several hours before cooking. However, cook hamburgers the same day, as ground meat does not keep well any longer.

STUFFED BREAST OF VEAL
Poitrine de Veau Farcie

Serves: 8 to 10

1 5½- to 6-lb. breast of veal, boned to yield about 3 to 3½ lbs. of meat (Have butcher bone the roast and make a pocket for stuffing.)

Stuffing

- 1 tablespoon butter
- 1 medium onion, minced
- 2 shallots, minced
- 1 clove garlic, minced
- ⅔ lb. lean veal, put through the grinder twice
- ⅓ lb. pork, put through the grinder twice
- 2 tablespoons Cognac
- 1 whole egg
- 1 egg yolk
- ¼ teaspoon ground rosemary
  Salt
  Freshly ground black pepper
  Freshly grated nutmeg

Cooking the meat

- 2 tablespoons butter
- 2 tablespoons oil
- 1 medium onion, cut in sixths
- 1 medium carrot, cut in sixths
- 3 tablespoons flour
- ½ cup dry white wine
- 4 cups quick chicken stock (see p. 20), warmed
- ½ teaspoon dried thyme
- 1 bay leaf
- 2 cloves garlic, crushed
- 1 medium tomato, peeled, seeded, and coarsely chopped, or 1
  tablespoon tomato paste
  Salt
  Freshly ground black pepper
- 1 tablespoon finely chopped parsley

✰Melt the butter in a small skillet and stir in the onion, shallots, and garlic. Cover and cook slowly, stirring occasionally, for 5 to 7 minutes, or until tender. Let cool slightly.

▫Put ground meats in a bowl and add the onion mixture, Cognac, egg and yolk, rosemary, and salt, pepper, and nutmeg to taste. Mix thoroughly and stuff veal with mixture. Close opening with skewers and string.

(continued)

Preheat oven to 350°.

Heat butter and oil in a flame-proof casserole until hot but not brown. Add stuffed breast and brown over moderate heat. This will take about 15 minutes. Remove veal and add onion and carrot. Cook for 5 minutes, or until they are lightly colored. Stir in flour and cook for 2 minutes, or until the flour is lightly colored. Pour in the wine and stock, bring to a boil, and boil for 1 minute, stirring. Return the veal to the casserole. The liquid should come three quarters of the way up the meat. Add more stock if necessary to bring the liquid to this level. Add bay leaf, thyme, garlic, and tomato. Season lightly with salt and pepper, if necessary. Cover, bring back to a boil, and bake for 1¾ to 2 hours, or until meat is fork-tender. Turn meat twice during cooking. (Cook in the pressure cooker for 50 minutes. Put a Flame-Tamer under the pressure cooker to prevent scorching.)

Transfer veal to a warm platter, cover loosely with foil, and let stand for 15 minutes in the turned-off oven.

Skim fat from sauce. Strain sauce through a fine sieve, pressing on the vegetables with the back of a spoon to extract all juices. Season with salt and pepper, if necessary. Pour sauce into a saucepan, bring to a simmer, and reduce until sauce is thick enough to coat a spoon.

Remove skewers from veal, cut it into ½-inch-thick slices, and arrange on a warm platter. Spoon a little of the sauce over the veal slices and sprinkle with parsley. Serve remaining sauce in a warm sauceboat.

Light variation

☆Omit 1 tablespoon butter in stuffing and replace with 3 tablespoons water.

▫Omit ⅓ lb. pork and replace with veal.

Notes

If preparing the veal breast a day in advance, return the meat and sauce to the casserole and cool uncovered. Cover and refrigerate. Reheat in a 325°oven for 35 minutes, turning meat and adding a little stock or water, if necessary.

This roast is delicious served cold with various vegetable sauces. Freeze leftover sauce and use it to enrich other sauces.

VEAL STRIPS IN LEMON SAUCE
Émincés de Veau au Citron

Serves: 6

6 veal scallops, ½ inch thick, about 5 oz. each
Salt
Freshly ground black pepper
2 tablespoons flour
Braised Mushrooms, made with ¾ lb. mushrooms, 1½ tablespoons butter, 3 tablespoons water, and 1½ tablespoons lemon juice (see p. 244 for directions)
2 lemons
2 tablespoons oil
3 tablespoons butter
3 shallots, finely chopped
½ cup dry white wine
2 tablespoons lemon juice
1 cup heavy cream
1 tablespoon finely chopped parsley

Cut the veal into strips about ⅜ inch wide and 2½ inches long. Put them on a platter and sprinkle with salt, pepper, and flour. Toss lightly with the hands to coat.

Prepare the mushrooms and drain, reserving the juice. Set mushrooms and juice aside separately. Peel off the thin yellow skin of 2 lemons in strips and cut lengthwise into the thinnest possible strands, or use a zester. Blanch the zest for 2 minutes in 1 qt. of boiling water. Drain, rinse under cold, running water, and set aside.

Add oil and 2 tablespoons butter to a skillet and heat until hot but not brown but starting to turn hazelnut. Add veal and cook over medium-high heat for 6 to 8 minutes, or until lightly golden, tossing the meat with a spatula.

Transfer meat to a warm platter. Cover loosely with foil and keep warm in a 200° oven while finishing the sauce. Discard fat left in skillet.

Melt remaining butter in skillet and add the shallots. Cook over moderate heat, stirring, for 1 minute. Add the wine and reduce to 4 tablespoons over moderate heat, scraping up brown glaze from bottom and sides of skillet.

Add lemon juice and reserved mushroom juice and reduce to ¼ cup over moderately high heat.

Add cream and boil down until the sauce has thickened slightly to a light creamy consistency. Taste and correct seasoning, if necessary.

Put veal and mushrooms into the sauce and simmer for 1 to 2 minutes to reheat. Transfer to a deep, warm serving platter and scatter lemon zest on top. Sprinkle with parsley.

Notes

Three whole chicken breasts may be substituted for the veal. Skin, bone, and halve them. Lay the breasts between 2 sheets of wax paper. Flatten lightly with a mallet until they are an even ¼ inch thick. Do not break the meat. Turkey scaloppine the same size and weight are an almost identical substitute.

Lemon juice and strips of zest give the dish and sauce a subtle piquancy.

VEAL WITH SAUERKRAUT
Choucroute de Veau

Serves: 8

    4½ lbs. sauerkraut, fresh
    ⅓ lb. seedless raisins
    12 whole black peppercorns
    20 juniper berries
       Salt
       Freshly ground black pepper
    8 round slices veal shank, about 1 inch thick (about 2½ lbs.)
    4 slices veal breast (about 2 lbs.)
    2 tablespoons butter
    2 tablespoons oil
    8 very thin slices salt pork
    8 small white onions, about 1½ inches in diameter
    8 medium carrots, peeled

1 bay leaf
½ teaspoon dried thyme
2 cups dry white wine or Champagne
⅔ cup water

Preheat oven to 375°.

Rinse and drain sauerkraut. Soak it in cold water for 15 to 20 minutes, rinse, and drain again. Squeeze out liquid. (These steps help remove salt and sourness.) Fluff sauerkraut with a fork and put it in a bowl with raisins, peppercorns, and juniper berries.

Season veal shank pieces and breast pieces with salt and pepper. Heat butter and oil in an ovenproof pot and lightly brown meat over medium-high heat in 2 or 3 batches without crowding meat. Transfer meat to a dish as it is browned.

Add onions to pot and cook over moderate heat for 4 minutes without coloring. Reserve onions and pour off fat. Line bottom of pot with slices of salt pork. Put 6 pieces of shank on the salt pork, top with one third of the sauerkraut, the onions and carrots, bay leaf, and thyme. Cover this with half of the remaining sauerkraut. Arrange breast slices and remaining shank pieces on top and add remaining sauerkraut.

Season with salt, if necessary; pour in wine and water. Cover and bring slowly to a boil on top of the stove. Bake for 1½ to 2 hours, or until liquid has been almost absorbed (35 to 40 minutes in pressure cooker). Remove from oven and let stand for 10 to 15 minutes. Remove peppercorns and juniper berries. Mound sauerkraut in center of a heated platter. Alternate overlapping slices of veal shank and breast and salt pork, if desired (otherwise discard), around sauerkraut. Arrange onions and carrots attractively.

Notes

Choucroute should be served with boiled or Mashed Potatoes (see p. 208).

It can be prepared 2 days in advance, but not more because carrots cause sauerkraut to ferment and spoil. Reheat slowly in the oven.

The lid on the ovenproof pot should be very tight. If not, place a piece of foil between pot and lid.

You can substitute turkey for veal.

STUFFED BREAST OF VEAL THE ENGLISH WAY
Poitrine de Veau Farcie à l'Anglaise

Serves: 6 to 8

1 4½-lb. veal breast which will yield about 2½ lbs. meat (Have butcher bone the breast and make a pocket for stuffing.)

Stuffing
⅓ lb. ground pork
½ lb. ground veal
½ cup cold cooked rice
5 leaves sorrel, well washed, stems stripped out, and chopped
¼ pound raw spinach leaves, well washed, thick stems removed, and chopped
2 shallots, minced
1 tablespoon minced mint leaves
1 clove garlic, minced
1 tablespoon finely chopped parsley
Salt
Freshly ground black pepper
⅛ teaspoon ground allspice
2 eggs

Cooking the meat
Salt
Freshly ground black pepper
2 bay leaves
½ teaspoon dried thyme
1 medium onion, halved and stuck with 3 whole cloves

Vegetables
8 medium carrots, peeled and tied together with kitchen string
8 small white turnips (the size of an egg), peeled (halve or quarter larger ones)
8 medium leeks (white part only), washed well and tied together with kitchen string
1 tight head Boston lettuce
1 tablespoon finely chopped parsley

☆Mix ingredients for stuffing thoroughly with wooden spatula. Stuff veal and close opening with skewers and string.

Put veal, enough water to cover, salt and pepper to taste, bay leaves, thyme, and onion in a stockpot. Cover and bring to a boil over moderate heat. Lower heat, uncover, and boil very slowly for 1½ hours (50 to 60 minutes in pressure cooker), skimming scum occasionally. Add carrots, turnips, and leeks. Cover and bring back to a boil. Uncover and continue to boil slowly for 15 to 20 minutes, or until vegetables are still *al dente.* Test them with a skewer. Add lettuce, bring to a boil, and boil slowly for 5 minutes. (Do not cook vegetables under pressure.) Total cooking time is about 2 hours. If meat needs more cooking, transfer vegetables to a warm platter, and keep warm, covered loosely with foil, in a 200° oven.

Transfer meat to platter and let it rest for 15 minutes before carving. Remove skewers and string. Carve roast into ½-inch-thick slices and arrange them lengthwise along one side of a platter, overlapping slightly. Halve the lettuce and arrange it and the other vegetables on other side of platter. Sprinkle with parsley.

Degrease broth, strain, and season with salt and pepper, if necessary. Serve 2 cups as a sauce in a warm sauceboat.

Light variation

☆In place of ⅓ lb. ground pork and ½ lb. ground veal, use 9 oz. ground veal.

Notes

Boiled potatoes are the best accompaniment.

Serve remaining degreased broth as a soup. Add a few tablespoons tapioca to thicken it, if desired, and sprinkle with chopped parsley. Broth may be frozen for use in other dishes. Cool uncovered and freeze.

This dish can be prepared 1 day in advance. Let veal cool in broth, cover, and refrigerate. Reheat veal in broth and when it is heated through add vegetables and heat for 5 minutes.

Veal may be served cold with a vinaigrette sauce and vegetable salads. Another way is to roast it in a buttered dish with 1 cup hot broth, basting occasionally, in 375° oven for 30 minutes. Slice and serve with Uncooked Tomato Sauce (see p. 48).

VEAL PATTIES
Subrics de Veau

Serves: 6

> 2 slices white bread, crusts removed
> Milk
> 2 tablespoons butter
> 2 large shallots, finely chopped
> 1⅓ lbs. lean ground veal
> ⅔ lb. lean ground pork
> 2 eggs
> Salt
> Freshly ground black pepper
> Freshly grated nutmeg
> 2 cloves garlic, minced
> 2 tablespoons finely chopped parsley
> Flour
> 1½ tablespoons oil

Put bread in a shallow bowl, cover with milk, and let soften for 2 to 3 minutes. Squeeze dry and put in a large bowl.

☆Heat half the butter in a small skillet, add the shallots, and cook briefly to soften. Transfer to bowl with bread, □ground meats, eggs, salt, pepper, and nutmeg to taste, garlic, and parsley. Blend well with a wooden spatula.

Dip palms of hands into flour, shape meat into balls about 2 inches in diameter, and flatten them slightly. Flour hands as necessary so that Subrics are lightly floured as they are formed.

Heat oil and remaining butter in a large skillet. Add Subrics and cook over moderate heat for 7 to 8 minutes, or until browned. Turn and cook for 7 to 8 minutes, or until browned and cooked through. Use the tip of a paring knife to prick center. Juice should run clear yellow with no trace of pink. A thermometer should register 170°.

Light variation

☆Omit butter and steam shallots in 1 to 2 tablespoons water until water has evaporated.

□In place of 1⅓ lbs. lean ground veal and ⅔ lb. pork, use 2 lbs. lean ground veal.

Notes

Make a meat loaf with mixture. Smear 1 tablespoon butter on a baking dish and form meat into loaf in center. Do not use a loaf pan. Bake for 50 minutes to 1 hour in a 400° oven, basting occasionally, until loaf registers 170° on a meat thermometer. Loaf will have a delicious crust.

Both the Subrics and loaf are delicious cold. They will keep refrigerated for 2 days.

ROAST LOIN OF VEAL WITH CELERY ROOT
Rôti de Veau au Céleri-Rave

Serves: 6

> 2 tablespoons butter
> 1 tablespoon oil
> 1 3-lb. boneless veal roast, rolled and tied (Ask butcher to cut bone in pieces and reserve it.)
> 2 medium onions, halved
> 3 medium carrots, cut into 3 pieces each
> 1 clove garlic, peeled
>   Salt
>   Freshly ground black pepper
> 1½ cups cider or dry white wine
> 1 cup chicken stock (see pp. 19–20)
> 4 qts. water
> 2 celery roots (3 lbs.), or several small ones
> 1 tablespoon finely chopped parsley

Preheat oven to 475°.

Put butter, oil, reserved bones, onions, carrots, and garlic into a roasting pan and bake for 5 minutes. Season veal roast lightly with salt and pepper. Push vegetables and bones to sides of roasting pan, and put roast in center.

Roast for 10 minutes, or until roast starts to brown lightly.

Scald cider or wine and pour half of it around roast. Baste, lower heat to 375°, and roast for 10 minutes. Add remaining cider or wine, baste, and roast for 10 minutes.

Scald stock and pour half of it around the roast. Baste and roast for 15 minutes. Add remaining stock, baste, and roast for 10 minutes.

While roast is cooking, bring 4 qts. water to a boil in a kettle. Wash celery roots, halve them, peel them deeply, and cut into 1-inch slices. Cut slices lengthwise into 1-inch sticks. Add 1½ tablespoons salt to boiling water and blanch celery root for 3 minutes. Drain.

Arrange celery root sticks around the roast, baste, and roast, tossing and basting them twice, for 20 minutes, or until meat thermometer registers 160°. Total cooking time is about 1 hour and 15 minutes. Remove bones and discard.

Let roast stand for 15 minutes, then carve into 9 to 12 slices. Arrange slices overlapping along one side of a heated platter. Arrange the celery root, onions, and carrots along the other side and sprinkle with parsley.

Notes

There is no sauce for this roast because the celery root (like potatoes) will have absorbed the juices almost completely. To prepare a sauce, leave bones, carrots, 2 to 3 pieces of celery root, and onions in the roasting pan and cook over medium-high heat. When sizzling, add 1 cup cider or wine. Reduce to ½ cup, stirring, and remove bones. Transfer vegetables and liquid to food processor and purée until smooth. Strain through a fine sieve and, if desired, add 1 to 2 tablespoons heavy cream. Season with salt and pepper, if necessary. Bring to a simmer in a saucepan and serve in a heated sauceboat.

VEAL CHOPS WITH MUSHROOMS AND GARLIC
Côtes de Veau aux Champignons à l'Ail

Serves: 6

4 veal chops, about 8 oz. each
Salt
Freshly ground black pepper

Flour for dredging
Braised Mushrooms (see p. 244)
2 tablespoons oil
2 tablespoons butter
8 garlic cloves, unpeeled, pierced twice with knife tip
½ cup dry white wine
⅔ cup heavy cream
1½ tablespoons finely chopped parsley

Sprinkle the chops with salt and pepper and dredge in flour.

☆Prepare the mushrooms and drain, reserving juice.

Add oil and butter to a skillet and heat until hot but not brown. Add chops and cook over medium-high heat for 4 minutes on each side, or until lightly golden, adding garlic cloves after 4 minutes.

Transfer meat to a warm platter. Cover loosely with foil and keep warm in a 200° oven. Keep garlic in skillet. Add wine and reduce to 4 tablespoons over moderate heat, scraping up brown glaze from bottom and sides of pan. Add mushroom juice. Reduce to ¼ cup.

□Add cream and reduce until sauce has a light creamy consistency. Season with salt and pepper, if necessary. Peel garlic, and add to sauce with veal and mushrooms, and reheat slightly.

Transfer to a warm platter and sprinkle with parsley.

Light variation

☆When braising mushrooms, omit butter and lemon juice (see p. 244).

□In place of ⅔ cup heavy cream, use 1 to 2 tablespoons heavy cream and ½ cup ricotta, blended in food processor. Remove juices from heat, add cream and ricotta, and correct seasoning, if necessary. Bring gently to first boil, stirring, and remove from heat immediately.

VEAL ROLLS WITH MUSTARD SAUCE
Roulades de Veau à la Moutarde

Serves: 6

6 veal scallops, ¼ lb. each

Stuffing

¼ lb. lean ground veal
¼ lb. lean ground pork
2 shallots, minced
2 cloves garlic, minced
1 tablespoon finely chopped parsley
Salt
Freshly ground black pepper
1 egg
3 medium onions, thinly sliced
¼ cup dry white wine
1 tablespoon butter
3 tablespoons Dijon mustard

Cooking the veal rolls

3 tablespoons flour
2 tablespoons butter
1½ tablespoons oil
1 cup dry white wine
2 to 3 cups chicken stock (see pp. 19–20)
3 egg yolks
1 tablespoon Dijon mustard
1½ teaspoons lemon juice
1 tablespoon finely chopped parsley

Preheat oven to 375°.

Pound the veal scallops lightly until very thin, using a flat mallet or rolling pin (or ask the butcher to do it).

✶Combine ground veal, ground pork, shallots, garlic, parsley, egg, and salt and pepper to taste. Mix thoroughly with a wooden spatula.

□Put onions, wine, and butter into a pan, cover, and cook, stirring occasionally, over medium-low heat without browning for 6 minutes, or until soft and wine has completely evaporated.

Lay veal slices on a flat surface and spread ½ tablespoon mustard on each. Divide onions and stuffing equally and put a portion in the center of each scallop. Roll and tie securely with 3 loops of kitchen twine or secure with toothpicks. Dredge the rolls in flour.

Heat butter and oil in an ovenproof pan, add the rolls, and brown. Remove and reserve. Pour off fat from pan, add wine, and reduce by half over moderate heat, scraping sides and bottom of pan to dissolve the cooking juices. Add stock, bring to a boil, and add reserved rolls. They should be half-covered with liquid. Season lightly with salt and pepper. Cover, bring back to boil, lower heat to 350°, and braise in the oven, turning occasionally, for 50 minutes to 1 hour (25 to 30 minutes in pressure cooker), or until a meat thermometer registers 170°. Transfer rolls to a platter and keep warm, loosely covered with foil, in a 200° oven.

Degrease pan juices, strain through a fine sieve, and return to pan (you should have about 1 cup). Bring to a boil. ✦Whisk egg yolks and mustard together in a bowl and add hot pan juices in a thin steady stream, whisking constantly. Add lemon juice and season with salt, pepper, and more mustard, if desired. Remove string or toothpicks, spoon sauce over the rolls, and sprinkle with parsley.

Light variation

☆In place of ground pork in stuffing, increase ground veal to ½ lb.

□Omit butter when cooking onions.

✦After returning juices to pan and boiling, remove from heat. Omit egg yolks and mustard and, instead, stir in 1 tablespoon cornstarch dissolved in 1 tablespoon white wine. Add just enough to the hot pan juices to make a light creamy sauce. Bring to a boil and cook for 1 minute. Remove from heat and stir in more mustard if desired.

(continued)

Notes

The veal rolls can be prepared 1 day in advance up through the point of cooking the meat. Leave the rolls in the juices and cool, uncovered. Then cover and refrigerate. Reheat in a 350° oven and finish the sauce as directed.

The dish can be cooked on top of the stove, but stir every now and then.

If the pot lid is not tight enough, put a piece of foil between the lid and the pot.

VEAL STEW
Ragoût de Viandes Blanches

Serves: 6 if meat is bone-in
8 if meat is boneless

3½ lbs. veal, cut into 1½-inch-square by ¾-inch pieces (Use veal shoulder and breast or a boneless cut, such as rump or round.)
1 medium-size onion, halved crosswise and stuck with 4 whole cloves
2 medium-size carrots, peeled and roughly sliced
3 medium-size celery stalks, roughly sliced
5 sprigs parsley
½ teaspoon dried thyme
2 bay leaves
Salt
Freshly ground black pepper
Braised Mushrooms (see p. 244)
1 slice white bread, crusts removed
Milk
⅔ lb. lean ground veal
½ lb. lean ground pork
1 egg
Freshly grated nutmeg

Rich Velouté Sauce (see p. 51) or Sauce aux Légumes (see p. 49), using veal cooking stock and juices from Braised Mushrooms

3 tablespoons finely chopped parsley

Put veal in a large pot and add enough cold water to barely cover. Cover and bring to a boil. Uncover and simmer for 5 minutes, skimming off any scum that rises to the surface.

Add the onion, carrots, celery, parsley, thyme, and bay leaves and season lightly with salt and pepper. Cover and simmer for 1½ hours (30 minutes in a pressure cooker), or until meat is tender.

While veal is cooking, prepare Braised Mushrooms, drain them, and reserve juices.

Using a slotted spoon, transfer veal to a warm platter and remove and discard any bones. Arrange reserved mushrooms around veal and cover with foil. Strain broth into a bowl and degrease if necessary. Reserve vegetables if you are preparing the Sauce aux Legumes for this recipe. Discard cloves.

Put bread in a shallow bowl, cover with milk, and let soften for 2 to 3 minutes. Squeeze dry and put in a mixing bowl. Add the ground veal and pork, egg, and nutmeg, salt, and pepper to taste. Blend well with a wooden spatula. Shape the mixture into balls about the size of a walnut. Poach the balls in simmering water for 7 minutes, or until thoroughly cooked. (Test by cutting one open to be sure that the color is even throughout.) Drain and discard the cooking liquid. Add meatballs to platter with veal and mushrooms and re-cover with foil.

While meatballs are cooking, preheat oven to 350°. Reheat the veal, mushrooms, and meatballs in the oven for 10 minutes. Pour off any juices that have accumulated on the platter. Ladle sauce over veal and sprinkle with parsley.

Notes

Serve the stew surrounded with Buttered Rice (see p. 203).

The veal, mushrooms, and meatballs can be prepared 1 day in advance. Cool and refrigerate covered. Reheating will take a little longer if the ingredients have been refrigerated. Add about 1 cup of stock when reheating to keep the meat moist.

COUNTRY TERRINE
Terrine de Campagne

Serves: 10

1 lb. lean veal, gristle and connective tissue removed, cut into 1½-inch cubes

1 lb. lean pork, gristle and connective tissue removed, cut into 1½-inch cubes

2 tablespoons Cognac

2 tablespoons Madeira

3 bay leaves

1 teaspoon dried thyme

4 cloves garlic, minced

2 shallots, minced

½ teaspoon freshly ground black pepper

3 teaspoons salt

1¼ lbs. fresh pork fat, plus 1 lb. pork fat, sliced paper thin

½ lb. pork liver, cleaned

¼ teaspoon freshly grated nutmeg

Special equipment
2½-quart terrine, or 2 smaller terrines.

Put veal and pork in a glass or porcelain bowl and add Cognac, Madeira, 2 bay leaves, half the thyme, garlic, shallots, pepper, and half the salt. Mix well, cover, and refrigerate overnight.

Preheat oven to 425°.

Discard bay leaf and put veal, pork, pork fat (not thin slices), and pork liver through the coarse blade of a meat grinder into a bowl. Add remaining salt and nutmeg. Mix well.

Line the terrine with some of the pork fat slices (do not overlap slices), covering bottom first, then building up sides, laying slices horizontally against the sides of the terrine. Pack meat mixture into the terrine evenly, smoothing the top. Cut the remaining pork fat slices into ⅓-inch-wide strips and top pâté with a lattice of fat. Sprinkle with remaining thyme and top with remaining bay leaf.

Cover terrine tightly with foil and the lid, put in larger pan, and add 1 inch of boiling water. Lower heat to 375° and bake for 1 hour and 50 minutes, or until fat which exudes is clear yellow and a meat thermometer registers 170°. Remove lid and foil. Put a dish, plate, or pan that fits inside terrine on top of pâté and put a 1-pound weight on it. Let stand at room temperature for several hours, or until cold. Remove weight, cover with lid, and refrigerate overnight before serving.

Notes

The pâté is weighted to compress it and make it easier to slice.

A food processor can be used to grind the meat. Make sure all gristle and connective tissue is trimmed from the meat as the blade does not cut or grind these.

Terrine will keep for 1 week in the refrigerator.

LAMB CHOPS WITH MINT SAUCE
Côtes d'Agneau Sauce Menthe

Serves: 6

    6 loin lamb chops, about ¾ to 1 inch thick
    1 tablespoon butter
 1½ tablespoons oil
      Salt
      Freshly ground black pepper
    2 cloves garlic, crushed
    2 shallots, minced
    1 cup concentrated quick chicken stock (see pp. 20) or all-purpose stock (see p. 18)
    ½ cup red wine
   12 mint leaves, finely chopped
    ⅔ cup heavy cream
    6 whole fresh mint leaves

Trim fat from lamb chops.

Heat butter and oil in a skillet until very hot but not smoking. Brown the chops for 5 to 7 minutes per side for medium-rare meat.

Season lightly with salt and pepper. Transfer the chops to a warm platter, cover loosely with foil, and keep warm in a 200° oven with the door open.

Pour the fat from the skillet and add the garlic, shallots, and 1 tablespoon stock. Cook over moderate heat for 1 minute, stirring with a wooden spoon to scrape up any brown bits clinging to the bottom and sides of the skillet. Add the wine and reduce to 3 to 4 tablespoons. Add half the chopped mint and the remaining stock and reduce to ⅓ cup.

☆Add the cream and boil slowly for 2 minutes, or until slightly thickened. Season with salt and pepper, if necessary. Strain the sauce through a sieve, pressing on the garlic and shallots with the back of a spoon to extract their juices. Return the sauce to the skillet and add any juices that have accumulated around the chops. Heat the sauce, remove from the heat, and add the remaining chopped mint. Coat the chops with the warm sauce and center a mint leaf on each chop.

Light variation

☆In place of the cream, use ½ cup ricotta, blended in a food processor, and 2 tablespoons heavy cream. After reducing the sauce to ⅓ cup, strain the sauce through a sieve, pressing on the garlic and shallots with the back of a spoon to extract their juices. Return the sauce to the skillet and add any juices that have accumulated around the chops. Stir in the blended ricotta and 2 tablespoons cream and season with salt and pepper, if necessary. Bring the sauce to a boil, stirring, remove from the heat and stir in the remaining chopped mint. Coat the chops with the warm sauce and center a mint leaf on each chop.

Notes

Shoulder chops or steaks, cut from the top of the leg, are also good for this recipe—and less expensive than loin chops.

BONED LEG OF LAMB WITH HERBS
Gigot d'Agneau Désossé aux Herbes

Serves: 10 to 12

1 7- to 8-lb. leg of lamb, boned and tied (reserve bones)

Stuffing

1 tablespoon butter
1 tablespoon oil
2 medium shallots, minced
2 cloves garlic, minced
¼ cup bread crumbs, preferably homemade (about 2 slices dried bread)
1 tablespoon minced parsley
½ teaspoon dried thyme, ground
3 large bay leaves, well crumbled and ground
½ teaspoon dried rosemary, ground
1 tablespoon Dijon mustard
   Salt
   Freshly ground black pepper
   Freshly grated nutmeg
1 egg, lightly beaten

Roasting the lamb

1 tablespoon butter
1 tablespoon oil
1 medium carrot, cut into 3 pieces
1 medium onion, quartered
   Salt
   Freshly ground black pepper
1 cup white wine
1 cup chicken stock (see pp. 19–20)
1 tablespoon finely chopped parsley
   Watercress sprigs

Preheat oven to 475°.

Have the butcher bone the lamb without cutting it open by boning out first the pelvic bone, then the leg bone. Leave the shank bone in to give the roast some shape. Scrape off the thin meat covering shank bone a few inches from the end to make a handle for the roast, which facilitates carving. Boning out the pelvic bone creates a flap of meat; the cavity is formed by the removal of the leg bone. (If butcher is unwilling to bone the lamb as suggested, let him slit the meat open and remove all the bones.)

Heat the butter and oil in a skillet. Add the shallots and cook slowly without browning for 1 minute, stirring occasionally. Add garlic and cook for 30 seconds. Remove from heat, add bread crumbs, parsley, thyme, bay leaves, rosemary, mustard, and salt, pepper, and nutmeg to taste. Add egg and mix thoroughly. If stuffing is too soft, add a few more bread crumbs. It should hold together. There will be only about ½ cup stuffing, but it is very flavorful.

Stuff the lamb and smear some on the meat flap, but do not come near the edges. (Or spread all over if opened completely.) Sew or skewer the cavity closed, squeezing and reshaping the meat around the cavity, then fold over the flap to cover the cut area where the pelvic and top of the leg bones were. Close shank opening if cut. The finished roast will look somewhat like a little fat ham. Tie roast.

Heat butter and oil in a roasting pan just large enough to hold lamb over moderate heat. Add the reserved bones, carrot, and onion and cook, stirring occasionally, until lightly colored. Remove from heat, push bones and vegetables to the sides, and put lamb in the pan. Turn lamb to coat evenly with fat. Rest it on its sewed side and sprinkle lightly with salt and pepper. Do not overseason or sauce will be too salty. The stuffing is well seasoned.

Put roast on the middle rack of the oven, lower heat to 450°, and roast for 15 minutes.

Bring wine to a boil and pour half of it around the roast. Roast for 10 minutes, add remaining wine, and roast for 10 minutes, basting occasionally. Scald stock and pour half of it around the roast. Roast for 20 minutes, basting occasionally. Lower heat to 425° if oven is too hot. Add remaining stock and roast until done, basting occasionally. Total cooking time is about 1¼ hours. Meat thermometer will register 135° to 145° for medium-rare or 155° to 160° for well done.

Transfer roast to a platter, cover with foil, and put it in a slow oven to sit for at least 15 minutes before carving.

Discard bones from roasting pan. Strain sauce through a fine sieve into a saucepan, degrease, and reduce for 1 to 2 minutes, or until thickened a little.

Carve lamb into thin slices and arrange on a warm platter. Spoon some of the sauce over the slices and sprinkle with parsley. Garnish with watercress sprigs.

Notes

Buttered Green Beans (see p. 225), Broiled Tomatoes (see p. 249), Sautéed Potatoes (see p. 210), and Braised Celery (see p. 233) are all good accompaniments.

If the lamb is roasted to medium-rare, the bones in a leg of lamb remain uncooked and, thus, give no flavor to the meat, so it is better to remove them and roast them in the pan with the meat to give added flavor to the sauce.

Wine and stock should be heated before adding to hot pan. This produces a better reduction. Flavor would be weak otherwise.

Lamb can be rolled and tied and roasted without stuffing. Cut 1 clove garlic into slivers and insert into small slits all over the meat.

ROAST BUTTERFLIED LEG OF LAMB
Gigot d'Agneau Rôti en Papillon

Serves: 10 to 12

> 1 tablespoon butter at room temperature
> 1 7- to 8-lb. leg of lamb, butterflied (reserve bones)
> Salt
> Freshly ground black pepper
> 1 carrot, quartered
> 6 garlic cloves, unpeeled, pierced with a knife tip
> ⅓ cup red wine
> ½ cup chicken stock (see pp. 19–20)
> ½ teaspoon dried thyme
> 1 tablespoon finely chopped parsley

Preheat oven to 500°.

Butter lamb lightly on both sides and season with salt and

pepper. Put lamb fat side down in a roasting pan and arrange reserved bones, carrot, and garlic around meat.

Put roast on middle rack of oven, lower heat to 450°, and roast for 10 minutes. Turn meat and toss vegetables. Roast for 10 minutes, pour in wine, and roast for 5 minutes.

Scald stock; pour half of it around the meat and roast for 10 minutes. Pour in remaining stock, sprinkle roast with thyme, and roast for 10 minutes. Total roasting time is about 45 minutes for pink, medium-rare meat, or 135° on a meat thermometer.

Transfer meat to a warm platter, cover loosely with foil, and let meat rest for at least 15 minutes in a warm place. This allows the juices to redistribute in the meat before carving.

Remove garlic from roasting pan, peel, and mash with a fork. Remove bones and carrot pieces and discard. Strain sauce through a fine sieve and degrease.

Cut lamb in half lengthwise and carve crosswise into ¼-inch-thick slices. Spread a little of the garlic purée on each slice and arrange the slices on a warm platter, overlapping slightly. Spoon a little sauce over each slice and sprinkle with parsley.

Notes

A 7- to 8-lb. leg of lamb will yield 4½ to 5½ lbs. trimmed meat after boning.

White Beans with Tomatoes (see p. 226) are a delicious accompaniment.

RACK OF LAMB PROVENÇAL
Carré d'Agneau à la Provençale

Serves: 4

  3 tablespoons olive oil
  2 shallots, finely chopped
  2 cloves garlic, finely chopped
  ¼ to ⅓ cup soft dry bread crumbs
  ¼ teaspoon ground thyme
  ½ teaspoon ground rosemary

2 tablespoons finely chopped parsley
Salt
Freshly ground black pepper
1 egg, lightly beaten
2 tablespoons Dijon mustard
1 2½- to 3-lb. rack of lamb (8 ribs), trimmed

Preheat oven to 525°.

Heat 2 tablespoons oil in a skillet. Add shallots and garlic and cook gently for 1 to 2 minutes, stirring. Do not let vegetables color. Off heat, add bread crumbs, thyme, rosemary, parsley, and salt and pepper to taste. Stir in egg then mustard. Stuffing should hold together in soft mounds.

Spread remaining oil over inside of roasting pan. Add lamb and turn to coat on all sides. Sprinkle lamb with salt and pepper and put fat side down in roasting pan. Roast for 9 minutes, turning over once so lamb browns on both sides. Remove from oven.

Spread stuffing over fat side of meat. Return to oven and roast for 8 minutes, or until a meat thermometer registers 130° to 135°. Meat will still be very pink inside. For well-done, cook 5 to 7 minutes longer.

Remove from oven, turn broiler to medium-high, and broil for 3 to 4 minutes, or until crumb crust turns golden brown. Transfer to a warm platter and let sit in a 200° oven for 5 to 10 minutes before carving.

Carve roast into 8 chops and arrange on a platter.

Notes

Tomatoes Provençal are superb with this. To make them, double the lamb stuffing. Spread the extra stuffing equally on 4 halved tomatoes. Put in a lightly buttered gratin dish big enough to hold them comfortably. Bake in a 400° oven for 10 to 15 minutes. Broil for 1 to 2 minutes, or until crumb crust turns a golden brown.

LAMB STEW WITH SPRING VEGETABLES
Navarin d'Agneau aux Primeurs

Serves: 6

3 lbs. lean lamb shoulder, cut into 1½-inch pieces
2 tablespoons butter
2 tablespoons oil
1 cup dry white wine
1 large onion, chopped
1 medium carrot, chopped
2 stalks celery, chopped
3 tablespoons flour
   Salt
   Freshly ground black pepper
¼ teaspoon dried thyme
2 bay leaves
3 cloves garlic, minced
3 parsley sprigs
3 cups water
2 medium tomatoes, peeled, seeded, and chopped, or 1 tablespoon tomato paste
1 tablespoon finely chopped parsley

Vegetable garniture
12 boiled small new potatoes, or 4 medium-size potatoes, cut
   into quarters
   Braised Turnips (see p. 251)
   Braised Onions (see p. 246)
1 tablespoon butter
2 shallots, finely chopped
1 lb. fresh peas shelled, or one 10-oz. package frozen peas,
   blanched until tender, depending on size
4 to 5 carrots, peeled, cut into 3 pieces, and blanched for 8
   minutes, or until tender-crisp

Preheat oven to 325°.
   Dry meat on paper towels.
   Heat half the butter and half the oil in each of two skillets.

Put lamb in skillets and cook over medium-high heat until brown. As pieces brown, transfer to an ovenproof pot or pressure cooker.

Discard all fat from one skillet, add 4 tablespoons of white wine, and reduce until syrupy, scraping the bottom and sides of the skillet with a wooden spatula. Add to the meat. Add onion, carrot, and celery to the second skillet and cook, stirring, over moderate heat for 2 to 3 minutes, or until the vegetables are lightly browned. Sprinkle flour over vegetables and cook, stirring, over moderate heat for 2 minutes to brown lightly. Add 1 cup water to the second skillet and bring to a boil, scraping the bottom and sides of the skillet with a wooden spatula. Add to the meat with the remaining wine, salt and pepper to taste, thyme, bay leaves, garlic, parsley, water, and chopped tomatoes. Meat should be barely covered by liquid. Cover, bring to a boil, and simmer for 1½ hours in the oven (35 to 40 minutes in pressure cooker), or until meat is fork-tender.

Pour contents of pot into a fine-mesh sieve set over a bowl. Discard bones. Return meat to pot. Press lightly on the vegetables in the sieve with the back of a spoon to extract their juice. Skim off the fat from the sauce and return sauce to the pot. Discard the vegetables. Bring sauce to a simmer, and add salt and pepper to taste. Add a little water if the sauce is too thick. The stew can be served at this point with just one of the suggested vegetable garnitures on the side, or with potatoes.

Add potatoes, cover, and cook over moderate heat, stirring occasionally, until heated through. Heat turnips and onions slowly. Melt butter in a skillet, add shallots, and cook, stirring, for 1 to 2 minutes. Add peas and carrots and toss over moderate heat for 2 minutes, or until heated through. Season with salt and pepper, if necessary.

Arrange the stew on a hot platter with potatoes, turnips, onions, peas, and carrots. Sprinkle with chopped parsley.

Notes

The stew and vegetable garnitures can be made 1 day in advance and stored together. Let cool uncovered and refrigerate covered. Reheat over low heat on top of the stove or in a 325° oven. Add a little water if needed while reheating.

The stew without the vegetable garniture freezes perfectly.

MARINATED PORK CHOPS WITH PINEAPPLE
Côtes de Porc Marinées aux Fruits

Serves: 4

4 pork chops (about 2 lbs.), cut 1 inch thick

Marinade
2 tablespoons oil
1 medium onion, thinly sliced
1 medium carrot, thinly sliced
1 medium stalk celery, thinly sliced
2 bay leaves
⅛ teaspoon dried thyme
4 sprigs parsley
½ teaspoon dried rosemary
½ teaspoon dried basil
4 whole black peppercorns
2 cloves
4 juniper berries
1 teaspoon sugar
1 tablespoon red wine vinegar
1 cup red wine

Cooking the pork chops
1 tablespoon oil
1 tablespoon butter
Salt
Freshly ground black pepper

Cooking the pineapple and sauce
1 4- to 5-lb. pineapple, 10 slices or one 20 oz. can,
unsweetened pineapple slices
1 tablespoon butter
3 tablespoons honey
1 tablespoon confectioners' sugar
⅔ cup heavy cream
Watercress or parsley sprigs

*Combine all the marinade ingredients and blend well. Pour half into a shallow non-aluminum dish, add the pork chops in 1 layer, and pour over remaining marinade. Marinate in the refrigerator for at least 6 hours.

Preheat oven to 450°.

Remove chops from marinade and dry on paper towels. Reserve marinade.

Heat oil and butter in a skillet until hot but not brown. Add pork chops and cook over medium-high heat for 2 to 3 minutes on each side, or until brown. Season the chops with salt and pepper to taste. Cover the skillet with a lid or foil and cook over medium-low heat for 10 minutes per side, turning the chops once or twice. Test the chops for doneness by pricking them near the bone with a skewer or the tip of a knife. The juices should run clear without any trace of pink. A meat thermometer should register 170°.

Cut off the top and stem ends of the pineapple, peel, halve lengthwise, and cut into ⅜-inch-thick slices. Remove core with a round biscuit cutter, or use a pineapple corer. Leave the slices whole and dry them on paper towels.

Use 1 tablespoon of butter to coat a flat baking dish. Arrange the pineapple slices in the dish in one layer. Brush the slices with a thin coating of honey and bake on the middle rack of the oven for 5 minutes. Dust lightly with confectioners' sugar and put under the broiler, about 2½ inches from the heat, for 1 minute, or until pineapple is golden brown.

Transfer the chops to a warm platter, cover loosely with foil, and put chops and pineapple in a turned-off oven with the door ajar.

Skim all the fat from the juices in the skillet and add half of the marinade (including all the vegetables) and reduce by half over medium-high heat, stirring with a wooden spoon to incorporate all of the browned cooking juices. Strain the sauce through a fine sieve, pressing on the vegetables to extract all juices, and return the sauce to the skillet.

□Add the cream and boil over moderate heat, stirring, until sauce reaches a creamy consistency. Season with salt and pepper, if desired.

Add any juices that have accumulated in the platter and blend well. Arrange the pineapple slices over the chops and garnish with watercress. Spoon some sauce over each chop.

Light variation

☆Omit the oil in the marinade.

□In place of the cream, use ½ cup ricotta, blended in a food processor with 6 tablespoons milk, and 2 tablespoons heavy cream. After returning the strained sauce to the skillet, stir in the blended ricotta and 2 tablespoons of heavy cream. Heat very gently, stirring, just to the boil. Remove from the heat immediately and season with salt and pepper, if desired.

Notes

Sautéed Apples (see p. 322) are a delicious accompaniment.

The marination gives the meat some of the "wild" flavor of game and tenderizes the meat.

The sauce can be thinned, if necessary, with stock.

A good way to cut and peel a pineapple is to halve it length-wise with the peel on. Cut into ¾-inch-thick slices. Remove peel by pressing a large cookie cutter on slice. Remove core with a smaller cookie cutter.

ROAST LOIN OF PORK WITH ONION PURÉE
Rôti de Porc à la Purée d'Oignons

Serves: 6–8

Cooking the pork

    1 4½-lb. loin of pork, boned to yield 2½ lbs. trimmed meat, tied (with bones reserved)
    Salt
    Freshly ground black pepper
    2 tablespoons oil
    2 medium onions, halved
    2 medium carrots, quartered
    1 clove garlic, peeled
    ⅛ teaspoon dried thyme

½ cup dry white wine

1 to 1⅓ cups concentrated chicken stock (see pp. 19–20)

The onion purée

8 medium onions (about 2 lbs.), thinly sliced, or Purée Soubise (see p. 245)

⅔ cup rice

⅛ teaspoon dried thyme

1 bay leaf

2 cups chicken stock (see pp. 19–20) or water

2 to 3 tablespoons heavy cream or 1 tablespoon butter

Preheat oven to 475°.

Season meat lightly with salt and pepper. Spread oil over bottom of roasting pan and add pork skin side down. Scatter reserved bones, onions, carrots, garlic, and thyme around pork. Put roasting pan on middle rack of oven and roast for 10 minutes. Turn pork, toss vegetables, and roast for 10 minutes. Lower heat to 375°, add half the wine, and roast for 10 minutes. Baste, pour in remaining wine, and roast for 10 minutes.

Scald the stock, pour ⅓ cup over pork, and roast for 10 minutes. Add remaining stock in 2 equal amounts at 10-minute intervals and baste often. Roast for 10 minutes after last addition of stock, or until meat thermometer registers 170°. (Total cooking time is about 1 hour and 20 minutes.) Turn off heat, cover meat loosely with foil, and let meat sit in warm oven for 15 minutes.

While meat is roasting, prepare Onion Purée: If you have a second oven, preheat to 400°. Otherwise prepare Onion Purée ahead. Bring 2 qts. water to a boil in a saucepan. Add sliced onions, cover, and bring to a boil. Uncover and boil for 2 minutes, drain, and return onions to pan. Add rice, thyme, bay leaf, salt and pepper to taste, and stock and bring to a boil, stirring occasionally. Cover and bake for 25 minutes, or cook over very low heat on top of the stove. (Use a Flame-Tamer so mixture will cook more evenly and will not stick to the bottom of the pan.) Remove bay leaf and force mixture through a sieve or food mill, or blend in a food processor until it is a smooth purée. Return purée to pan and cook over moderate heat, stirring with a wooden spoon to evaporate extra moisture and dry purée until it has a firmer consistency. Remove from heat, beat in cream, and keep warm in a larger pan of warm water.

Cut roast into ⅓-inch-thick slices and arrange them lengthwise along one half of a warm platter. Fill other half with onion purée. Garnish top with cooked vegetables from roast.

Degrease liquid in roasting pan, heat over moderate heat, stirring occasionally, and coat meat with sauce.

Notes

Purée may be prepared in advance through puréeing step. Beat in butter or cream just before serving.

If roast is prepared more than 1 to 2 hours in advance, let cool, then cover and refrigerate. It will keep for 1 to 2 days. Reheat, wrapped in foil, in a 375° oven for 35 to 40 minutes. Sauce may be degreased, cooled, refrigerated, and reheated as well.

The wine and stock are added in portions to allow a portion to reduce somewhat before the next addition. This allows a better emulsion. If all the liquid is added at once, the sauce will have a very weak flavor and color. It is the reduction that produces a concentrated flavor.

For an attractive presentation, spread a little of the purée on each slice and rebuild roast. Cover all over with purée and sprinkle with ½ cup grated Swiss cheese. Reheat in a 375° oven for 30 minutes, and put under broiler until cheese is golden.

BONED FRESH HAM STUFFED WITH SPINACH
Jambon Frais Désossé aux Épinards

Serves: 12

1 8½-lb. fresh ham (half a ham), boned to yield about 6½ lbs., with bone reserved, skin left on, and tied (Have the butcher remove the bone without cutting the meat open, if possible.)
1 large onion, sliced
2 stalks celery, sliced

2 carrots, sliced
Coarse salt
1 teaspoon dried thyme
5 or 6 sprigs parsley
3 bay leaves
15 whole black peppercorns
Creamed Spinach, regular or light version (see p. 247)

For the sauce

1 tablespoon butter
1 carrot, minced
1 medium onion, minced
2 teaspoons flour
½ cup white wine
1 cup hot concentrated chicken stock (see pp. 19–20)
Salt
Freshly ground black pepper

Make several slashes through the skin and fat of the ham so it melts while cooking. Put ham and bones in a kettle with onion, celery, carrots, salt, thyme, parsley, bay leaves, and peppercorns. Add water to cover, cover, and bring to a boil. Uncover and boil slowly for 3 hours, or until a meat thermometer registers 170°. Let the ham cool in the broth.

When ready to assemble the dish, carefully take the ham out of the broth and lay it on a board. Remove the string. Cut off the rind and fat, leaving about a ¼-inch-thick layer of fat on the meat. Discard rind and fat. Carve the meat, cutting very thin slices at a 60° angle two thirds of the way through the meat, leaving the bottom third of the ham uncut. As each slice is cut, lay it on the board next to the roast, keeping the order so that the ham can be reassembled into its original shape.

Put the uncut bottom third of the ham on a platter and spread with a thin layer of spinach. Spread the first slice of ham with 1½ tablespoons of the spinach and begin to reassemble the roast, slice by slice, on top of the uncut "bed." When all the slices are back in place, stick a small skewer through to fasten the slices together. (A few ham slices may not fit back because of the room taken up by the spinach.)

(continued)

Preheat the oven to 375°.

Melt the butter in a skillet large enough to hold the ham. Add carrot and onion and cook, over moderate heat, stirring and tossing, until lightly brown. Add flour and cook for 1 to 2 minutes to color it lightly. Add wine and stock, stirring, and season lightly with salt and pepper to taste. Put re-formed ham into the sauce and bake for 35 to 40 minutes, basting occasionally. Remove ham to a warm serving platter, strain sauce, and coat ham with strained sauce.

Notes

The ham is composed of three large muscles. Once the bone is removed, there is nothing to hold them together, so tie the roast securely at 1- or 2-inch intervals. As meat firms up during cooking, it can be carved and stuffed without falling apart.

The roast can be fully prepared up to the final baking and refrigerated for 1 day. To store leftovers, scrape the spinach from the ham slices, because it will not keep as long as the meat. Wrap the two separately and refrigerate. The ham will keep for 3 days; the spinach for only 1 to 2 days.

Serve with Mashed Potatoes (see p. 208), which look especially nice piped around the ham.

A delicious variation is to stuff the ham with Duxelles (see p. 243). Double the recipe and proceed as for the spinach stuffing.

CHICKEN WITH CIDER
Poulet au Cidre

Serves: 6

1 4½-lb. chicken, cut into serving pieces
  Flour
2 tablespoons butter
1 tablespoon oil
¼ cup Calvados or applejack
  Salt
  Freshly ground black pepper
1¾ cups cider
¼ teaspoon dried thyme
1 bay leaf

3 parsley sprigs
⅔ cup heavy cream
1 tablespoon finely chopped parsley

Dredge chicken pieces in flour. Heat butter and oil in a skillet until hot but not brown. Add chicken pieces skin side down, and cook over moderate heat until slightly golden brown. Turn and brown lightly on the other side. Add Calvados to the skillet and ignite it with a match. (Protect face and hair while doing this or tilt skillet.) Let flame die. Season with salt and pepper to taste. Add cider, thyme, bay leaf, and parsley. Bring to a simmer, cover, and simmer for 35 to 40 minutes. Check breasts for doneness after 20 minutes. Remove if cooked, and cook legs and thighs for 10 minutes longer. Chicken flesh should be springy and juicy. Transfer chicken to a warm platter, cover loosely with foil, and keep warm in a 200° oven.

Degrease sauce. ☆Add cream and boil over moderate heat, stirring, for 1 to 2 minutes, or until sauce has a light creamy consistency and colors lightly. Add any juices that have accumulated around chicken. Season sauce with salt and pepper, if necessary. Strain sauce over the chicken and sprinkle with parsley.

Light variation

☆In place of the cream, use ½ cup ricotta, blended in a food processor, and 2 tablespoons heavy cream. Degrease sauce and reduce it to ⅓ cup over moderate heat. Remove from heat and beat in processed ricotta, 2 tablespoons cream, and any juices that have accumulated around the chicken. Heat gently, stirring, just to the boil. Remove from the heat immediately and season with salt and pepper, if necessary. Strain sauce over the chicken and sprinkle with parsley.

Notes

Sautéed Apples (see p. 322) are a delicious accompaniment.

The dish can be partially prepared 2 to 3 hours in advance. Finish it up to the point that the chicken is cooked. Reheat slowly, adding 2 to 3 tablespoons water to compensate for evaporation. Finish the sauce just before serving.

The chicken can also be served with just the pan juices and not the cream sauce.

CHICKEN WITH TOMATO AND MUSHROOM SAUCE
Poulet Sauté avec Sauce Tomate aux Champignongs

Serves: 4

> Sautéed Mushrooms (see p. 245)
> Tomato Fondue (see p. 50)
> 1 3-lb. chicken, cut into serving pieces, or 3 whole chicken breasts, split
> Salt
> Freshly ground black pepper
> 1 tablespoon butter
> 1 tablespoon oil
> ½ cup dry white wine
> ⅓ cup heavy cream
> 1 tablespoon finely chopped parsley

Add drained Sautéed Mushrooms to Tomato Fondue and reserve. Season chicken pieces with salt and pepper. Heat butter and oil in a skillet and add chicken skin side down. Cook, uncovered, over moderate heat for 8 minutes. Turn pieces and cook for 15 to 17 minutes (breasts for 12 minutes), turning the pieces occasionally to brown evenly all over and lifting the pieces to let the butter run underneath so they do not stick. Total cooking time should be about 25 minutes (20 minutes if using breasts). Transfer chicken to a warm platter, cover loosely with foil, and keep warm in a low oven.

Pour off fat from the skillet, add wine, and reduce to 3 tablespoons, scraping up the browned juices from the bottom and sides of the pan with a wooden spatula. Add the tomato-mushroom mixture. ☆Add cream, and bring to a boil over moderate heat, stirring occasionally. Boil slowly for 1 to 2 minutes, or until sauce is smooth and thick. Spoon sauce over the chicken. Sprinkle with parsley.

Light variation

☆Omit cream and bring sauce just to a boil over moderate heat, stirring occasionally. Spoon sauce over the chicken. Sprinkle with parsley.

Notes

Sautéed chicken is at its best when eaten immediately. It can, however, be sautéed several hours ahead and reheated, loosely covered with foil, in a preheated 350° oven for 10 to 15 minutes.

Serve with Buttered Noodles (see p. 215) or Buttered Rice (see p. 203).

CHICKEN WITH GARLIC AND RED PEPPERS
Poulet à l'Ail et Poivres Rouges

Serves: **4**

20 medium cloves garlic, unpeeled
 2 sweet red peppers (about ½ lb.)
 1 3½-lb. chicken, cut into serving pieces
   Salt
   Freshly ground black pepper
 1 tablespoon oil
 4 tablespoons butter
 1 cup dry white wine
 2 tablespoons white wine vinegar
 ⅛ teaspoon dried thyme
 1 bay leaf
1½ cups chicken stock (see pp. 19–20)
 1 tablespoon butter, softened
 1 tablespoon flour
 2 tablespoons finely chopped parsley

Preheat broiler.

Poke each clove of unpeeled garlic twice with the tip of a paring knife or a skewer and reserve.

Put peppers on a foil-lined baking pan and broil, turning frequently, 5 inches from the flame, until charred almost all over. Put the peppers in a bowl, cover, and, when cool enough to handle, pull off the skin with a paring knife. Core and halve the peppers lengthwise, remove the seeds, and cut lengthwise into ⅜-inch-wide strips.

(continued)

Season chicken with salt and pepper. Heat oil and 1 tablespoon butter in a skillet until hot but not brown and add the chicken skin side down. Cook, uncovered, over moderate heat for 8 minutes, or until golden brown. Turn and cook for 15 to 17 minutes, turning the pieces so they brown all over and cook evenly. Lift the chicken pieces occasionally to let the butter run underneath so they do not stick. Remove breast pieces after 12 minutes.

Transfer the chicken to a deep serving platter. Add the red pepper strips. Cover loosely with foil and keep warm in a 200° oven.

Add garlic to the skillet and sauté over moderate heat, tossing and stirring, for 2 to 3 minutes, or until the skin becomes a little dry and crisp. Pour off fat but keep garlic in the skillet. Add wine, vinegar, thyme, and bay leaf and slowly reduce to ¼ cup. Add stock and slowly reduce to ¾ cup. Strain sauce into a small saucepan.

When garlic is cool enough to handle, peel and pass half of the garlic through a sieve into the sauce. Scatter the remaining garlic over the chicken and pepper strips.

Use a fork to knead the flour and 1 tablespoon of soft butter together to make a beurre manié. Bring the sauce to a simmer and remove from the heat. Beat in enough of the beurre manié to give a light creamy consistency. (The sauce should be thick enough to coat a spoon.) Season with salt and pepper, if necessary, and bring to a boil. Boil for 1 minute. ☆Remove from the heat and swirl in the remaining butter.

Spoon the sauce over the chicken and pepper strips and sprinkle with parsley.

Light variation

☆Use only 2 tablespoons of butter: one to sauté the chicken and one to make the beurre manié. Do not swirl in any butter after the beurre manié is added to the sauce.

Notes

Sautéed Mushrooms (see p. 245) are a delicious garniture for this dish.

The sauce will have a pleasant, distinctly garlicky, but not strong, flavor. The cooking moderates the strength of the garlic without making it insipid.

CHICKEN SAUTÉ GEORGE SAND
Poulet Sauté George Sand

Serves: 4

2 tablespoons butter
2 tablespoons oil
1 small carrot, finely chopped
1 very small onion, finely chopped
1 clove garlic, minced
1 bay leaf
⅛ teaspoon dried thyme
⅔ lb. medium shrimp, shelled and deveined
  Salt
  Freshly ground black pepper
2 tablespoons Cognac
½ cup dry white wine
1 cup chicken stock (see pp. 19–20)
½ lb. Sautéed Mushrooms (see p. 245), or
  Braised Mushrooms (see p. 244)
1 3-lb. chicken, cut into serving pieces
1½ tablespoons flour
⅓ cup heavy cream
1 egg yolk
2 tablespoons parsley, finely chopped

Heat 1 tablespoon butter and 1 tablespoon oil in a skillet and add carrot and onion. Cook over moderate heat, stirring with a wooden spatula, for 5 minutes, or until tender and lightly colored. Add garlic, bay leaf, thyme, shrimp, and salt and pepper to taste. Cook, stirring and tossing shrimp, for 2 minutes. Add Cognac and ignite. (Protect face and hair.) Add wine and stock, bring to a simmer, and cook for 2 to 3 minutes. Remove shrimp with a slotted spoon and reserve on a warm platter.

Reduce pan juices to 1 cup. Strain through a sieve into a saucepan, pressing on the vegetables with the back of a spoon to extract all juice. Discard vegetables and reserve liquid in the pan.

Prepare Sautéed or Braised Mushrooms. Drain and reserve with the shrimp.

(continued)

Season chicken with salt and pepper. Heat remaining butter and oil in the skillet and add the chicken skin side down. Cook, uncovered, over moderate heat for 8 minutes, or until golden brown. Turn and cook for 15 to 17 minutes, turning occasionally so chicken browns and cooks evenly. Check breasts for doneness after 12 minutes. Remove if cooked, and cook legs and thighs 5 minutes longer. Lift chicken occasionally to let butter run underneath so the chicken does not stick. Total cooking time should be about 25 minutes. Transfer chicken to the platter with the shrimp and mushrooms. Cover loosely with foil and keep warm in a low oven.

Heat reserved broth in the saucepan.

Pour off all but 1½ tablespoons of fat in the skillet. ☆Add flour and cook over moderate heat, stirring with a wooden spatula, for 1 to 2 minutes. Remove from heat, wait 10 seconds, and add hot broth all at once, stirring rapidly. Boil slowly for 1 to 2 minutes, stirring constantly.

Strain sauce into a saucepan. Gradually stir in ▢cream and boil slowly for 1 to 2 minutes, stirring occasionally. Season with salt and pepper, if necessary. Sauce should lightly coat a spoon. Thin with chicken broth, if desired, and remove from heat.

✦Beat egg yolk in a bowl and add ¼ cup of sauce in a thin steady stream, stirring. Add this mixture to the remaining sauce, stirring rapidly. Add any juices that have accumulated in the platter. Season with salt and pepper, if necessary. Spoon sauce over chicken, shrimp, and mushrooms and sprinkle with parsley.

Light variation

☆Use only 1 tablespoon of flour to make sauce.

▢Omit cream.

✦Omit egg yolk.

After adding hot broth, boil sauce slowly for 1 to 2 minutes, stirring constantly. Add any juices that have accumulated in the platter. Season with salt and pepper, if necessary. Strain sauce over chicken, shrimp, and mushrooms and sprinkle with parsley.

Notes

Serve the chicken surrounded with Buttered Noodles (see p. 215).

If dish is not to be eaten immediately, film sauce with 2 to 3 tablespoons stock, or rub surface with a piece of chilled butter held on a knife tip. This will prevent a skin from forming.

This dish can be prepared 2 hours in advance. Reheat in a 250° oven covered with foil.

CHICKEN STANLEY
Poulet à la Stanley

Serves: 6

  1 4½-lb. chicken, cut into serving pieces
     Salt
     Freshly ground black pepper
     Flour
  4 tablespoons butter
  3 medium onions, thinly sliced
  ½ to 1 cup concentrated chicken stock (see pp. 19–20)
  1 cup heavy cream
  1 teaspoon lemon juice
  ¼ teaspoon curry powder
  1 teaspoon tomato paste
  1 truffle, cut into thin strips (optional)
 12 croutons (see p. 63), optional
  1 tablespoon finely chopped parsley
  ½ lb. Braised Mushrooms (see p. 244), optional

Preheat oven to 350°.

Season the chicken pieces with salt and pepper and dredge lightly in the flour.

☆Heat the butter in a skillet until hot but not brown. Add the chicken skin side down. Cook over moderate heat for 2 minutes on each side. (This is just to stiffen the flesh a bit, not to give it a deep browning.) Transfer the chicken to a platter.

Add the onions to the butter remaining in the skillet and cook over moderate heat, stirring, for 5 to 7 minutes, or until soft.

□Add ½ cup concentrated stock and return the chicken to the skillet.

(continued)

✧Add the cream, season lightly with salt and pepper, cover, and bring to a simmer. Transfer to the oven and bake for 35 minutes, or until tender. Check the breasts for doneness after 25 minutes, remove if cooked, and cook legs and thighs about 10 minutes longer. The chicken flesh should remain springy.

Transfer the chicken to a warm platter. Cover loosely with foil and keep warm in a 200° oven.

Put the pan with the sauce over moderate heat and add the curry powder and tomato paste. Simmer, uncovered, stirring.

When the sauce has a nice creamy consistency and coats a spoon, strain it through a sieve, pressing hard with the back of a spoon to force as much of the onions through the sieve as possible. Return the sauce to the pan and heat over moderate heat, stirring. Remove from the heat and add the lemon juice.

Stir in any juices that have accumulated around the chicken and season the sauce with salt and pepper, if necessary.

Pour the sauce over the chicken. If using the truffle, place a thin strip on each piece of chicken and garnish the platter with the croutons. (Dip one corner of each crouton in the sauce and then into the chopped parsley before adding them to the platter.) Heat and drain the Braised Mushrooms and arrange them between the chicken pieces.

Light variation

☆In place of the 4 tablespoons butter, use 2½ tablespoons butter to cook the chicken.

▢In place of ½ cup concentrated chicken stock, use 1½ cups chicken stock.

✧Omit cream. Season the chicken lightly with salt and pepper, cover, and bring to a simmer. Transfer to the oven for 35 minutes, or until cooked. Check for doneness after 25 minutes, remove the breasts if cooked, and cook the legs and thighs for about 10 minutes longer. The chicken flesh should remain springy.

Transfer the chicken to a warm platter. Cover loosely with foil and keep warm in a 200° oven. Add curry powder and tomato paste to the sauce and simmer to reduce the liquid to ⅓ cup. Blend ½ cup ricotta in a food processor. Add 2 tablespoons cream. Remove sauce from heat and stir in the blended ricotta and the cream. Strain sauce through a sieve, pressing hard with the back of a spoon to force as much of the onions through the sieve as possible. Heat over moderate heat to first boil, stirring.

Notes

This dish can sit for one hour and be reheated gently. The sauce can be thinned, if necessary, with a little stock.

The light variation can be finished up to the point where the chicken is cooked. Reheat gently, adding a little more stock or water, if necessary. Finish the sauce just before serving.

SAUTÉED BONED CHICKEN BREASTS WITH GREEN PEPPERCORNS
Suprêmes de Volaille aux Poivres Verts

Serves: 4

> 2 whole chicken breasts, about 1¼ lbs. each, skinned, boned, and split
> Salt
> Freshly ground black pepper
> Flour
> 2½ tablespoons butter
> 1 tablespoon oil
> 1 tablespoon minced shallots
> ½ cup dry white wine
> 1 tablespoon Cognac
> 1 cup chicken stock (see pp. 19–20)
> ⅔ cup heavy cream
> 2 tablespoons green peppercorns, drained and roughly chopped
> Chopped parsley

Place the suprêmes between sheets of wax paper, skin side down, and pound them lightly with a flat mallet. Sprinkle on both sides with salt and pepper and dredge lightly in flour.

Heat 1½ tablespoons of butter and the oil in a skillet until hot but not brown. Add suprêmes in one layer and cook over moderate heat for 2 to 3 minutes, or until golden brown. Turn and cook until lightly brown on the other side. Transfer to a warm platter, cover loosely with foil, and keep warm.

Pour off fat from skillet. Add remaining butter and shallots and sauté over moderate heat for 1 minute. Add wine to skillet and reduce until slightly syrupy, stirring and scraping the sides and bottom of the pan to dissolve any browned juices. Add Cognac and cook for 1 minute.

Add stock and reduce to ⅓ cup. ☆Add cream and green peppercorns and boil until sauce is reduced to a creamy consistency. Spoon sauce over chicken and sprinkle with parsley.

Light variation

☆In place of cream, use ⅓ cup ricotta, blended in food processor, and 2 tablespoons cream. After adding stock and reducing to ⅓ cup, remove from heat and stir in ⅓ cup ricotta, 2 tablespoons cream, and the green peppercorns. Reheat gently just to a boil. Remove from the heat immediately. Spoon sauce over chicken and sprinkle with parsley.

Notes

Prepare a different sauce by substituting 2 tablespoons well drained chopped capers and 3 tablespoons thinly sliced cornichons (small sour pickles, preferably imported) for the green peppercorns. Prepare as directed in the recipe. Remove from the heat and stir in 1 tablespoon Dijon mustard.

Adding green peppercorns with the cream or ricotta produces a sauce which is not too hot. If a hotter sauce is preferred, add the peppercorns with the wine.

BONED CHICKEN BREASTS WITH MUSHROOM SAUCE
Suprêmes de Volaille aux Champignons

Serves: 4

 2½ tablespoons butter
 2 whole chicken breasts (about 1½ lbs. each), skinned, boned, and split
 Salt
 Freshly ground black pepper

Lemon juice
¾ lb. mushrooms, sliced thick
⅓ cup water
⅔ cup heavy cream
1 tablespoon finely chopped parsley

Preheat the oven to 400°.

Melt 1½ tablespoons butter in a skillet and remove skillet from heat. Add the suprêmes in one layer and turn to coat with the butter, leaving skin side up. Season with salt and pepper to taste and ☆sprinkle with 1 tablespoon lemon juice. Cover with foil and bake for 8 to 10 minutes. The breasts should be shiny, springy, and plump.

While the chicken is baking, prepare the mushrooms: □Melt 1 tablespoon butter in a saucepan and add the mushrooms, 1 table-spoon lemon juice, water, and salt and pepper to taste. Stir, cover, and bring to a boil. Boil slowly for 2 to 3 minutes, or until the mushrooms give up their juices. Strain the mushrooms and reserve the mushrooms and juices separately.

Transfer the chicken to a warm platter, cover, and keep warm. Add the mushroom juices to the pan juices in the skillet. Bring to a boil and reduce to ¼ cup. ✧Add cream and cook over moderate heat, stirring, until the sauce thickens to a light creamy consistency. Add lemon juice and salt and pepper to taste. Spoon sauce over suprêmes and sprinkle with parsley.

Light variation

☆Do not sprinkle lemon juice on chicken.

□Omit lemon juice and butter when preparing the mush-rooms.

✧In place of cream use ⅓ cup ricotta, blended in a food proces-sor, and 2 tablespoons heavy cream. Reduce the combined mush-room and pan juices to ⅓ cup. Remove from heat and stir in the processed ricotta and cream. Heat sauce just to the boiling point over moderate heat. Add lemon juice and salt and pepper to taste. Spoon sauce over suprêmes and sprinkle with parsley.

Notes

This dish is attractive and delicious when served surrounded by Buttered Noodles (see p. 215) or Buttered Rice (see p. 203).

CHICKEN LEGS STUFFED WITH LEEKS AND SPINACH
Cuisses de Poulet Farcies aux Poireaux et Épinards

Serves: 4

    4 whole chicken legs, unskinned but boned

Maceration

    3 cloves garlic, minced
    3 shallots, minced
    3 tablespoons finely chopped parsley
    1 tablespoon finely chopped fresh tarragon, or ½ teaspoon dried
    ¼ teaspoon dried thyme
    1 bay leaf
    Freshly ground black pepper
    ½ teaspoon salt
    1 cup dry white wine

Stuffing

    4 leeks (white part only), well washed and trimmed
    ⅔ lb. spinach, washed and trimmed
    2 tablespoons butter
    ⅓ lb. lean ground veal
    ½ cup soft bread crumbs, preferably homemade
    Salt
    1 egg yolk

Cooking the chicken and the sauce

    1 tablespoon oil
    Salt
    Freshly ground black pepper
    12 medium cloves garlic, unpeeled and pierced with the tip of a knife
    ½ cup dry white wine
    ⅓ cup water
    1 tablespoon finely chopped parsley

Mix maceration ingredients together. Pour half into a non-aluminum dish and add the legs in a single layer. Pour the remaining maceration over the legs. Macerate in the refrigerator for at least 2 hours or overnight.

Preheat oven to 375°.

Cut leeks into thin matchstick strips about 2½ inches long, or slice very thinly. Melt 1 tablespoon butter in a saucepan. Add the leeks, cover, and cook slowly until tender, stirring occasionally. Add maceration from chicken and the spinach. Cook over moderate heat, stirring occasionally, until liquid has completely evaporated. Remove bay leaf and cool. Put mixture into the container of a food processor with the veal and bread crumbs. Blend until mixed. Season with salt, add egg yolk, and blend.

Stuff the legs equally with the stuffing mixture, wrap the skin around, and tie with string.

Heat remaining butter and oil in an ovenproof pan over moderate heat. Add legs and cook for 15 minutes, or until golden. Discard fat. Season lightly with salt and pepper. Add garlic and half the wine and cook for 2 minutes. Add remaining wine, cover, and bake for 30 to 35 minutes, turning legs twice and adding the water after 15 minutes. Check for doneness by pricking the legs with a skewer or the tip of a paring knife. It should go in easily.

Transfer the chicken to a heated platter, cover loosely with foil, and keep warm. Peel the garlic cloves and return them to the sauce in the pan. Spoon juices over the chicken legs and sprinkle with parsley.

Notes

This dish can be prepared 1 day in advance and reheated in a 325° oven. Add a little water to compensate for evaporation.

BONED CHICKEN BREASTS WITH GARLIC
Suprêmes de Volaille à l'Ail

Serves: 4

2 whole chicken breasts, about 1¼ lbs. each, skinned, boned, and split
1 qt. water
12 medium-size cloves garlic, unpeeled

Stuffing
1 tablespoon butter
¼ lb. mushrooms, finely chopped
1 tablespoon finely chopped parsley
½ teaspoon dried rosemary, or ¼ teaspoon ground
Salt
Freshly ground black pepper
1 tablespoon dry bread crumbs
1 tablespoon heavy cream

Cooking the chicken and the sauce
Flour
2½ tablespoons butter
1 tablespoon oil
½ cup dry white wine
1 cup heavy cream
Salt
Freshly ground black pepper
1 tablespoon finely chopped parsley

Butterfly chicken breasts. Using a thin sharp knife, cut breasts horizontally in from the thick edge toward the thin part of the suprême to within ¼ inch of the edge.

Bring 1 qt. of water to a boil. Poke 2 holes in each garlic clove with the tip of a paring knife or a thin skewer to prevent their skin from exploding. Drop garlic cloves into boiling water and boil for 12 minutes.

Heat butter for stuffing in a large skillet, add chopped mushrooms, and sauté over moderately high heat, stirring and tossing, for 5 minutes, or until lightly browned and moisture has evaporated. Remove from heat.

Drain garlic cloves, peel, and purée by forcing through a fine sieve or blending in food processor until smooth. Set aside 2 teaspoons of purée for sauce. Add remainder to skillet with mushrooms and add the rest of the stuffing ingredients.

Divide stuffing into 4 portions and spread one on each suprême, leaving a ½-inch border so that stuffing does not leak out when closed. Close by folding and pressing edges lightly together. Season lightly with salt and pepper and dredge in flour.

Heat remaining butter and oil in the skillet. Add suprêmes and sauté over moderate heat for 6 to 8 minutes on each side, lifting them occasionally to let butter run underneath so they do not stick. Test for doneness by opening suprêmes lightly to make sure there is no sign of rawness inside.

Transfer suprêmes to a warm platter and keep them warm in a very low oven. Pour off fat in skillet, add wine, and reduce to 3 tablespoons over moderate heat, scraping up brown bits from the bottom and sides of the skillet with a wooden spatula. Stir in reserved garlic purée.

☆Add cream and reduce over moderate heat, stirring until sauce has a light creamy consistency. Season with salt and pepper to taste. Spoon sauce over suprêmes and sprinkle with chopped parsley.

Light variation

☆In place of cream in sauce mixture, use ½ cup ricotta, blended in a food processor with 6 tablespoons milk, and 2 tablespoons heavy cream. After adding the garlic purée to the sauce, remove the sauce from the heat. Stir in the processed ricotta and 2 tablespoons heavy cream. Heat very gently just to a boil, stirring constantly. Remove from heat immediately. Season with salt and pepper to taste. Spoon sauce over suprêmes and sprinkle with chopped parsley.

Notes

The suprêmes can be stuffed 1 day in advance. Cook and prepare sauce just before serving.

The food processor is useful to chop mushrooms, but do not mush them. They should remain in small pieces.

STUFFED CHICKEN FESTIVAL
Poulet de Fête

Serves: 8

2 3- to 3½-lb. chickens, boned, with carcasses reserved

Stuffing
1½ teaspoons butter
1 tablespoon water
3 shallots, minced
⅓ cup Madeira
2 slices bread, crusts removed
Milk
2 tablespoons Cognac
1 2¾-ounce can pâté de foie gras
¾ lb. lean ground veal
⅔ lb. lean ground pork
2 eggs
Livers from chickens, cleaned and chopped
1 truffle, minced (optional)
¼ teaspoon freshly grated nutmeg
Salt
Freshly ground black pepper

Cooking the chicken and sauce
4½ tablespoons butter
1 medium onion, peeled and quartered
1 carrot, quartered
⅓ cup Madeira
1½ cups all-purpose stock (see pp. 17–18) or chicken stock (see pp. 19–20), heated
1 bunch watercress
1½ teaspoons cornstarch dissolved in 2 teaspoons Madeira

Preheat oven to 400°.

Prepare stuffing: Melt butter in a small skillet over moderate heat. Add shallots and cook for 2 minutes, stirring, without browning. Transfer to a bowl. Add Madeira to skillet and reduce to 2 tablespoons. Add to bowl with shallots. ☆Add remaining stuffing ingredients, season to taste with salt and pepper, and blend well with a spatula.

Lay chickens flat open, skin side down, and spread with stuffing, using the back of a spoon to spread it evenly. Close chickens like a book and use skewers to hold the skin edges together, pinning them together like 2 pieces of fabric. Turn chickens on their backs and truss.

Cook the chickens: Melt 2 tablespoons butter in a roasting pan. Put chickens in on their sides and scatter carcasses, onion, and carrot around the chickens. Roast for 20 minutes, turn on other side, and roast for 20 minutes. Heat stock.

Add Madeira to roasting pan, cook for 5 minutes, and add ⅓ of the hot stock. Turn chickens, breast side up, baste, and roast for 15 minutes. Add remaining stock, ½ cup at a time at 10-minute intervals. A meat thermometer inserted into center should register 170°. Total roasting time is about 1 hour and 20 minutes.

Transfer chickens to a warm platter and keep warm in a low oven for 15 minutes.

Strain juices into a saucepan and degrease. Bring to a boil. Remove from heat and stir in enough of the cornstarch mixture to reach a light creamy consistency. Return to a boil and boil for 1 minute. Remove from heat, □swirl in the remaining butter, and season with salt and pepper, if necessary.

Cut thighs and legs from chickens and carve each body into 8 slices. Arrange in the center of a heated platter, slightly overlapping. Arrange the legs and thighs around the slices and surround with watercress. Spoon a little of the sauce over the chicken and serve the remainder in a warm sauceboat.

Light variation

☆In place of ground veal and pork, use 1⅓ lb. ground veal only in the stuffing mixture.

□Swirl in 1 tablespoon of butter only and season the sauce with salt and pepper, if necessary.

Notes

Chickens can be stuffed several hours in advance.

Leftovers are delicious cold, served with a cold vegetable salad.

ROAST CHICKEN WITH TARRAGON
Poulet Rôti à l'Estragon

Serves: 4

   ½ tablespoon oil
   ½ tablespoon butter
  1 3½-lb. chicken
     Salt
     Freshly ground black pepper
 1½ teaspoons dried tarragon, or about 8 sprigs fresh (keep 5 sprigs whole, mincing rest finely)
  2 shallots, finely chopped
  ½ cup dry white wine
  ⅔ cup heavy cream
     Watercress sprigs

Preheat oven to 425°.

Heat oil in a roasting pan. Cut off and discard lumps of fat from skin flaps of chicken. Season cavity with salt and pepper and put half the dried tarragon (or 5 sprigs) inside. Truss chicken and put in roasting pan on its side. Roast for 20 minutes on each side and for 20 minutes breast up, or until juices inside cavity run a clear yellow. Baste every 15 minutes.

Remove chicken from oven. Cut into serving pieces, and transfer to a warm platter. Keep warm in a 200° oven.

Pour off most of the fat from the roasting pan. Add shallots and sauté over moderate heat for ½ minute, stirring. Add wine and remaining tarragon and reduce to 3 tablespoons, stirring and scraping up any brown bits from the bottom and sides of the pan. Drain juices from chicken into roasting pan.

☆Add cream and reduce over moderate heat, stirring, until sauce has a creamy consistency and coats a spoon. Season with salt and pepper, if necessary.

Arrange chicken on heated individual plates. Garnish with bunches of watercress and spoon sauce over chicken.

Light variation

☆In place of cream, use ½ cup ricotta, blended in a food processor with 6 tablespoons milk and 2 tablespoons heavy cream. Remove the reduced pan juices from the heat and stir in the processed ricotta and 2 tablespoons heavy cream. Heat very gently just to first boil, stirring constantly. Remove from heat and season with salt and pepper, if necessary.

Notes

Chicken can be roasted 1 to 2 hours in advance. Reheat alone, covered loosely with foil, in a 350° oven for 15 minutes. Finish sauce just before serving.

CHICKEN WATERZOOI
Waterzooi de Poulet

Serves: 6

    3 tablespoons butter
    2 leeks (white part only), cut into julienne strips
    2 or 3 celery hearts, cut into julienne strips
    1 large onion, cut into julienne strips
    1 bunch parsley roots, quartered or halved lengthwise, de-
      pending on size, and tied together with string
    1 cup dry white wine
    1 4- to 4½-lb. chicken, cut into serving pieces
    3 cups chicken stock (see pp. 19–20)
      Salt
      Freshly ground black pepper
    4 egg yolks
    1 cup heavy cream
 1½ tablespoons finely chopped parsley

Melt the butter in a large pot and add the julienned leeks, celery hearts, and onion. Put the parsley roots on top and pour in the wine. Cover and cook slowly over moderate heat, stirring occasionally, for 10 minutes, or until the vegetables are slightly softened.

Arrange the chicken pieces over the bed of vegetables, add stock to barely cover, and season with salt and pepper to taste. Cover and bring to a boil. Simmer slowly for 30 to 40 minutes, or until the chicken is cooked. Transfer chicken to a dish and cover loosely with foil to keep warm. Remove the parsley roots and degrease the broth.

Put the parsley roots in the container of a blender or food processor. Add a little of the cooking liquid and blend until smooth.

Skin and bone the chicken and put the meat in a warm soup tureen.

☆Beat the egg yolks and cream together. Add the parsley purée and beat well. Add the mixture to the degreased broth and stir well. Season with salt and pepper, if necessary, and heat, stirring, over moderate heat. Do not let it boil as the yolks will curdle.

Ladle the soup over the chicken and sprinkle with parsley.

Light variation

☆Omit the egg yolks and cream. Add the parsley purée to the degreased broth and stir well. Season with salt and pepper, if necessary, and heat, stirring, over moderate heat.

Notes

To prepare 1 day in advance, stop at the point where the chicken is cooked. Let cool, cover, and refrigerate. Degrease and reheat to a simmer over moderate heat and continue with the recipe.

To prepare the recipe in a pressure cooker, cook the butter, vegetables, and wine under pressure for 4 minutes. Add the chicken and cook under pressure for 12 to 15 minutes. Remove from heat, take out chicken and remove skin and bones.

Degrease broth. Blend or process the vegetables with the broth in batches until it is smooth. Return purée and chicken to pot and bring back to a simmer. Remove from heat. Ladle about 1 cup of the puréed soup in a thin stream over the egg yolk cream mixture.

Pour back into soup while stirring. Taste for seasoning. Reheat to just under a boil.

ROAST TRUFFLED TURKEY WITH MUSHROOM SAUCE
Dinde Rôtie aux Truffes aux Champignons

Serves: 8

- 2 truffles, cut into thin slices, optional
- 1 7- to 8-lb. turkey, thawed if frozen
  Salt
  Freshly ground black pepper
- 1 7-inch stalk celery, roughly chopped
- 1 lb. mushrooms, stems removed and reserved whole and caps sliced
- 2 tablespoons butter
- 1 tablespoon oil
- 2 medium carrots, thickly sliced
- 2 medium onions, peeled and halved
- ¼ teaspoon dried thyme
- 1 bay leaf
- 1½ cups white wine (not too dry)
- 1½ cups chicken stock (see pp. 19–20)
- 2 tablespoons Madeira, or 1 tablespoon Cognac
- 1 bunch watercress

If using the truffles, one day before cooking slide the truffle slices under the breast and thigh skin, using a finger to push the slices under, and being very careful not to tear the skin. Refrigerate the turkey so that the flesh will absorb the subtle truffle flavor.

Preheat the oven to 450°.

Season the turkey cavity lightly with salt and pepper and stuff with the celery and mushroom stems. Close the cavity with skewers and kitchen twine and truss the bird.

Heat the butter and oil in a roasting pan, add carrots and onions, and cook over moderate heat, stirring, for 5 minutes, or until lightly browned. Add thyme and bay leaf and set turkey on its side in the pan. Lower oven heat to 400° and roast for 15 minutes. Turn bird onto other side and roast for 15 minutes.

Heat wine and stock in separate pans.

Pour off any fat from the roasting pan and pour ¾ cup hot wine around turkey. Turn turkey breast up and roast, basting occasionally, for 15 minutes. Add remaining hot wine and roast for 15 minutes, basting occasionally. Pour in ¾ cup hot stock and roast, basting occasionally, for 20 minutes. Pour in remaining hot stock and roast, basting occasionally, for 20 minutes, or until done. If turkey browns too much, lower oven temperature to 375°. After about an hour and a half of roasting, scatter sliced mushrooms around turkey. Turkey is done when juices from inside cavity run clear yellow with no trace of pink. Total cooking time is about 1 hour and 40 minutes.

Transfer turkey to a warm platter, cover loosely with foil, and keep warm. Let stand for at least 20 minutes before carving.

Using a slotted spoon, transfer the sliced mushrooms to a warm dish and cover. Discard carrots, onions, and bay leaf. Degrease the cooking juices in the roasting pan. Remove mushroom stems from inside turkey's cavity. Transfer to the container of a blender or food processor with the cooking juices. Blend the mixture until smoothly puréed, strain through a fine sieve, and pour into a small saucepan. Bring to a boil, stirring, and season with salt and pepper, if necessary. If too thick, thin with a little stock. Add Madeira or Cognac and boil for 1 minute.

Remove trussing strings from turkey. To carve turkey, first cut off legs and cut meat from thighs and drumsticks in lengthwise slices. Carve each breast half into 8 thin slices and arrange with the meat from the thighs and drumsticks in the center of a heated platter. Put half of the reserved sliced mushrooms at either end of the platter, garnish with watercress, and serve sauce in a warm sauceboat.

Notes

To make a more elaborate and festive presentation, surround the sliced turkey with a garnish of several vegetables, such as braised chestnuts, celery, and onions in addition to the mushrooms.

ROAST DUCK WITH ORANGE SAUCE
Canard à l'Orange

Serves: 6

2 4- to 5-lb. fresh or frozen ducklings, thawed if frozen
Salt
Freshly ground black pepper
2 tablespoons oil
Zest of 2 oranges
Zest of 1 lemon
6 to 8 juice oranges (enough to make 2 cups of juice)
Juice of ½ lemon

For the sauce and garnish

4 oranges, preferably navel
½ cup sugar
2 cups water
Juice of ½ lemon
1 tablespoon cornstarch dissolved in 1 tablespoon lemon juice
1 tablespoon Cointreau or Grand Marnier
Watercress sprigs

Preheat oven to 525°.

Pull excess fat from duck cavities and sprinkle inside of each duck lightly with salt and pepper. Truss and pat dry with paper towels.

Oil a shallow baking dish big enough to hold the 2 ducks and lay them in it on their sides. Roast in the oven for 15 minutes. Pour off all but 2 tablespoons of fat from the pan and lower heat to 450°. Turn ducks on their other sides and roast, basting, for 20 minutes.

Use a zester (see p. 10) or cut zest from oranges and lemon in hair-thin strips. Blanch the orange and lemon zest in 1 qt. boiling water for 2 minutes. Drain and sprinkle with cold running water. Squeeze the juice oranges and ½ of the lemon. Strain juice through a fine sieve into a saucepan, and heat until hot.

When ducks have roasted for a total of 35 minutes, pour off all the fat in the roasting pan. Turn ducks breast sides up, pour in hot juice and the blanched zest, and roast, basting, for 40 minutes, or until juice inside the cavities runs clear yellow and there is no trace of blood. (The total cooking time is about 1¼ to 1½ hours.)

Peel and section navel oranges, removing pith and membranes. Boil sugar, water, and juice of ½ lemon in a large skillet, stirring occasionally. When sugar is completely dissolved, add orange sections and poach them for 1 minute. Remove orange sections with a slotted spoon and reserve. Reserve 1 to 2 tablespoons of syrup for the sauce and discard the rest of the syrup.

Drain juices from cavities into pan juices and transfer ducks to a heated platter. Put ducks in the turned off oven while preparing the sauce.

Degrease pan juices, pour into a small saucepan, and bring to a boil. Remove from heat and stir in just enough of the cornstarch mixture to get a light creamy consistency. Season with the reserved syrup and salt and pepper to taste. Boil for 1 to 2 minutes, stirring, and add the Cointreau.

Carve the ducks (see p. 123) and arrange pieces on a heated platter. Scatter the orange sections attractively over the duck. Spoon a little of the sauce over the dish and surround with watercress. Serve remaining sauce in a warm sauceboat.

Notes

To prepare ahead, put cooked, carved ducks and oranges in an ovenproof dish and pour sauce over. Let cool and cover. They will keep for 1 day refrigerated. Reheat in an oven preheated to 325° for 20 to 30 minutes.

Crisp French Fried Potatoes (see p. 209) are the best accompaniment.

The zest of a citrus fruit is the outer colored portion of the skin that contains all the flavorful oils. Pare it off the fruit thinly, being careful not to get any of the bitter white pit underneath. A zester will do a fast and perfect job, but you can also use a vegetable peeler. Roll up each strip of zest, then cut crosswise into pieces as fine as pine needles. Or stack the strips and cut lengthwise into pine needles.

BROILED DUCK
Canard Grillé

Serves: 2

1 5-lb. fresh or frozen duck, thawed if frozen
Salt
Freshly ground black pepper
Green Peppercorn Butter (see p. 53)

Preheat broiler to high.

Discard excess fat from the duck's cavity. Split the duck down the back with a pair of poultry shears by cutting down one side of the backbone. Cut down the other side of the backbone and discard it. Open up the duck and spread it flat skin side up. Pound it with the side of a cleaver so that it will lie as flat as possible. Make diagonal slashes about 3 inches long on the breast and around the body to help release the fat while the bird is cooking. Cut through the skin into the fat but not down to the flesh. Cut through the joint of the drumstick and thigh so they will cook more thoroughly.

Sprinkle duck with salt and pepper and put skin side down on a foil-lined baking dish. Broil 5 inches from the heat for 20 minutes. Turn duck skin side up and broil for 20 minutes. If not brown enough, raise duck closer to heat for 1 minute. Let stand for 10 minutes. Carve off each breast and serve topped with a slice of cold green peppercorn butter.

Notes

Save the legs and thighs for a ragoût (see p. 194). Let cool, wrap, and refrigerate for 1 day. The legs and thighs can also be broiled as directed, then separated from breasts and broiled for 5 to 7 minutes longer.

Chicken and Cornish Game Hens can also be cooked this way, 25 to 30 minutes for chicken, 20 to 25 minutes for game hen. There is not the same problem with the leg and thigh meat.

DUCK LEG STEW WITH PINEAPPLE AND PRUNES
Ragoût de Cuisses de Canard à l'Ananas et Pruneaux

Serves: 4

 1 cup red wine
 ½ teaspoon cinnamon
 ½ lb. pitted prunes
 1 2- to 3-lb. pineapple
 4 duck legs with thighs attached
   Salt
   Freshly ground black pepper
 1 tablespoon butter
 1 tablespoon oil
 4 yellow onions, 2 inches in diameter
 4 medium mushrooms, or 8 small, stems trimmed
 2½ tablespoons brown sugar
 1 cup concentrated chicken stock (see pp. 19–20) or all-purpose stock (see p. 17–18)
 1 tablespoon cornstarch mixed with ¼ cup Madeira or Port
 4 croutons (see p. 63), optional

Combine wine and cinnamon and let prunes soak overnight in the mixture. Drain and reserve wine and prunes separately.

Peel pineapple, remove eyes, and halve lengthwise. Cut crosswise into ⅜-inch-thick slices, remove core with a small round biscuit cutter, or use a pineapple corer, and reserve juice.

Season duck legs lightly with salt and pepper. Heat butter and oil in a pan over moderate heat. Add legs, skin side down, and onions and cook slowly for 15 to 20 minutes, turning pieces occasionally.

Pour off all but 2 tablespoons of the fat, add mushrooms and half the sugar. Cook for 7 minutes, or until nicely browned.

Transfer legs, onions, and mushrooms to a warm platter and cover with foil to keep warm.

Add remaining sugar and pineapple slices to pan and cook gently for 4 to 5 minutes, or until golden. Remove and keep warm. Pour wine into the pan and reduce to ⅓ cup over moderately high heat, stirring with a wooden spatula. Add pineapple juice and reduce by half. Add stock and bring to a boil. Remove from heat and stir in enough cornstarch mixture to get a light creamy consistency. Season with salt and pepper to taste.

Add duck legs, onions, mushrooms, and prunes, bring to a simmer, and simmer for 15 minutes, or until legs are tender and cooked through. Put ragoût in a deep heated dish and surround it with pineapple slices. Garnish with croutons, if desired.

Notes

Duck can be prepared 1 day in advance and reheated covered. Reheat in a 325° oven. Do not make sauce too thick.

This is a good way to use the legs of Grilled Duck. Either sever them from the duck before broiling, or, if using them broiled, omit the first step in this recipe for browning the duck legs. A whole duck can be used. Cook as directed, but remove breasts before final 15 minutes of cooking. Reheat breasts in the sauce just before serving. They should be eaten slightly pink.

DUCK WITH GRAPES
Canard aux Raisins

Serves: 6

    2 4- to 5-lb. fresh or frozen ducklings, thawed if frozen
      Salt
      Freshly ground black pepper
1½ tablespoons oil
1½ lbs. ripe seedless green grapes
    1 cup concentrated chicken stock (see pp. 19–20)
    3 teaspoons cornstarch mixed with 3 teaspoons cold water

Preheat oven to 525°.

Pull excess fat from duck cavities. Sprinkle inside of each duck lightly with salt and pepper. Truss and pat dry with paper towels.

Oil a shallow roasting pan and put ducks in it on their sides. Roast on middle rack of oven for 15 minutes. Pour off all but 2 tablespoons of fat from the pan and lower heat to 450°. Turn ducks on their other sides and roast, basting, for 25 minutes. Turn ducks breast up and roast for 20 minutes. Cover breasts with foil and roast for 15 minutes, discarding all but a bit of the fat in the pan while roasting.

Using a paring knife, peel ½ lb. of the grapes and put them in a small saucepan. Put remaining grapes through a food mill into a bowl and reserve.

Ducks are cooked when juices run clear from cavity. Drain juices from cavities into pan juices and transfer ducks to a heated platter. Keep warm in a 180° oven, covered loosely with foil.

Degrease pan juices. (A degreaser is especially useful. See p. 12.) Bring juices to a boil over moderate heat with half of grape juice, using a wooden spoon to scrape in any brown bits which cling to the bottom and sides of the pan. Reduce slightly. Add remaining purée and reduce again, stirring. Add stock and boil for 5 minutes, stirring. Remove from heat and stir in just enough of the cornstarch mixture to get a light creamy consistency. Bring sauce to a boil and boil, stirring, for 1 to 2 minutes. Season with salt and pepper, if necessary. Pour sauce into a saucepan and keep it warm in a larger saucepan of warm water.

Add 2 tablespoons of sauce to the reserved peeled grapes. Bring slowly to a simmer and simmer for 2 to 3 minutes to heat thoroughly.

Carve ducks and arrange pieces attractively on a warm platter. Glaze with a little sauce and surround with grapes. Serve remaining sauce in a warm sauceboat.

Notes

To make this dish in advance, roast ducks in the morning and keep at room temperature. Reheat whole, covered loosely with foil, in a 350° oven. Also prepare sauce in advance, adding cornstarch just before serving.

DUCK PÂTÉ
Pâté de Canard

Serves: 10 to 12

1 5-lb. duck, skinned, boned, and tendons removed to yield about 1 lb. 2 oz. lean meat
1 duck liver, cleaned
1 lb. lean pork
1¼ lbs. fresh pork fat
2 large shallots, finely chopped
2 or 3 cloves garlic, finely chopped
2 teaspoons salt
3 tablespoons Cognac
½ teaspoon freshly ground black pepper
2 eggs, lightly beaten
Grated zest of 2 oranges
2 tablespoons finely chopped parsley
3 tablespoons white wine
1 lb. unsalted fresh pork fat back, sliced paper thin
⅛ teaspoon dried thyme
2 bay leaves or orange slices

Special equipment
2-qt. terrine with lid or smaller ones with lids

Preheat oven to 425°.

Put duck meat, liver, pork, and pork fat through the coarse blade of a meat grinder. Put the ground mixture into a bowl and add the shallots, garlic, salt, Cognac, pepper, eggs, orange zest, parsley, and wine. Mix well.

Line the terrine with fat back. Do not overlap the slices. First cover the bottom and build up sides, laying slices horizontally against the sides of the mold. Pack ground mixture into terrine. Cut the remaining fat back into ⅓-inch-wide strips and top pâté with a lattice of fat. Sprinkle with thyme and top with bay leaves. Or decorate the top with 3 or 4 half moons of orange.

Cover terrine tightly with foil and the lid. Put terrine in a large baking pan and add 1 inch of boiling water. Bake for 1½ hours, or until a meat thermometer registers 170°.

Put a small plate or dish that fits inside the terrine on top of the pâté and weight it down with a 1-lb. weight. Let sit at room temperature for several hours until cool. Remove the weight and refrigerate overnight before serving.

Notes

Pâté will keep for 1 week in the refrigerator.

A food processor can be used to grind the meat. All gristle and tendons must be removed as the blade will not grind them.

Instead of orange zest, use ½ cup natural blanched pistachios. Leave them whole and layer them with the pâté so that when the finished pâté is sliced the nuts will give it a pretty look.

For a third flavor, use 2 tablespoons chopped green peppercorns and omit the zest.

7
RICE, POTATOES, AND PASTA

A cereal, a vegetable, and flour made into a dough and cut into various shapes . . . what can these very different foods have in common besides whiteness? Plenty. All three are high in carbohydrates, and all are markedly hospitable to other flavors, going well with almost every sort of food except one another. And all are inexpensive. Being economical, filling, and nutritious, they are staples in the diets of whole populations, two of them—rice and potatoes—ranking with wheat, the basis of pasta, as the world's most important sources of nourishment.

RICE

More than half of humankind subsists principally on this grain, the seeds of a tall grass that grow in water. Rice is 98 percent digestible, and requires only an hour to digest compared with the two to four hours most foods require. Its eight percent of protein is of exceptional quality. It is low in sodium, and it contains neither cholesterol nor gluten.

In the United States—now the world's leading exporter of rice—two types predominate, the long grain and the short grain. In both, the hulls and bran have been removed and the rice grains polished, but the resulting loss of nutrients has been partly made up for by the addition of minerals and vitamins. We prefer the long grain variety for most uses. When cooked, it is fluffier and drier and its grains separate better and remain firmer. On the other hand stickier, moister short grain rice binds puddings well and soaks up sauces nicely.

POTATOES

The white or Irish potato, the swollen underground stem of a flowering plant, is probably the most popular of all vegetables in Western countries within the temperate zones. It is also the most versatile of vegetables, being prepared in many different ways and served in infinite variations and combinations.

There isn't much we can add to this except to say that we are both exceedingly fond of potatoes. Chef Jorant, who cherishes them above all other vegetables, likes his peeled and boiled with nothing on them, not even butter. By contrast Isabelle Marique has been converted since she moved to America to potatoes baked in their skins.

The flesh of potatoes tends toward either waxiness or mealiness, the former type being suited to boiling and the latter type to baking. Both types, however, can be prepared in many other ways, with just a few reservations. Thus, while crumbly baking potatoes can be boiled, the firmer boiling potatoes aren't much good for mashing as they don't bind well. Then there are the little new potatoes, with their delicate skins ranging from pink to light red or brown; they are always waxy and invariably delicious.

Choose potatoes that are well shaped, firm, and smooth, without soft spots, knobs, or cracks. Never buy one that has begun to sprout, as sprouting makes it shrink in size. And don't expose them to sunlight or they will turn greenish and acquire a slightly bitter flavor. Potatoes, which after all have lived out most of their existence underground, need darkness, so store them in some cool, dark place; they will keep there for several months. (Don't refrigerate them or they will turn sweet.)

Scrub potatoes with a Teflon sponge or a vegetable brush. To conserve their nutrients, chiefly located in a thin layer just beneath the skin, leave the skin on when cooking. If you must peel them, at least try to cook them whole. Immediately after peeling, drop them in cold water or they will darken, but don't leave them to soak too long or nutrients will be lost.

Potatoes provide potassium, phosphorus, and iron, and an abundance of Vitamin C. There's as much Vitamin C in a medium-sized potato as in an orange.

PASTA

Pasta (Italian for paste) was probably brought to Europe from China by Mongol invaders in the thirteenth century, but it is only now that French people venturing abroad are learning how to prepare this marvelous food, so long esteemed by their neighbors to the south. But was it Italians who finally broke them of their habit of boiling spaghetti or noodles for twenty minutes or more? For Isabelle Marique it was Americans.

"It was in New York that I had my first taste of properly prepared pasta," Ms. Marique relates. "The spaghetti was cooked *al dente* and covered with a superb sauce made with fresh basil, an herb I didn't know much about either. What a revelation that meal was!"

Pasta fits in all around the menu: in soups and salads, as a side dish, as a main course garnished with a sauce and grated cheese. When you boil it, keep testing strands, stirring occasionally, until they approach that state, tender yet still firm, known as *al dente* ("to the tooth," with "firm" implied). Use plenty of water—at least a gallon per pound—to prevent the strands from sticking together. And when it is done don't rinse it as this washes out the starch, the element that makes pasta taste so smooth when immediately combined with its sauce.

The best factory-made pasta is made with flour milled from hard durum wheat. Pasta made from semolina, the gritty, coarse particles left after the finer flour has passed through the bolting machine, is firm and chewy and binds well with sauces. If there is an Italian grocery near you, buy imported factory-made pasta rather than domestic.

Some American pastas do well enough if you stop cooking them the instant they are *al dente*; in general, however, they are

softer and blander than the Italian kind, and lack character by comparison. As you will find, some brands take longer to cook than
others do.

All types of pasta are easy to reheat in a skillet with either oil,
butter, or a sauce.

Of late, it seems, growing numbers of home cooks have taken
to making their own pasta, from soft-wheat flour and eggs. Pasta is
made either the ancient way, by hand, which we prefer (see various cookbooks on Italian cuisine), or with simple machines obtainable in specialty hardware stores, well-stocked cookware shops, and
the kitchen-equipment departments of big department stores. These
machines are of two types, but both the hand-cranked and electric
pasta-makers work like wringers, extruding thin bands or ribbons
of dough from between cylindrical rollers. Most authorities prefer
the electric model because of its speed in flattening the dough. Its
rollers are covered with textured nylon, turning out pasta with a
slightly uneven surface like that of handmade pasta, whereas the
hand-cranked machine's polished steel rollers produce a surface
that is smooth and slippery.

HOW FATTENING ARE RICE, POTATOES, AND PASTA?

Starchy foods are filling, and when we eat them our bodies leave us
in no doubt of the fact. But are they, then, fattening? Even in this
day of heightened awareness of nutrition some people may still be
surprised to learn that a gram of carbohydrate (as in rice, potatoes,
or pasta) contains the same number of calories as a gram of protein
(as in lean meat or fish)—namely, four—whereas a gram of fat contains nine. Here's how the three foods covered in this chapter stack
up in terms of calories; the amounts of rice and pasta represent
about the same bulk as the medium-size potato:

Rice	½ cup cooked	112 calories
Potatoes	1 medium-size, boiled then pared	122 calories
Pasta	½ cup cooked	93 calories

Enough said.

BUTTERED RICE (PILAF)
Riz au Naturel

Serves: 4

2½ tablespoons butter
1 medium onion, finely chopped
1 cup rice
2 cups water or chicken stock (see pp. 19–20)
Salt
Freshly ground black pepper

Preheat oven to 400°.

Melt butter in an ovenproof pan, add onion, and cover. Cook over low heat, stirring occasionally, for 5 minutes, or until onion is soft and translucent. Add rice and stir to blend well. Add water and salt and pepper to taste. Bring to a boil, stirring occasionally. Cover and cook for 18 minutes in oven or over a very low flame on top of the stove. Let stand a few minutes before serving.

Notes

Leftover rice keeps for 2 days in a covered container in the refrigerator.

This rice may be used cold in salads, such as Vegetable Salad with Rice (see p. 206) or Rice with Seafood (see p. 204).

Allow ½ cup raw rice per person when serving as a side dish.

CREOLE RICE
Riz Créole

Serves: 4

3 qts. water
Salt
1 cup rice
2 tablespoons butter, softened (optional)
2 tablespoons chopped parsley (optional)
Freshly ground black pepper

Bring 3 qts. water to a boil in a large pot. Add 4 teaspoons salt. Sprinkle rice gradually into boiling water so the water does not stop boiling. Boil, stirring occasionally, for 18 minutes, or until rice is tender. Drain in a colander and put in a serving bowl. Fluff and add butter and parsley. Season with salt and pepper to taste, if necessary.

Notes

This is a very simple, practical, and digestible way to cook rice. Unlike the Pilaf, which absorbs water and keeps its starch, Creole Rice absorbs less water and rejects its starch.

Serve the rice plain with any sauced dish, such as Veal Stew (see p. 150) or Sole Fillets with Seafood (see p. 86), or use it cold in salads.

RICE WITH SEAFOOD
Pilaf de Fruits de Mer

Serves: 4

- 4 shallots, finely chopped
- 1 cup dry white wine
- 3 tablespoons finely chopped parsley
- 2½ lbs. mussels, scrubbed and bearded
  Freshly ground black pepper
- 1 lb. fish fillets, such as sole, flounder, or any fresh, non-oily fish
- ¼ lb. shrimp, shelled and deveined
- ¼ lb. bay scallops, or sea scallops, cut in half crosswise
  Salt
  Buttered Rice (Pilaf), made with 1⅓ cups rice, substituting fish cooking liquid for chicken stock (see p. 203)
- 3 egg yolks
- ½ cup heavy cream
- ½ tablespoon lemon juice

Preheat oven to 400°.

Put 1 tablespoon of the shallots, ½ cup wine, 1 tablespoon parsley, the mussels, and pepper to taste in a kettle. Cover tightly and cook over moderate-high heat, shaking the kettle occasionally, for 6 minutes, or until the mussels are opened. Using a slotted spoon, transfer the mussels to a bowl. Steam any unopened mussels for a few minutes more. If they still do not open, discard them. Shell the mussels and reserve them. Strain the cooking liquid through a fine sieve that has been lined with a dampened and squeezed-out linen or cotton towel and reserve.

Sprinkle remaining shallots over the bottom of a gratin dish. Arrange fish fillets over shallots in a single layer, overlapping them slightly where the fillet ends are thinner. Scatter shrimp and scallops over fillets. Sprinkle lightly with salt and pepper, and pour over mussel liquid, remaining wine, and enough water to cover. Cover tightly with foil or a lid and bake for 15 to 20 minutes, or until fish just starts to flake.

Using a slotted spatula, carefully remove fish fillets and seafood. Drain well and transfer to a platter. Let cool. Strain the cooking liquid through a fine sieve into a bowl. Reserve 1 cup for the sauce. Use the remaining liquid to prepare the Rice Pilaf. (Make up any required liquid with water.) Prepare the Rice Pilaf and transfer it to a serving bowl. Let cool. Cut shrimp in half lengthwise. Cut fillets into 1¼-inch pieces. Arrange the fish and seafood attractively on top of the rice. Just before serving spoon sauce over. Sprinkle with remaining parsley.

In a small bowl, beat the egg yolks.

Reduce the reserved cooking liquid to ¼ cup over high heat. ☆Add the cream, return to a boil, stirring over moderate heat, and boil for 2 to 3 minutes, or until the sauce has a light creamy consistency. (It should remain thin and transparent.) Whisk the boiling mixture rapidly into the beaten egg yolks in a thin steady stream. Add the lemon juice.

Light variation

☆In place of the cream, use ½ cup ricotta, blended in a food processor, and 2 tablespoons heavy cream. Reduce the reserved cooking liquid to ⅓ cup over high heat. Remove from the heat and stir in the processed ricotta and 2 tablespoons heavy cream. Return just to the boil.

VEGETABLE SALAD WITH RICE
Salade de Légumes aux Riz

Serves: 8

Buttered Rice, made with 1⅓ cups rice (see p. 203)

2 qts. water

Salt

½ lb. green beans, trimmed and halved

½ lb. fresh peas, or one-half of a 10-oz. package frozen tiny peas

½ lb. carrots, cut into ¼-inch-thick slices

Sauce

¼ lb. imported cornichons (gherkins) or sour pickles, roughly chopped

2 shallots, roughly chopped

2 tablespoons Dijon mustard

Salt

Freshly ground black pepper

3 tablespoons wine vinegar

4 tablespoons oil

3 tablespoons olive oil

3 tablespoons very finely chopped chives

3 tablespoons finely chopped parsley

Preparing the salad

2 grapefruit

½ lb. mushrooms

Lemon juice

2 large tomatoes (¾ lb.), peeled, seeded, and cut into ⅜-inch cubes

20 tiny black olives, preferably French or Italian, pitted and halved

1 tablespoon finely chopped parsley

Prepare the rice and let it cool.

Bring 2 qts. water to a boil in a kettle. Add 2½ teaspoons salt and beans. Cover to bring water back to a boil as fast as possible.

Uncover and boil for 5 to 6 minutes, or until beans are tender-crisp. Drain in a colander and run cold water over beans so they retain their bright green color. Boil and refresh peas and carrots in the same manner. Boil peas for 4 to 6 minutes depending on their size (for the tiny frozen ones, drain them as soon as water reaches boil). Boil carrots for 4 to 5 minutes. Let vegetables cool.

Blend shallots, cornichons, and mustard in a blender or food processor until smoothly puréed. Add salt and pepper to taste, vinegar, and *oils and blend until well combined. Stir in chives and parsley.

Peel grapefruit, separate into segments, and halve them. Slice mushrooms and toss with 2 tablespoons lemon juice. Put beans, peas, carrots, mushrooms, tomatoes, grapefruit, and olives in a bowl. Add dressing and toss. Add more lemon juice to taste.

Arrange vegetables in the middle of a deep platter, circle with rice, and sprinkle with parsley.

Light variation

*In place of oil and olive oil, use ½ cup heavy cream and ½ cup ricotta blended in a food processor with ¼ cup skim milk. Blend shallots, cornichons, and mustard in a blender or food processor until smoothly puréed. Add ½ cup heavy cream and ½ cup ricotta to skim milk mixture, salt and pepper to taste, and vinegar. Blend until just combined, 1 or 2 quick on-off turns. Stir in chives and parsley.

Notes

Rice, all vegetables (except mushrooms), and standard dressing can be made 1 day in advance. It is best to slice the mushrooms and toss vegetables with dressing just before serving, but this may be done 1 hour in advance, if necessary.

The base for Light Dressing may be prepared in advance and combined with cream and ricotta just before serving.

MASHED POTATOES
Purée de Pommes de Terre

Serves: 6

2 lbs. baking potatoes (about 6 or 7 medium)
Salt
1 cup milk
3 tablespoons butter, cut in pieces, at room temperature
Freshly ground black pepper
Freshly grated nutmeg

Wash, peel, and rinse potatoes. Cut them into thirds crosswise. Put in a large saucepan, cover with cold water by 1 inch, and add 1¼ teaspoons salt per quart of water. Cover and bring to a boil. Boil slowly for 15 to 20 minutes, or until tender. (Test by piercing with a thin skewer so they do not break.) Potatoes must not be overcooked and mushy or the purée will be watery.

Drain and return potatoes to saucepan. Put over very low heat, uncovered, for 30 seconds to dry the potatoes, shaking the pan gently to prevent sticking.

Bring milk to a boil in a small saucepan.

Force potatoes through a food mill into a heavy saucepan. ☆Beat in butter and return to low heat. Vigorously beat in enough boiling milk to give a thick, soft texture. (The potatoes should neither run easily from the spatula nor mound on it, but fall in large drops.) Season with pepper and nutmeg to taste and add salt, if necessary. Continue beating until heated through. Transfer to a warm serving bowl, or use a pastry bag with a large star tube to pipe swirls around any dish the potatoes are to garnish.

Light variation
☆Omit butter.

Notes
Reheat potatoes in a larger pan of boiling water.

For additional flavor, thinly sliced braised onions or diced carrots can be stirred into the prepared potatoes. For 2 lbs. potatoes, use ½ lb. onions or carrots. To cook onions, slice them and cook, covered, in 1½ tablespoons butter and 2 to 3 tablespoons water in a heavy pan over low heat until very soft. Uncover and cook until lightly browned. To cook carrots, see recipe on page 230, dicing carrots instead of slicing them.

FRENCH FRIED POTATOES
Pommes Frites

Serves: 6

2 lbs. baking potatoes (Idaho are best)
Oil for deep frying
Salt

Special equipment
Electric deep fryer

Heat oil to 320°.

Wash and peel the potatoes and drop them into cold water so they do not discolor. Cut lengthwise into ⅜-inch-thick slices. Cut each slice into ⅜-inch-thick sticks. Return to cold water and rinse. (This removes some of the starch so they do not stick together while frying.) Drain and dry well in a towel.

Put about 2 or 3 handfuls of potato sticks (do not crowd deep fryer) into fry basket and plunge them into the hot oil. Cook for 5 minutes and check for doneness. They should be soft inside. Drain and turn out onto a plate lined with paper towels. Cook remaining potatoes. Let cool for 10 minutes.

Just before serving, heat oil to 340°. Plunge the fries into the oil a second time, stirring occasionally. They will turn a beautiful, crisp, golden brown in 1 to 2 minutes. Drain on paper towels and transfer to a warm platter. Sprinkle with salt.

Notes

The preliminary frying can be done several hours or even 1 day in advance. Keep the potatoes covered in the refrigerator.

PARSLEYED POTATOES
Pommes de Terre Persillées

Serves: 6

> 2 lbs. small new potatoes, or 6 to 7 large ones, cut into thirds or quartered
> Salt
> Freshly ground black pepper
> 2½ tablespoons butter, at room temperature
> 1 tablespoon lemon juice
> 2 to 3 tablespoons minced parsley

Wash and peel potatoes and drop into cold water so they do not discolor. Put potatoes in a saucepan and add cold water to cover potatoes by ½ inch. Add 1¼ teaspoons salt per quart of water. Bring to a boil and boil slowly for 10 to 15 minutes, or until tender. (Test by piercing with a thin skewer so they do not break.)

Drain and return potatoes to saucepan. Put over moderate heat for 30 seconds to dry the potatoes, shaking the pan to prevent sticking. Remove from heat. Add salt and pepper to taste, ☆butter, lemon juice, and parsley, and swirl pan until potatoes are well coated.

Light variation
> ☆Use 3 tablespoons heavy cream in place of butter.

SAUTÉED POTATOES
Pommes de Terre Sautées

Serves: 6

> 12 small red- or white-skinned new potatoes (about 2 lbs.), not larger than 2 in. in diameter (If only larger potatoes are available, quarter or dice them.)
> 2 tablespoons oil
> Salt
> Freshly ground black pepper

Wash and peel potatoes and trim them into smooth rounds so they will cook evenly. Drop into cold water so they do not discolor. Drain and dry well in a towel.

Heat the oil in a skillet over moderate heat. Add potatoes and shake the skillet back and forth to make potatoes roll. Cook until a thin, hard pale crust forms all over. Cover the skillet loosely with foil or leave lid slightly ajar and cook over very low heat for 15 to 20 minutes, shaking pan every now and then to make sure potatoes do not stick and are cooking evenly. (Use a Flame-Tamer on a gas range.) Season with salt and pepper to taste.

Notes

The potatoes can wait, partially covered, for 30 minutes to 1 hour before serving. Reheat gently over medium-low heat.

Diced potatoes will take only 7 to 10 minutes to cook. A Flame-Tamer will not be necessary.

SAND POTATOES
Pommes de Terre Sablées

Serves: 6

- 2 lbs. boiling (waxy) potatoes (about 6 or 7 medium)
  Salt
- 2 tablespoons oil
- 6 tablespoons butter
- ¾ cup fine dry bread crumbs, preferably homemade
  Freshly ground black pepper

Preheat oven to 475°. Scrub potatoes. Put in large pot and add cold water to cover by ½ inch. Add 1¼ teaspoons salt per quart of water. Bring to a boil and boil slowly for 15 to 20 minutes, or until just tender. (Test with a thin skewer so potatoes do not break.) Drain, peel, and cut into ⅜-inch cubes.

✶Heat half the oil and half the butter in a skillet until hot but not brown. Add half the potatoes and cook, tossing with a spatula, until lightly colored. Transfer to a gratin dish and keep warm, loosely covered with foil, while cooking the remaining potatoes.

Sprinkle crumbs over potatoes and season with salt and pepper to taste. Toss to coat well with crumbs. Bake on middle rack of the oven for 15 minutes, or until heated through.

Put gratin dish under the broiler, 4 inches from flame, for 1 minute, or until nicely golden.

Light variation

☆Heat 2 tablespoons butter and 2 tablespoons oil in a skillet. Remove from heat and add all the potatoes. Toss to coat.

Notes

Potatoes can be made 1 day in advance up to the point of baking. Let cool, cover, and refrigerate.

POTATOES MONT-D'OR
Pommes de Terre Mont-d'Or

Serves: 6

    2 lbs. baking potatoes (about 6 to 7 medium)
    Salt
    1 cup milk
    4 tablespoons butter, at room temperature
    2 eggs, separated
    ⅛ teaspoon freshly grated nutmeg
    Freshly ground black pepper
    1 cup grated imported Swiss cheese

Wash, peel, and rinse potatoes. Cut them into thirds crosswise. Put in a large saucepan and add cold water to cover by ½ inch. Add 1¼ teaspoons salt per quart of water, cover, and bring to a boil. Boil slowly, covered, for 15 to 20 minutes, or until tender when pierced with a thin skewer. (The potatoes should not be overcooked and mushy or the purée will be watery.) Drain and return the potatoes to the saucepan. Put the pan over very low heat, uncovered, for 30 seconds to dry the potatoes, shaking the pan gently to prevent sticking.

Bring the milk to a boil in a small saucepan.

Force the potatoes through a food mill into a saucepan. ☆Beat in 3 tablespoons butter, the egg yolks, nutmeg, and salt and pepper to taste. Beat vigorously. Beat in enough hot milk to give the purée a thick, smooth texture. (The mixture should neither run easily from the spoon nor mound on it, but fall in large drops.) □Blend in the cheese.

Preheat the oven to 375°.

Beat the egg whites until stiff (see p. 271), and fold them into the potatoes. Spoon the potato mixture into a baking dish. Smooth the top and dot with the remaining ✧butter. Bake for 15 to 20 minutes. Then put under the broiler until golden brown.

Light variation

☆Omit the 3 tablespoons of butter when adding the egg yolks, nutmeg, and salt and pepper to taste.

□Use 1 cup grated Jarlsberg cheese in place of the Swiss cheese.

✧Do not use the remaining 1 tablespoon of butter to top the potato mixture before baking.

Notes

The potatoes can be prepared several hours in advance up to the point of being ready to bake. Cool, cover, and refrigerate if the kitchen is very warm.

POTATOES LYONNAISE-STYLE
Pommes de Terre Lyonnaise

Serves: 8

 3 lbs. boiling (waxy) potatoes (about 10 medium)
   Salt
 4 tablespoons butter
 1 lb. yellow onions, thinly sliced
 2 cloves garlic, crushed
 2 bay leaves
   Freshly ground black pepper
 4 tablespoons oil
 4 tablespoons finely chopped parsley

Scrub potatoes, put in a large pot, and add cold water to cover by ½ inch. Add 1¼ teaspoons salt per quart of water. Bring to a boil and boil slowly for 15 to 20 minutes, or until potatoes are tender. (Test with a thin skewer so the potatoes do not break.) Let cool briefly, peel, and cut into ¼-inch-thick slices.

Melt 2 tablespoons butter in a saucepan and add onions, garlic, bay leaves, and salt and pepper to taste. Cover and cook over medium-low heat for 6 to 7 minutes, stirring occasionally, or until wilted. Uncover and cook over moderate heat for 3 to 4 minutes, or until onions start to color lightly.

☆Heat 1 tablespoon butter and 2 tablespoons oil in a large skillet until very hot but not brown. Put half the potato slices flat in the skillet in one layer, season with salt and pepper, and brown lightly on both sides. Remove and cook the second batch of potatoes, using the remaining butter and oil.

Combine the potatoes, onions, and 2 tablespoons of parsley. Transfer to a warm serving dish and sprinkle with the remaining parsley.

Light variation

☆Instead of browning the potatoes in butter and oil, combine the potatoes and onions and put them into a gratin dish. Bake in a 425° oven for 10 minutes. Gently mix in 4 tablespoons heavy cream and 2 tablespoons parsley. Sprinkle with remaining parsley.

Notes

Cooked potatoes do not keep well, as they get sour. Do not keep them for more than 1 day refrigerated. If it is necessary to reheat them, put them into a gratin dish and bake, uncovered, in a 350° oven.

BUTTERED NOODLES OR SPAGHETTI
Nouilles ou Spaghetti au Beurre

Serves: 4 as a side dish

    4 qts. water
    5 teaspoons salt
    ½ lb. thin or broad noodles or spaghetti
    3 tablespoons butter at room temperature
    Freshly ground black pepper

Bring water to a boil in a kettle. Add salt and noodles. Cover, return to a boil, and boil uncovered for 8 to 10 minutes, or until tender. The noodles should be *al dente* (with a slight resistance to the bite).

Drain noodles immediately and return to the kettle. ✮Add butter and salt and pepper to taste and toss well.

Light variation

✮In place of butter, use ½ cup ricotta, blended in food processor until smooth, and ½ cup concentrated chicken stock or skim milk. After draining the noodles and returning them to the kettle, add processed ricotta and stock and salt and pepper to taste. Toss to coat well and heat. Add more stock if too dry. Do not overheat or ricotta mixture will curdle.

NOODLES OR SPAGHETTI WITH MUSHROOMS
Nouilles ou Spaghetti aux Champignons

Serves: 6

    6 qts. water
    Salt
    1 lb. noodles or spaghetti
    3½ tablespoons butter
    1½ lbs. fresh mushrooms, sliced thick
    2 or 3 cloves garlic, finely chopped
    Freshly ground black pepper
    1½ to 1¾ cups heavy cream
    3 tablespoons finely chopped parsley

Bring 6 qts. water to a boil, add 2½ tablespoons salt, and cook pasta until *al dente* according to package directions.

(continued)

☆Heat butter in skillet until hot but not brown. Add mushrooms and sauté over medium-high heat, tossing and shaking pan and stirring for 6 to 8 minutes, or until lightly brown. Add garlic during the last minute of cooking. Season lightly with salt and pepper. ☐Add cream and cook over moderate heat, stirring, for 2 minutes, or until cream starts to thicken lightly. Remove from heat and stir in parsley.

Drain pasta. Divide among 4 heated soup plates and top with sauce.

Light variation

☆Omit butter when cooking mushrooms. Put mushrooms, garlic, salt and pepper to taste, and ½ cup water in a saucepan. Cook over moderate heat, stirring occasionally, until mushrooms render their juice. Drain and reserve juice.

☐In place of cream, use 1 cup ricotta, blended in food processor with 1 cup milk (or skim milk), and 2 tablespoons heavy cream. Add ricotta, milk, and cream to the pan with the mushrooms. Season with salt and pepper. Bring gently to a boil, stirring. Remove from the heat immediately. Drain the pasta, put it back in its pot, and toss with sauce. Add just enough of the reserved mushroom juice to bind them smoothly. Heat gently. (You'll usually need all of the reserved mushroom juice if you are using good-quality pasta.) Stir in parsley.

Notes

The pasta should be topped with the sauce, tossed, and eaten as soon as it has been drained, so have the sauce ready. The sauce can be prepared during the time it takes to bring the water to a boil and cook the pasta.

If the pasta is made from durum wheat or semolina, which is more starchy than other flour, it absorbs more liquid. The light sauce should be thinned with more milk, if necessary.

A delicious variation is to sauté 1½ lbs. asparagus, which have been cooked until tender and cut into 1-inch pieces (see p. 224), in the butter for 1 to 2 minutes, add cream, and cook until sauce starts to thicken lightly. To prepare the light sauce, blend ricotta with 1⅓ cups concentrated chicken stock (see pp. 19–20) or milk and prepare as with mushrooms.

8
VEGETABLES

Fresh vegetables are crammed with valuable nutritional substances, in particular mineral salts and vitamins. They are virtually free of fat and easy to digest. And cooking them is a simple affair, quickly done. These features all commend them to busy home cooks seeking to promote their own and their families' health and well-being. But two additional attributes of vegetables assure them the favor of cooks and diners alike: their appealing colors and shapes and, above all, their delicate flavors and inviting textures.

Vegetables, traditionally relegated to subordinate roles in cuisine, are today being treated by home cooks with new respect.

By now everyone who cares about food is surely aware that vegetables must not be overcooked.* The object is no longer to reduce a vegetable to sodden submission but instead to bring it to a state at which it is both tender and crisp, the test for crispness being that the tines of a fork go into it but meet a certain resistance. Vegetables taste best, look best, and retain a maximum of their nutritive values when cooked just this long.

But how long is "just long enough"? Leaving aside differences in the times required for cooking vegetables of various types, depending on their firmness and thickness, we differ with some

---

* It was American chefs, impressed by Chinese ways with vegetables, who brought this message to France. A few French chefs listened, tried fast-cooking and liked the results; the word spread, and now home cooks throughout France are happily atoning, with never a backward glance, for the sins of their mothers in this regard.

home cooks on this point. In our view these people overdo a good idea by underdoing their vegetables, serving them up almost raw and imbued with their sometimes harsh natural taste. Raw or near-raw vegetables have their place, but that place is not, we feel, in the harmonious blend of compatible and complementary flavors making up a fine meal.

Other home cooks steam vegetables instead of boiling them. *Chacun à son goût.* While steaming does keep more of a vegetable's nutrients from escaping it tends to steal away some of its color and flavor. On balance, we feel that with most vegetables boiling—for a very limited time, clearly specified in our recipes—brings out the best they have to offer in terms of taste, texture, and appearance.

BOILING AND PARBOILING

As with pasta, you need plenty of water to boil vegetables—at least a gallon (with 5 teaspoons salt) for each pound of vegetables—so that when you drop in the vegetables the water will return almost at once to a rapid boil. Letting vegetables steep for minutes until the water comes to a second boil leaches out taste, color, and vitamins. Incidentally, boiling does more than take the edge off the naturally rough taste of vegetables and make them more digestible, it also extracts water from them when they are to be combined with other foods as in a quiche or a vegetable pie.

In parboiling, also called blanching, vegetables are boiled briefly and only part-way through. Onions and cabbage, for example, are usually parboiled before braising to neutralize their strong flavors.

After being boiled, vegetables must instantly be refreshened to halt the cooking process and preserve their color. But how? Dropping them in ice cold water, as some authorities suggest, gives us the shivers, as we're convinced that doing so washes out retained nutrients. Instead, we plop boiled vegetables in a colander and sprinkle them with cold water by holding a finger over the tap. This keeps the inevitable loss of minerals and vitamins to a minimum.

BRAISING

Braising is done with vegetables that require more time than most to cook and that are usually cooked whole, such as onions, leeks, celery, endive, and cabbage. Often, they are first browned lightly in butter. They should fit snugly into the pot—ideally, a heavy enameled cast-iron one—for with too much liquid swirling around them they can become "washed out." The pot is filled with stock or water to the depth of one third of the vegetables' height, its lid clamped on and the whole put in the oven; there, the liquid boils gently, suffusing the vegetables with heat and steam. They should be turned occasionally so that they cook evenly and so that exposed surfaces don't dry out.

Braised vegetables, which incidentally lose very little of their nutritive values in the process, have a delicious concentrated taste. More *fondant*—softer—than boiled vegetables, they take readily to reheating.

ÉTUVER OR À L'ÉTOUFFÉE:
A KIND OF QUICK-BRAISING

This method is employed mostly with young vegetables, in particular young carrots, peas, and pearl onions. Only a few tablespoons of liquid are added to them, just enough to provide a little steam that will force them to release their own water. Again the cooking vessel should be a covered heavy pot to lessen the chance of scorching; the vegetables cook over moderately low heat and ultimately reabsorb their own juices, retaining two to three tablespoons of liquid. It's a meticulous kind of cooking, requiring the cook to keep a close watch on things lest the delicate young plants scorch. This method conserves nearly all the vitamins and imparts an exquisite aroma and flavor. Once done, they, too, are easy to reheat.

RAW VEGETABLES

Raw vegetables are a prime source of vitamins and minerals. Shredding and thin-slicing them improves their flavor, and macerating them in lemon and oil for anything from half an hour to an hour makes them more tender, hence easier to eat.

We recommend that you buy all of your vegetables fresh or not at all. However, once you get them home there are certain things that are often overlooked in the washing and storage of vegetables.

ON WASHING VEGETABLES

Your object is to get rid of insecticide sprays, parasites, and dirt adhering to vegetables while removing as little as possible of the nutrients. With lettuce, we recommend that you discard the outer leaves and with other leafy vegetables all blemished ones. Then plunge the greens into a large tub or pan of water to which you have added distilled vinegar or salt at a proportion of approximately one to two tablespoons per quart. The first washing should take no more than ten or fifteen seconds, after which you again wash the vegetables to rinse them. Retrieving them from the water, you spin dry them and pack them in a plastic bag lined with a paper towel to soak up the last moisture. Don't close the bag tightly but let some air circulate in it. Finally, put the bag in the refrigerator. This procedure works well for spinach, string beans, Brussels sprouts, broccoli, cauliflower, mushrooms, and salad greens.

For other vegetables—including leeks, artichokes, endive, corn, asparagus, cucumbers, tomatoes, onions, potatoes, turnips, carrots, and celery stalks—you should rub them clean under cold running water, then dry and peel those with skins. (You will, to be sure, lose vitamins this way, but then which would you rather eat, vitamins together with the wax and/or spray that usually coats the skins of vegetables or fewer vitamins and no wax or spray?) Trim and pare as suggested in the pertinent recipe and store as above.

GARLIC

Deep fry unpeeled garlic cloves for 2 minutes, and peel them. Scatter them whole, chopped, or puréed on vegetables or meat. They are divine!

BOILED ARTICHOKES
Artichauts Bouillis

Serves: 6

6 whole artichokes
1 lemon, halved
6 qts. water
2½ tablespoons salt
2 tablespoons finely minced parsley
   Hollandaise Sauce (see p. 43), Lemony Hollandaise (see p. 42), or Isabelle's Vinaigrette (see p. 46)

Wash the artichokes and cut or break off the stems as close as possible to the base. Rub the cut surfaces with the lemon to prevent discoloration.

Break off the bottom round of little leaves at the base of each artichoke. Use scissors to cut off the pointed top of the leaves in the bottom rows. Leave the top closed and untrimmed as the artichokes cook faster this way.

Bring the water to a boil in a large kettle and add the salt. Plunge the artichokes into the boiling salted water, stems down, cover, and bring rapidly back to a boil. Partially cover and boil rapidly for 25 to 35 minutes, depending on the size of the artichokes, or until a leaf pulls loose easily. A thin skewer or paring knife should pierce the middle of the base easily.

Remove the artichokes with a slotted spoon and drain them upside down in a colander.

Gently spread apart the top leaves. Reach down into the center of the artichoke and firmly grasp the small center leaves between your thumb and first two fingers (a pastry pinch does a fantastic job). The leaves will all come loose at once (they look like a small funnel), exposing the furry choke underneath. Scrape out the choke with a spoon.

Put the artichokes on individual plates or on a serving platter and replace center leaves upside down with the narrow points inside. Garnish the center of each artichoke with chopped parsley.

Serve warm with Hollandaise Sauce or Lemony Hollandaise Sauce, or cold with Isabelle's Vinaigrette.

(continued)

Notes

The artichoke heart often has thick fibers extending through it from the stem. To remove these, bend and twist the stem all around in a circle without actually breaking it. This breaks the fibers. Bend the stem to break it off and the fibers can then be pulled out easily. Trim the base so the artichoke stands straight.

To store, cool, cover, and refrigerate. The artichokes will keep for 1 to 2 days. If serving cold, remove from the refrigerator at least 1 hour before serving. If serving warm, cook, set aside without removing the choke, and boil for 2 to 5 minutes to reheat.

Do not discard the stems. They are good to eat. Peel off the tough outer skin and boil with the artichokes until tender.

PLAIN ARTICHOKE HEARTS
Coeurs d'Artichauts Bouillis

Serves: 6

> 1½ qts. cold water
> 6 tablespoons lemon juice or vinegar
> 6 artichokes
> 1 lemon, halved
> 1 tablespoon flour per quart water
> 1¼ teaspoon salt per quart water
>   Enough water to cover artichoke hearts

Put the cold water into a mixing bowl and add 3 tablespoons lemon juice or vinegar.

Cut off the artichoke stems as close as possible to the base. Rub the cut surface with a lemon half to prevent discoloration. Break off the bottom-most leaves of the artichokes, until some white begins to show at the bottom. Squeeze the artichoke; the narrower top portion will give to pressure, while the bottom remains firm. Cut off the narrow top at the point it begins to give, usually about one quarter to one third of the way up from the base. Pull away any violet-colored leaves left in the center and expose the choke, but do not remove the choke.

Peel the bottoms of the artichokes as you would an apple, cutting around the circumference and base with a knife or a vegetable peeler to remove all the green surface. Drop the trimmed bottoms into the bowl of acidulated water as each is finished.

Put the prepared artichokes in a large saucepan. Cover them with cold water. Remove the artichokes and set them aside. Measure the water and set it aside. Put 1 tablespoon of flour for each quart of reserved water into a saucepan and gradually whisk in about ⅓ cup of reserved water until the flour is completely dissolved. Add the remaining water and lemon juice and bring to a boil, stirring occasionally. Add the reserved artichokes and 1¼ teaspoons of salt for each quart of water. Cover, bring to a boil, and simmer for 25 to 30 minutes, or until the artichokes are tender when pierced with a thin skewer. Remove artichokes with a slotted spoon and refresh under cold running water. (Do not let the water run too hard.)

Drain the artichokes cut side down in a colander. Scrape out the chokes with a teaspoon and pat the artichokes dry with paper towels.

Notes

The cooked artichokes will keep for 1 day in the refrigerator. Let cool and cover.

This method of cooking (adding flour to the artichoke cooking water) is called *à blanc*. Its purpose is to keep the artichokes as white as possible; it also makes them mellower.

Artichoke hearts may be served warm with Hollandaise Sauce (see pp. 42–43) or Béarnaise Sauce (see p. 45). They may also be served cold with Isabelle's Vinaigrette (see p. 46) or Uncooked Tomato Sauce (see p. 48), or stuffed with a salad, such as the Vegetable Salad with Rice (see p. 206), or Poached Shrimp (p. 112) tossed with Isabelle's Vinaigrette.

BOILED ASPARAGUS
Asperges en Branche

Serves: 6

2 lbs. large asparagus of uniform size, about
   2 to 2½ inches around
About 2 qts. water
Salt

Wash the asparagus and cut off about 1 inch of the woody part of the bottom of each stalk. Peel the stems beginning 3 to 4 inches down from the tip. Peel off a second layer 6 inches down from the tip. This makes the asparagus more evenly tender.

Bring the water to a boil in a skillet with deep sides and add the salt. Lay the asparagus in the skillet, cover, and return to a boil. Uncover and boil for 5 to 7 minutes. Do not overcook. The asparagus should remain firm. A longer cooking time makes them taste bitter.

Carefully lift the asparagus out of the water using a slotted spatula. Put them on a folded towel to drain, then transfer them to a platter.

If serving the asparagus hot, cook them just before serving. If serving them cold, let them cool on the towel and serve at room temperature.

Notes

Serve the asparagus hot with Hollandaise Sauce (see pp. 42–43) or Lemon Butter Sauce (see p. 52), or cut into 1½-inch pieces and toss with 1½ tablespoons melted butter and a minced shallot. Sprinkle with 1 tablespoon minced parsley. (This is known as Asperges Poulette.)

Serve cold with Isabelle's Vinaigrette (see p. 46) or Mayonnaise (see pp. 39–42).

BUTTERED GREEN BEANS
Haricots Verts au Beurre

Serves: 6–8

2½ lbs. green beans
5 qts. water
Salt
2 tablespoons butter
2 shallots, finely minced, or 3 garlic cloves, finely minced
¼ cup heavy cream
Freshly ground black pepper
2 tablespoons finely minced parsley.

Snap, string, and wash the beans.

Bring water to a boil in a large kettle. When boiling, stir in 2 tablespoons salt. Plunge the prepared beans into the boiling salted water. Cover and bring back to a boil as fast as possible. Uncover and boil for 5 to 6 minutes. Do not overcook. The beans should still be quite crisp and green. Drain immediately and sprinkle cold running water over them to stop the cooking and to help retain the bright green color. Drain again.

Heat the butter in a large skillet. Add the shallots and cook for 1 minute, stirring occasionally. Add the beans, cream, and salt and pepper to taste. Cook over moderate heat for 3 to 4 minutes, shaking the pan so the beans and shallots are well mixed and coated. Sprinkle with parsley.

Notes

Sauté just before serving. The beans may be blanched several hours in advance. They can be cooled, covered, and refrigerated. They will keep for 1 or 2 days in the refrigerator.

WHITE BEANS WITH TOMATOES
Haricots aux Tomates

Serves: 6 to 8

Cooking the beans

    1 lb. dried white beans, such as Great Northern

    12 cups water

    1 medium onion, halved crosswise, each half stuck with 2 cloves

    2 medium carrots, coarsely sliced

    1 clove garlic, crushed

    ⅛ teaspoon dried thyme

    1 bay leaf

    1 stalk celery, coarsely sliced

    Salt

    Freshly ground black pepper

Sauce for the beans

    2 tablespoons butter or oil

    4 medium onions, thinly sliced

    1½ lbs. ripe but firm tomatoes, peeled, seeded, and roughly chopped, or 2¼ cups drained canned Italian plum tomatoes, roughly chopped

    1 clove garlic, minced

    1 bay leaf

    ⅛ teaspoon dried thyme

    Salt

    Freshly ground black pepper

    1 tablespoon finely chopped parsley

Sort beans carefully, removing all foreign matter. Rinse the beans carefully under cold running water and soak them overnight in 6 cups cold water. (Or use the quick method: Drop the rinsed beans into boiling water, bring back to a boil, and boil gently, uncovered, for 3 minutes. Cover and soak for 1 hour. Drain and rinse.)

    Drain the beans and put them in a large heavy pot. Add 6 cups water, the onion halves, carrots, garlic, thyme, bay leaf, celery, and salt and pepper to taste. Cover and bring to a boil over moderate heat. Simmer, covered, for 1½ to 1¾ hours, or until tender.

Prepare the sauce for the beans: ☆Melt the butter in a saucepan. Add the onions, cover, and cook slowly, stirring occasionally, for 5 to 6 minutes, or until the onions are tender but not browned. Add tomatoes, garlic, bay leaf, thyme, and salt and pepper to taste. Stir to mix well, cover, and cook over moderate heat for 3 minutes, or until tomatoes have released their juice. Uncover and cook over moderate heat, stirring, for 20 minutes, or until juice has evaporated.

Drain the beans and combine with the tomato mixture in the pot in which the beans were cooked. Heat slowly. Season with salt and pepper, if necessary. Serve in a warm serving dish. Sprinkle with parsley.

Light variation

☆Use only 1½ tablespoons butter to cook the onions for the sauce. Melt the butter in a saucepan. Add the onions and ⅓ cup water, cover, and cook slowly, stirring occasionally, for 5 to 6 minutes, or until the onions are tender but not browned.

Notes

The beans are an excellent, nutritious main dish. They can also be served as an accompaniment with lamb, pork, chicken, veal, or beef.

This dish will keep, covered, for 1 to 6 days in the refrigerator. Let cool uncovered before refrigerating. Reheat slowly on top of the stove, adding 2 to 3 tablespoons water to compensate for evaporation.

Leftover beans keep very well in the freezer.

BROCCOLI OR CAULIFLOWER SOUFFLÉ
Soufflé de Brocoli ou Chou-fleur

Serves: 6

- 1½ tablespoons butter
- 4 qts. water
  Salt
- 1 bunch broccoli, stems peeled and broken into flowerets, or
  1 medium cauliflower, broken into flowerets
- 4 egg yolks
  Freshly ground black pepper
  Freshly grated nutmeg
- 5 egg whites
  Lemon juice
- ½ cup grated imported Swiss or Parmesan cheese, or
  a combination of both

Special equipment
  6-cup soufflé dish

Preheat oven to 450°. Spread butter evenly over the inside of the soufflé dish.

Bring the water to a boil in a large kettle. When boiling, stir in 1½ tablespoons salt. Plunge the broccoli into the boiling water, cover, and bring back to a boil. Uncover and boil for 3 to 5 minutes (boil cauliflower for 5 to 7 minutes). Drain.

Purée by forcing through a food mill or blending in a food processor until smooth. Put purée into a saucepan and cook over moderate heat, stirring with a wooden spatula, for 1 to 2 minutes to dry and evaporate any excess moisture. Remove from heat. Beat in the egg yolks one at a time and season with salt, pepper, and nutmeg to taste.

Beat the egg whites with a pinch of salt and a few drops of lemon juice until smooth, shiny, and stiff (see p. 271). Spoon them over the vegetable mixture and fold in rapidly with a whisk, while sprinkling in the ☆grated cheese. Pour into the prepared dish (the dish should be no more than two thirds full).

Put in the oven, lower the oven temperature to 400°, and bake for 20 to 22 minutes, or until puffed and golden. Serve immediately, using 2 spoons to lift out portions gently.

Light variation

☆Use ½ cup grated Jarlsberg cheese instead of the imported Swiss or Parmesan.

Notes

The unbaked soufflé can wait for 1 hour before baking. There is no need to refrigerate it if the kitchen is not too hot.

BROCCOLI PURÉE
Purée de Brocoli

Serves: 4

1½ lbs. broccoli
4 qts. water
   Salt
3 tablespoons heavy cream
   Freshly ground black pepper
⅛ teaspoon freshly grated nutmeg
   Parsley sprigs

Cut off 1½ inches of the tough end of each stalk of broccoli. Halve or quarter the stalks lengthwise, depending on their thickness. Peel the stem of each piece down to the pale green inner flesh. Wash thoroughly.

Bring the water to boil in a large pot. When boiling add 5 teaspoons of salt. Plunge the broccoli into the boiling water. Cover and bring back to a boil. Uncover and boil for 3 minutes. Drain.

Purée the broccoli by forcing it through a food mill or blend it in a food processor until smooth. Return the purée to the pot, add the ☆cream, and season with nutmeg and salt and pepper to taste.

Bring the purée slowly to a simmer over moderate heat, stirring with a wooden spatula. Simmer for 2 minutes. Remove from the heat. If the purée seems too dry, add a little more cream. Mound the purée in a warm bowl and garnish with parsley.

(continued)

Light variation
    ☆In place of the cream, use milk or half-and-half.

Notes
    The purée may be made up to the addition of the cream a few hours or as much as 1 day in advance. Let the purée cool to room temperature, transfer to a bowl, cover, and refrigerate if holding more than an hour or so.

    A purée can be made with many vegetables, although some are better than others because they purée and bind better. Carrots, celery root, broccoli, cauliflower, and spinach make the best purées. Leeks and asparagus are stringy and should be bound with potato to obtain the proper consistency.

BRAISED CARROTS
Carottes Étuvées

Serves: 6

    2 tablespoons butter
    2 teaspoons minced shallots or scallions
    2 lbs. carrots, cut into ¼-inch-thick slices or julienne strips
    Salt
    Freshly ground black pepper
    1 bay leaf
    ¼ teaspoon dried thyme
    ¼ teaspoon sugar
    ½ cup water
    1 tablespoon minced parsley

Melt the butter in a heavy pan and add the shallots. Sauté for 2 minutes over moderate heat. Add the carrots, salt and pepper to taste, bay leaf, thyme, sugar, and water and stir. Cover and cook over moderately low heat, stirring occasionally, for 5 to 7 minutes, or until the carrots are just tender but still crunchy. (The water should have evaporated but the carrots should still be moist. If the carrots are not cooked by the time the water has evaporated, add 2 tablespoons of water to finish the cooking.) Sprinkle with parsley.

Notes

Carrots cooked this way will keep for 1 to 2 days in a covered container in the refrigerator. Reheat slowly on top of the stove, stirring several times. Add a little water if the carrots are too dry.

CARROT PURÉE
Purée de Carottes

Serves: 4

  1½ lbs. carrots
   3 qts. water
     Salt
   3 tablespoons heavy cream
     Freshly ground black pepper
   5 parsley sprigs

Peel the carrots and cut each into 3 pieces.

Bring the water to a boil and add 4 teaspoons salt. Add carrots, cover, and bring back to a boil. Uncover and boil for 7 to 10 minutes, or until tender. Drain.

Purée the carrots by forcing them through a food mill or blending them in a food processor until smooth. Return purée to pot and add ☆cream, and season with salt and pepper to taste.

Bring purée slowly to a simmer over moderate heat, stirring with a wooden spoon. Simmer for 2 minutes. If purée seems too dry, add a little more cream.

Mound the purée in a warm bowl and garnish with the parsley sprigs.

Light variation

☆In place of the cream, use milk or half-and-half.

Notes

The carrots are cut in 3 pieces because the more surface area exposed to the water the more water they absorb and the more watery the purée.

CARROT SOUFFLÉ
Soufflé aux Carottes

Serves: 6

>   1 lb. carrots, sliced
> 1½ tablespoons butter
>   Salt
>   2 tablespoons flour
>   ½ cup heavy cream
>   3 egg yolks
>   5 egg whites
>   ½ teaspoon lemon juice or vinegar
>   Freshly ground black pepper

Special equipment
   6-cup soufflé dish or gratin dish

Preheat oven to 450°. Spread ½ tablespoon butter evenly over the inside of the soufflé dish.

Put carrots in a saucepan with the remaining butter and sprinkle lightly with salt. Add water to cover by half. Cover, bring to a boil, and cook over moderate heat for 6 to 10 minutes, or until carrots are tender but not mushy. Uncover and let excess water evaporate. Purée in a food mill or food processor and transfer purée to a saucepan.

Whisk flour and ⋆2 to 3 tablespoons of cream together in a small bowl until smooth. Then whisk in remaining cream. Add to the carrot purée and cook, stirring, over moderate heat for 2 to 3 minutes, or until thick and creamy. Remove from heat and season with salt and pepper, if necessary.

□Beat in egg yolks one at a time with a wooden spoon. Cover and set aside.

In a large bowl beat egg whites with a pinch of salt and the lemon juice until smooth and shiny but stiff (see p. 271). Immediately turn carrot purée into egg whites and stir gently 3 times with a whisk, folding until well mixed. Do not overfold.

Pour into prepared dish and smooth the top. Make a shallow indentation around the edge of the soufflé with the handle of a spoon. (This will prevent the soufflé from toppling over.) Make a crosshatch on the top of the soufflé so that it will not crack while cooking.

Put in oven, lower oven temperature to 400°, and bake for 20 to 22 minutes, or until puffed and golden. Serve immediately, using 2 spoons to lift out portions gently.

Light variation

☆In place of cream use ½ cup ricotta, blended in a food processor with 2 tablespoons flour. Transfer carrot purée to a saucepan and stir in processed ricotta. Bring to a simmer over medium-low heat, stirring. Remove from heat and season with salt and pepper, if necessary.

▫Use only 2 egg yolks to thicken the purée.

Notes

The unbaked soufflé can wait for 1 hour before baking. There is no need to refrigerate it if the kitchen is not too hot.

BRAISED CELERY
Céleris Braisés

Serves: 4

    2 whole celery hearts
    3 tablespoons butter
    1 small onion, thinly sliced
    1 cup chicken stock (see pp. 19–20) or water
    1 bay leaf
    ¼ teaspoon dried thyme
      Salt
      Freshly ground black pepper

Break off 2 or 3 outer green stringy stalks from the celery hearts (keep them for soup). Trim the stem ends of the hearts.

☆Melt the butter in a pressure cooker and add the onion. Cover (do not secure the lid of the pressure cooker) and steam over moderate heat for 4 to 5 minutes, or until the onion is softened. Add the celery hearts, stock, bay leaf, thyme, and salt and pepper to taste. Secure the lid of the pressure cooker and cook for 15 to 20 minutes.

(continued)

Light variation

☆Use only 1½ tablespoons butter and 2 tablespoons of water to steam the onions.

Notes

The celery can be prepared 1 day in advance. Reheat in its juice, adding a little water or stock, if necessary.

GRATINÉED CELERY ROOT MOUSSELINE
Mousse de Céleri-Rave au Gratin

Serves: 4

    1½ tablespoons butter
    1 qt. water mixed with 2 tablespoons vinegar
    2 lbs. celery root
    3 qts. water
      Salt
    ½ cup milk
    1 egg yolk
      Freshly ground black pepper
      Freshly grated nutmeg
    2 egg whites
      Lemon juice
    ¼ cup freshly grated Parmesan cheese

Preheat oven to 425° Spread 1 tablespoon butter evenly over the inside of a 6-cup gratin dish.

Put the water and vinegar into a large bowl. Wash the celery root, quarter, and peel deeply. Drop immediately into the acidulated water to prevent discoloration.

Bring three quarts of water to a boil in a kettle and add 1 tablespoon salt.

Cut the celery root into 1-inch cubes, rinse, and drop into the boiling salted water. Cover and bring back to a boil. Uncover and boil slowly for 15 to 20 minutes, or until tender. Drain. (The cooking liquid can be used in a soup, if desired.)

Transfer the drained celery root to a food processor. Add the milk and blend until smooth. (Do this in 2 or 3 batches, if necessary.) The purée should remain firm. Add the egg yolk and blend. Transfer the purée to a mixing bowl and season with salt, pepper, and nutmeg to taste.

Beat the egg whites with a pinch of salt and a few drops of lemon juice until they hold straight shiny peaks when the beater is lifted (see p. 271). Fold immediately into the purée with a whisk. Scoop the mixture into the prepared gratin dish and smooth the surface with the back of a spoon. Sprinkle with cheese and dot with remaining butter. Put in oven, lower temperature to 400°, and bake on the middle rack for 15 to 20 minutes, or until puffed and golden.

Notes

Unbaked mousseline can be prepared several hours in advance and reserved loosely covered with foil.

BRAISED CHESTNUTS
Marrons Braisés

Serves: 6

  4½ lbs. chestnuts
   3 tablespoons butter
   1 tablespoon light brown sugar
   2 stalks celery, finely chopped
     Salt
     Freshly ground black pepper
   1 cup red or white wine
   ½ cup concentrated quick chicken stock (see p. 20)

Preheat oven to 475°.

Make a shallow gash in the shell on the flat side of each chestnut. Put the chestnuts in one layer in roasting pans or cookie sheets. Add about ½ cup water to each pan and bake for 8 minutes. Remove and lower oven temperature to 375°. While chestnuts are still warm, remove shell and inner skin with a paring knife.

(continued)

Melt butter in a skillet large enough to hold the chestnuts in one layer. Add chestnuts and cook over moderate heat, stirring and tossing, until chestnuts are completely coated with butter. Sprinkle sugar over them evenly and cook, stirring, for 3 minutes, or until they are golden. Add celery and cook for 2 minutes. Season with salt and pepper to taste. Add ½ cup wine and reduce by half over medium-high heat. Add remaining wine and reduce by half. Add stock, cover, and bring to a boil on top of the stove. Put in the oven and bake for 15 to 20 minutes, or until tender.

CREAMED CUCUMBERS
Concombres à la Crème

Serves: 6

    3 cucumbers, each about 8 inches long
    3 qts. water
    Salt
    ⅔ cup heavy cream
    2 shallots, minced
    15 mint leaves, minced
    Freshly ground black pepper

Wash the cucumbers, dry, and peel them thinly. Halve them lengthwise and scrape out the seeds with a teaspoon. Cut each half into thirds crosswise and cut each third into 4 or 5 pieces lengthwise to obtain matchsticks about ⅜ inch thick.

Bring the water to a boil in a kettle and add 4 teaspoons salt. Drop the cucumber matchsticks into the boiling salted water, cover, and bring back to a boil. Uncover and boil for 2 minutes. Drain and refresh under cold running water and drain again.

Put 2 tablespoons of the cream into a heavy saucepan. Add the shallots and half of the minced mint. Cover and steam over low heat for 2 minutes, stirring occasionally.

☆Add the remaining cream and the cucumbers and boil over moderate heat until smooth and creamy. Stir in remaining mint and salt and pepper to taste.

Light variation

☆In place of remaining cream, use ½ cup ricotta, blended in a food processor with 5 tablespoons milk. Add to the sauce with the cucumbers, salt and pepper to taste, and remaining mint. Heat slowly just to a boil, stirring constantly.

Notes

The cucumbers can be blanched 1 day in advance. Finish the dish just before serving.

Zucchini can be prepared in the same way. Tarragon is a delicious substitute for the mint. Steam using ½ teaspoon dried or 1 teaspoon fresh. At the end add ¼ teaspoon ground dried tarragon or 1 teaspoon fresh tarragon.

COLD CREAMED CHOPPED CUCUMBER
Concombres Froids Hachés à la Crème

Serves: 4

   2 cucumbers, each about 8 inches long
     Juice of 1 lemon
½ cup heavy cream
   1 tablespoon finely chopped parsley
   1 tablespoon finely chopped chives
   2 mint leaves, finely chopped
     Salt
     Freshly ground black pepper

Wash cucumbers and peel them. Halve lengthwise and scrape the seeds out with a spoon.

Cut the halves crosswise into chunks the size of a food processor feeding tube. Lay them flat in the tube and process through the thick shredder disk. Divide among 4 individual plates.

Combine the lemon juice, ☆cream, parsley, chives, mint, and salt and pepper to taste. Mask each portion of cucumbers with the sauce.

(continued)

Light variation

☆In place of the cream use ⅓ cup ricotta, blended in a food processor, and 2 tablespoons yogurt or skim milk. Combine the lemon juice, processed ricotta, yogurt, parsley, chives, mint, and salt and pepper to taste. Thin out sauce with more milk if necessary. Mask each portion of cucumbers with the sauce.

Notes

The salad can be prepared up to 2 hours in advance. Serve chilled.

EGGPLANT TART WITH VEGETABLES
AND FRESH CHEESE
Galette d'Aubergines aux Légumes et Fromage Frais

Serves: 8

> 1½ tablespoons butter, softened
> 4 eggplants, about 2½ lbs.
> 4 qts. water
> Salt
> 5 leeks (white and pale green parts only), about 2½ lbs. untrimmed
> 3 to 4 tablespoons oil
> 2 medium onions, finely chopped
> 6 or 7 tomatoes, about 2½ lbs., peeled, seeded, and roughly chopped
> 3 tablespoons finely minced parsley
> 2 cloves garlic, finely chopped
> ¼ teaspoon ground thyme
> ¼ teaspoon ground rosemary
> 1 bay leaf
> Freshly ground black pepper
> 1 15-oz. container ricotta, blended in food processor

Special equipment

9-inch round cake pan, 1½ inches deep

Preheat oven to 500°.

Butter pan generously, line bottom with parchment paper, and butter paper.

Wash eggplants and cut crosswise into ¼-inch-thick slices. Put slices in a large bowl and toss with 1 tablespoon salt. Cover and let stand for 30 minutes, so they can exude their moisture.

Bring 4 quarts of water to a boil in a kettle. Add 1½ tablespoons of salt and plunge the leeks into the boiling water. Cover, bring back to a boil, and cook for 10 minutes, or until the leeks are tender-crisp. Drain and refresh the leeks under cold running water. Dry in a towel. Cut the leeks crosswise into 1½-inch chunks and halve each chunk lengthwise.

✭Heat 2 tablespoons oil in a pan and add the onions. Cook over moderate heat, stirring, for 5 to 7 minutes, or until soft. Add the tomatoes, 2 tablespoons parsley, garlic, thyme, rosemary, bay leaf, and salt and pepper to taste and cook, covered, for 5 minutes, or until the tomatoes have released some juice. Uncover and cook, stirring occasionally, for 10 to 15 minutes, or until the juices have evaporated and the mixture is thick. Remove bay leaf and set vegetable mixture aside.

Put the eggplants in a colander and rinse under cold running water. Drain and dry on a towel.

Oil 2 baking sheets and arrange eggplant slices in one layer on the sheets. Brush the tops of the eggplant slices with oil and bake for 3 to 5 minutes, or until golden underneath. Turn, brush with oil, and bake for 3 to 5 minutes, or until golden on other side.

Arrange a circle of eggplant slices around the bottom of the prepared pan, overlapping the slices slightly. Cut some of the slices in half and line the sides of the pan. Do not overlap these slices.

Fill the empty space in the center of the pan with pieces of leek. Mask the eggplant and leeks with a layer of tomato sauce. Add a layer of ricotta over the tomato sauce, and sprinkle with salt and pepper. Continue to alternate layers of vegetables, sauce, and cheese, finishing with a layer of vegetables. (Do not go over the top of the eggplant slices lining the pan, or the cheese and sauce will leak in.)

Lower oven temperature to 400° and bake tart for 40 to 50 minutes, or until a thin skewer inserted in the center comes out clean. Let stand for 5 to 7 minutes, unmold onto a warm platter, peel paper off, and sprinkle with remaining parsley.

(continued)

Light variation

☆Omit oil and cook onion in ¼ cup water, steaming for 5 minutes, or until onion is soft. Add the tomatoes, 2 tablespoons parsley, garlic, thyme, rosemary, bay leaf, and salt and pepper to taste and cook, covered, for 5 minutes, or until the tomatoes have released some juice. Uncover and cook, stirring occasionally, for 10 to 15 minutes, or until the juices have evaporated and the mixture is thick. Remove bay leaf and set vegetable mixture aside.

Notes

The tart can be eaten warm or cold. It can be prepared 1 day in advance. Let cool unmolded, cover, and refrigerate. To reheat, bake, covered in foil in a 325° oven for 20 minutes, or until it is heated through. Let stand for 5 minutes and sprinkle with 1 tablespoon minced parsley.

If there are leftover vegetables and sauce, use them to make a sauce to accompany the tart. Put them in a blender or food processor, purée, and add enough chicken stock or water to make a thick sauce. Stir in 1 to 2 tablespoons cream, season with salt and pepper, and heat.

Eggplant and tomato sauce should be kept as the base of the tart, but other vegetables, such as zucchini, mushrooms, peppers, or cauliflower, could be used with or instead of the leeks. Cut and blanch as directed in the recipe.

STUFFED BRAISED BELGIAN ENDIVES
Endives Farcis Braisés

Serves: 4

8 large (about 2 lbs.) Belgian endives
1 slice bread, crust removed
½ cup milk
¼ lb. lean ground pork
¼ lb. lean ground veal
1 tablespoon finely chopped parsley

1 egg
   Salt
   Freshly ground black pepper
   Freshly grated nutmeg
3½ tablespoons butter
   1 shallot, finely chopped
   ½ cup freshly grated Parmesan cheese (optional)

Preheat oven to 400°.

Remove any blemished leaves and trim off the bottoms of the endives. Cut ⅛ inch off the tips to help open the leaves. Wash the endives one at a time, holding them tip up under the faucet. The pressure of the water will open the leaves. Remove the core very carefully without going too close to edge so leaves are not cut off. Drain.

Put bread in a soup plate, cover with milk, and let soak for 5 minutes, or until soft. Squeeze dry and discard milk. Put bread in a mixing bowl, and add ☆pork, veal, parsley, egg, and salt, pepper, and nutmeg to taste.

Melt ½ tablespoons butter in a small skillet and sauté the shallot over moderate heat for ½ minute, stirring. Transfer to the bowl with the pork and veal and blend ingredients thoroughly with a spatula or wooden spoon.

Stuff the endives, using the hands to push the stuffing between the center leaves. Squeeze endives lightly to close the leaves back over the stuffing.

Melt the remaining butter in a heavy pot or pressure cooker. Add the endives in one layer and turn to coat with butter. Sprinkle lightly with salt and pepper. Add enough water to cover the endives by one third (add only 1 cup water if using a pressure cooker). Cover tightly and bring to a boil on top of the stove. Transfer to the oven and bake for 45 minutes to 1 hour, turning the endives over after 25 minutes. Add more water if too much has evaporated. (Or pressure cook for 20 to 25 minutes.)

Uncover and boil down any liquid left in the pot over moderate heat and cook to lightly brown the endives, turning them as necessary. Transfer to a warm serving platter and sprinkle the endives with Parmesan.

(continued)

Light variation

☆Omit the pork and use ½ lb. lean ground veal for the stuffing.

Notes

Serve with creamy Mashed Potatoes (see p. 208).

The endives can be cooked 1 day in advance. Let them cool uncovered. Cover and refrigerate. Reheat either in a 350° oven or on top of the stove, adding a little more water to prevent them from sticking or burning.

Endive is a vegetable that should be cooked until quite tender rather than until tender-crisp. It is important to remove the core because it is bitter.

CREAMED BELGIAN ENDIVES
Endives a la Crème

Serves: 4

   2 lbs. Belgian endives (about 8 to 10)
   3 tablespoons butter
      Salt
      Freshly ground black pepper
   ½ to ¾ cup water, more or less
      Snow Sauce (see p. 52)

Preheat oven to 300°.

Wash and trim ends of each endive. Discard any blemished leaves.

☆Melt the butter in a heavy pot or pressure cooker and arrange the endives in one layer. Turn to coat with butter. Add salt and pepper to taste and ¾ cup water, or enough so that the endives are at least half immersed in water.

Cover and bring to a boil on top of the stove. Transfer to the oven and bake for 45 minutes to 1 hour (pressure cook for 15 to 20 minutes), turning endives over after 25 minutes. Add more water if too much has evaporated.

Drain endives well, arrange upside down in a sieve, and let drain for 15 minutes.

Pour about one third of the sauce into the bottom of a dish. Arrange endives on top and cover with remaining sauce. Put in oven and bake for 10 to 15 minutes to heat through.

Light variation

☆Use only 1½ tablespoons butter to melt and coat the endives.

Notes

Endives are the only vegetables that should be cooked until quite tender rather than until tender-crisp. The texture should be soft so they melt in the mouth.

Each endive can be wrapped in a thin slice of boiled ham before being sauced and reheated.

Endives can also be served plain.

DUXELLES

Yield: 1 cup

    2 tablespoons butter
    3 tablespoons oil
    ½ cup (scant) finely chopped shallots
    ½ cup (scant) finely chopped onion
    1 lb. mushrooms, finely minced
       Juice of 1 lemon
       Salt
       Freshly ground black pepper

Melt butter and oil in a heavy skillet and add shallots and onion. Cover and cook over low heat, stirring occasionally with a wooden spatula for 10 minutes, or until soft. Do not brown.

Add mushrooms and cook, uncovered, over medium-high heat, stirring, until all liquid has completely evaporated. The Duxelles must be dry but not brown. (The total cooking time is 5 to 7 minutes after the mushrooms have exuded their liquid and started to boil.) Add salt and pepper to taste.

(continued)

Notes

To store, let cool and pack in a covered jar. Duxelles keeps for 4 to 5 days in the refrigerator. It also freezes well.

The food processor is very good for chopping the mushrooms. While chopping them, either by hand or with the processor, sprinkle some lemon juice over them to prevent darkening.

The flavor of Duxelles can be varied with nutmeg and chopped fresh or dried herbs. Or other ingredients, such as boiled ham or cooked rice, may also be added. Since Duxelles is easy to make and store well, it should always be on hand.

You can use Duxelles to stuff meat, chicken, or fish. The proportion is usually one third onion and shallots to two thirds mushrooms.

BRAISED MUSHROOMS
Champignons à Blanc

Serves: 6 to 8

2 tablespoons butter
1 lb. mushrooms, thickly sliced
2 tablespoons lemon juice
⅓ cup water
Salt
Freshly ground black pepper

☆Melt the butter in a saucepan and add the mushrooms, lemon juice, water, and salt and pepper to taste. Stir, cover, and bring to a boil. Boil slowly for 2 to 3 minutes, or until mushrooms give up their juices.

Light variation

☆Omit the butter and cook the mushrooms with lemon juice, water, and salt and pepper to taste.

Notes

If using these mushrooms in a dish which calls for ricotta, eliminate the lemon juice in this recipe.

SAUTÉED MUSHROOMS
Champignons Sautés

Serves: 4

   2 to 2½ tablespoons butter
   ½ lb. mushrooms, whole if very small, or halved or quartered
      if larger
   Salt
   Freshly ground black pepper

Melt butter in a heavy skillet large enough to hold the mushrooms
in one layer. Add the mushrooms and cook over medium-high heat
for 3 minutes, stirring and tossing until they are light brown. Season with salt and pepper to taste.

Notes

   The mushrooms can be cooked several hours ahead or 1 day
in advance. Cover and refrigerate if holding more than 2 or 3
hours.

ONION PURÉE
Purée Soubise

Yield: 2 cups

   2 qts. water
   1 lb. large yellow onions, sliced
   3 tablespoons butter
   ½ cup rice
   1 cup concentrated quick chicken stock (see p. 20)
      Salt
      Freshly ground black pepper

Bring water to a boil and blanch onions for 2 minutes. Drain well.
   ☆Melt the butter in a saucepan, add onions, cover, and cook
over low heat for 15 minutes, or until very tender but not brown.
   Add rice and stir to coat with butter. Add stock and salt and

pepper to taste. Bring to a boil, stirring, cover, lower heat, and simmer slowly for 35 to 40 minutes, or until liquid has been absorbed and mixture is soft and tender.

Purée mixture in a food processor or force through a food mill. If mixture is watery, put it over low heat and cook gently, stirring, until liquid has evaporated and mixture has thickened.

Light variation

☆Omit butter and cook blanched onions with rice and stock only. Add salt and pepper to taste.

Notes

The purée will keep for 1 to 2 days in the refrigerator. Let cool, uncovered, then cover and store.

Reheat in a heavy saucepan over low heat, adding a little stock so the purée does not scorch.

This purée is delicious with chicken or turkey, veal, and pork.

BRAISED SMALL WHITE ONIONS
Petits Oignons Blancs Braisés

Serves: 4

    2 qts. water
    1 lb. small white onions (about 1½ inches in diameter), unpeeled
    1½ tablespoons butter
    2 teaspoons sugar (optional)
    ⅓ cup dry white wine
    1 cup concentrated chicken stock (see pp. 19–20), more or less
        Salt
        Freshly ground black pepper

Preheat oven to 375°.

Bring water to a boil and drop in unpeeled onions. Bring back to a boil and boil slowly, uncovered, for 3 minutes. Drain and cool under cold running water. Cut a thin slice off the root end of each onion and squeeze gently. Onions will slip out of their skins.

Melt the butter in a saucepan large enough to hold the onions in one layer. Add the onions and sauté them over medium heat until golden, turning them as necessary. Sprinkle the sugar over the onions and cook, stirring, for 1 to 2 minutes, or until the sugar colors slightly. Add the wine and reduce to 2 tablespoons. Add enough stock to cover the onions by one third. Sprinkle with salt and pepper, cover, and bring to a simmer on top of the stove. Transfer to the oven and bake for 35 to 40 minutes, or until tender, turning the onions occasionally so they cook evenly and the exposed surfaces do not dry out.

Notes

Tiny onions about ½ inch in diameter, called pearl onions, are available occasionally. Braise as directed, but watch onions carefully. They take very little time to cook and are as sweet as candy.

Onions, turnips, and celery are good examples of braised vegetables. Very little fat is added, but an excellent concentrated chicken stock will be almost completely absorbed by the vegetables, which makes them succulent.

CREAMED SPINACH
Épinards à la Crème

Serves: 6 to 8

8 qts. water
Salt
4 lbs. spinach, washed and picked over, with stems removed
2 tablespoons butter
1 tablespoon chopped shallot
2 cloves garlic, minced (optional)
Freshly ground black pepper
¼ teaspoon freshly grated nutmeg
⅓ to ½ cup heavy cream

Bring water to a boil in a large kettle and add 3 tablespoons of salt. Drop in the spinach. As soon as it wilts, drain it immediately, refresh under cold running water, and squeeze dry. Chop the spinach finely by hand or in a food processor and set aside.

Melt the butter in a saucepan and add the shallots and garlic. Cook slowly for 1 to 2 minutes, stirring. Add the chopped spinach and season with salt, pepper, and nutmeg. ☆Stir in the cream and cook over moderate heat, stirring, until the mixture is heated through and holds together smoothly.

Light variation

☆In place of the cream, use ⅓ to ½ cup milk.

Notes

The spinach can be blanched and chopped 1 day in advance. Finish cooking just before serving. Remember, spinach loses color and taste if heated too long.

SAUTÉED CHERRY TOMATOES
Tomates Naines Sautées

Serves: 4

    1½ qts. water
    1 pt. cherry tomatoes, not too ripe
    1½ tablespoons butter
       Salt
       Freshly ground black pepper
    1 shallot, finely minced
    1 tablespoon finely minced parsley or fresh basil

Bring water to boil in a saucepan. Add the cherry tomatoes and poach for 10 seconds. Refresh immediately under cold water and drain on paper towels. Slip off the skins with a paring knife.

Melt the butter in a skillet. Add the tomatoes and cook over moderate heat for 2 minutes, or until heated through, shaking and tossing the tomatoes so they cook evenly. (Do not overcook or they will get mushy.) Season with salt and pepper to taste. Add the shallot and cook for 1 minute, tossing and shaking the pan. Remove from the heat and toss with the parsley.

Notes

Peel the tomatoes ahead of time so that the final preparation takes just a few minutes.

The flavor of the dish can be changed by adding 1 minced garlic clove, or ½ teaspoon dried rosemary, or oregano to taste.

BROILED TOMATOES
Tomates Grillées

Serves: 6

> 3 medium, ripe but firm, tomatoes
> 2 cloves garlic
>   Salt
>   Freshly ground black pepper
> ¾ teaspoon dried rosemary
> 2 tablespoons oil

Preheat broiler to high.

Wash and dry the tomatoes and halve them crosswise. Squeeze the garlic through a garlic press (you do not have to peel it first). Spread a little garlic on the cut side of each tomato half. Sprinkle with salt, pepper, and rosemary. Spoon the oil over the top. Arrange the tomatoes cut side up in a baking pan large enough to hold them snugly.

Put under the broiler at least 5 inches from the flame and broil for 5 to 10 minutes, or until tender but not mushy. The tomatoes should hold their shape.

Notes

The tomatoes can be prepared several hours in advance up to the point where they are ready to go under the broiler.

STUFFED TOMATOES ATLANTA
Tomates Farcies Atlanta

Serves: 6

6 qts. water
4 to 6 ears corn
12 medium, firm but ripe, tomatoes, about 2½ to 3 inches in
    diameter
    Salt
3 tablespoons butter
½ lb. cooked ham, cut into ¼-inch cubes
2 shallots, finely chopped
    Freshly ground black pepper
½ cup heavy cream
2 tablespoons finely chopped parsley
1 cup grated imported Swiss or Parmesan cheese, or
    a combination of both

Preheat oven to 400°.

Bring water to boil in a covered kettle. Add shucked corn, cover, and bring back to a boil. Uncover and boil for 5 minutes. Drain. When cool enough to handle, cut and scrape the kernels from the cobs. Set the kernels aside.

Cut out the core of each tomato. Cut a thin slice off the bottom of each tomato and carefully hollow them out, using a teaspoon, being careful not to break the flesh. Sprinkle the insides lightly with salt and invert the tomatoes on a rack. Let drain for 15 minutes. Bake the tomatoes, still inverted on the rack in a roasting pan, for 6 minutes. Set them aside.

Spread 1 tablespoon of butter on the inside of a gratin dish large enough to hold the tomatoes comfortably. Turn the broiler to high.

Melt the remaining butter in a skillet. Add the ham and sauté over medium-high heat for 1 minute, tossing and shaking the pan. Add the shallots and toss for 30 seconds. Add the corn kernels and pepper to taste, and toss for 1 minute.

☆Add the cream and simmer over moderate heat, stirring, until the mixture thickens a little and blends together. Remove from the heat and stir in the parsley.

Stuff the tomatoes evenly and arrange them in the prepared gratin dish. Sprinkle with the cheese, and put under the broiler until golden.

Light variation

☆In place of the cream, use ½ cup ricotta, blended in a food processor with 4 tablespoons of milk. Remove the ham mixture from the heat and add the ricotta mixture. Mix well. Heat gently just to the boil over moderate heat, stirring. Stir in the parsley.

Notes

The tomatoes can be prepared through the filling step several hours before serving. Reheat in a 325° oven and run under the broiler until golden.

Cooking the tomatoes alone inverted on a rack helps them render part of their juices which would make the stuffing soggy.

Prepare this dish when tomatoes and corn are at their peak.

Onion Purée (see p. 245) and Duxelles (see p. 243) also make delicious fillings for tomatoes.

BRAISED WHITE TURNIPS
Navets Braisés

Serves: 4

1 lb. small white turnips, peeled (leave whole if small; halve or quarter if large)
1½ tablespoons butter
1 teaspoon sugar (optional)
⅓ cup dry white wine
1 cup quick chicken stock (see p. 20), more or less
Salt
Freshly ground black pepper

Preheat oven to 375°.

Melt butter in a large heavy pot. Add turnips and sauté over medium heat until golden, turning as necessary. Add sugar and cook, stirring, for 1 to 2 minutes, or until sugar colors lightly. Add wine and reduce to 2 to 3 tablespoons. Add enough stock to cover turnips by one third. Sprinkle with salt and pepper. Cover and bring to a simmer on top of the stove. Transfer to the oven and cook for 20 to 30 minutes, or until tender, turning turnips occasionally so they cook evenly and exposed surfaces do not dry out. Season with salt and pepper, if necessary. (If the cooking liquid boils away before the turnips are cooked, add a little more stock to prevent their burning. If cooking liquid has not evaporated and turnips are tender, remove turnips and reduce liquid to 4 to 5 tablespoons.)

VEGETABLE TART
Tourte aux Légumes

Serves: 6

Vegetables
> 1 head Savoy cabbage
> Salt
> ¼ lb. celery stalks
> 1 lb. leeks
> ½ lb. Swiss chard
> ¼ lb. green beans
> 1 tablespoon butter, softened

Custard filling
> ½ cup ricotta, blended in a food processor, or ½ cup plain yogurt
> 1 whole egg
> 1 egg yolk
> ½ cup heavy cream
> Salt
> Freshly ground black pepper
> ½ cup freshly grated Swiss or Parmesan cheese, or a combination of both

Special equipment

6-cup round cake pan, 8 inches in diameter and 1½ inches deep (a charlotte or savarin mold will do, but the name of the dish would change to pain de légumes or turban de légumes respectively)

Preheat oven to 425°.

Core cabbage and discard blemished outer leaves. Separate remaining leaves, cutting away coarse inner ribs.

Bring a large kettle of water to a rapid boil and add 1¼ teaspoons salt per quart of water. Blanch the cabbage leaves for 2 minutes, or until just limp. Remove with a slotted spoon and put in a colander. Refresh under cold running water and put on a towel to dry.

When all cabbage leaves are blanched, add the cabbage heart to the water and boil for 4 to 5 minutes, or until cooked but still crisp. Remove with a slotted spoon, drain, and refresh under cold running water. Dry and chop coarsely. Keep water boiling to blanch remaining vegetables.

Peel outer stalks of celery with a swivel-blade vegetable peeler. Drop whole stalks into water and boil for 3 to 4 minutes, or until cooked but still crisp. Drain and refresh under cold running water. Dry and cut crosswise into 1½-inch pieces.

Cut off the dark green part of the leeks, remove the outer layer, and trim roots closely so leaves stay together. Drop whole leeks into boiling water and blanch for 5 to 7 minutes, or until cooked but crisp. Drain and refresh under cold running water. Dry and cut crosswise into 1½-inch pieces.

Trim the Swiss chard and cut off the stringy parts from the ribs. Blanch in boiling salted water until just wilted. Refresh under cold running water. Dry on paper towels and cut into 1½-inch strips.

Snap ends and string green beans. Blanch in boiling salted water for 5 minutes. Drain and refresh under cold running water. Dry on paper towels.

Butter the cake pan, line the bottom with parchment paper, and butter the paper.

Blend the ricotta in a food processor until smooth. Transfer to a bowl and add the egg, egg yolk, cream, and salt and pepper to taste. Beat until blended.

(continued)

Completely line the bottom and sides of the prepared pan with the cabbage leaves, leaving enough overhanging so the mold can be completely covered when filled. Arrange the beans, leeks, celery, and Swiss chard attractively in the mold. Cover with the chopped cabbage and the remaining leaves. Pour the ricotta mixture over the vegetables, sprinkle with cheese, and cover the filling with the overhanging cabbage leaves.

Put the pan in a larger pan and add boiling water to a depth of ¾ inch. Lower the oven temperature to 375° and bake the tart for 1 hour, or until a small knife inserted in the center comes out clean.

Remove the tart from the oven and larger pan. Cover with foil to keep warm and allow to stand for 5 to 7 minutes. Invert onto a warm serving dish and peel off paper. If the tart is to be served cold, unmold, peel off paper, cool, cover, and refrigerate.

Notes

This tart can accompany white meat entrées, such as chicken, pork, veal, or turkey. It can be eaten warm with a tomato sauce, or cold with a vinaigrette.

The recipe can be doubled easily, using 2 pans.

This is an excellent example of a light, well-balanced vegetable main course.

COUNTRY-STYLE VEGETABLES
Ragoût de Légumes

Serves: 6

- ½ lb. green peppers (about 2 medium)
- ½ lb. red peppers (about 2 medium)
- 2 tablespoons butter
- ¾ lb. yellow onions (about 3 medium), thinly sliced
- 2 lbs. tomatoes (about 5 medium), peeled, seeded, and roughly chopped
- 1 teaspoon minced garlic
- ¼ teaspoon dried thyme
- 2 small bay leaves
- Salt

Freshly ground black pepper
1 tablespoon finely minced parsley

Preheat broiler to high.

Put the red and green peppers on a foil-lined pan and broil about 4 inches from the heat, turning frequently, until the skins char almost all over.

Put the peppers in a bowl and cover them with foil until they are cool enough to be handled. Peel the charred skin off the peppers with a paring knife. Be sure to remove all the blackened skin as it can give a burnt taste to the dish. Halve the peppers, remove the seeds and pith, and cut them lengthwise into ⅜-inch-thick strips.

Melt the butter in a large skillet over moderate heat. Add the onions and cook, stirring occasionally, for 7 minutes, or until they are soft but not brown. Add the tomatoes, garlic, thyme, bay leaves, and salt and pepper to taste. Cook, uncovered, over medium-high heat, stirring occasionally, for 10 to 15 minutes, or until all the juices have evaporated.

Combine the peppers with the vegetables in the skillet and heat them gently over low heat. Add salt and pepper, if necessary. Transfer to a warm dish and sprinkle with parsley.

Notes

Vegetables will keep for 1 to 2 days in the refrigerator. Let cool uncovered, cover, and store. Reheat slowly on top of the stove in a skillet. Add a little water if the vegetables get too dry. The vegetables freeze very well.

This dish is superb with Poached Eggs (see p. 60), broiled chicken, broiled fish, steaks and roasts of all sorts.

CARROT AND APPLE SALAD
Salade de Pommes et Carottes

Serves: 6

> 2 tablespoons lemon juice
> Salt
> Freshly ground black pepper
> 2 tablespoons oil
> 2 large carrots, washed and peeled thinly
> 2 large tart apples, such as Granny Smiths or McIntosh, peeled and cored

In a salad bowl, mix the lemon juice with salt and pepper to taste, using a small whisk. Add the oil and mix well again.

Shred the carrots and apples, using the shredding disk of a food processor, and put them into a salad bowl. Toss immediately with dressing so the apples do not discolor. Season with more salt and pepper, if necessary.

GRATED CARROT SALAD
Carottes Rapées

Serves: 6

> 6 medium carrots
> 2 to 3 tablespoons lemon juice
> 1 to 2 tablespoons oil
> Salt
> Freshly ground black pepper

Wash the carrots and peel thinly. Shred them, using the shredding disk of a food processor. Transfer the shredded carrots to a serving bowl.

Combine the lemon juice and oil with salt and pepper to taste. Pour over the carrots and toss lightly until all shreds are coated with dressing. Marinate in the refrigerator for at least 1 hour.

Notes

This salad will keep for 2 to 3 days, covered and refrigerated.

The crisp sweet taste of the fresh carrots is enhanced by the simple dressing. Each serving has only about 55 calories.

CUCUMBER SALAD
Salade de Concombres

Serves: 6

2 cucumbers, each about 8 inches long
  Isabelle's Vinaigrette (see p. 46), strong version
1 tablespoon very finely minced fresh dill (optional)

Wash cucumbers, dry, and peel thinly. Cut in half crosswise and remove seeds by piercing core of cucumber all the way through with a sharp paring knife. Using the dull edge of the blade, twist within the core until all seeds are removed.

Slice the cucumbers thinly and put them into a serving bowl. Pour in the dressing, add the dill, and mix thoroughly. Macerate in the refrigerator for at least ½ hour.

Notes

The thin slicing disk of a food processor works very well for slicing the cucumbers. Put the cucumbers straight in the feed tube. (Since the seeds are removed, the cucumbers can be squeezed a little to fit into the tube.) Press the pusher down firmly to obtain perfect wheels.

The salad keeps for at least 2 days, covered and refrigerated.

GREEN AND WHITE SALAD
Salade Verte et Blanche

Serves: 6

    4 Belgian endives (about ¾ lb.)
    1 bunch watercress
    2 to 3 tablespoons vinegar
    1 qt. water
    ½ lb. mushrooms
       Isabelle's Vinaigrette (see p. 46)
       Lemon juice, if needed

Rinse endives under cold running water. (Do not let them soak in the water or they will become very bitter.) Trim off the ends of the endives, remove any blemished leaves, and pat dry with paper towels. Halve the endives lengthwise, slice each half lengthwise again, and cut each into ¼ inch julienne strips. Arrange the strips standing up around the sides of a salad bowl.

Cut the thick stems off the watercress, wash it, and spin dry or dry thoroughly in a towel. Arrange in the middle of the salad bowl.

In a bowl mix together the vinegar and water.

Trim the ends off the mushrooms and rub them quickly in the acidulated water, rinse, and dry thoroughly. Slice the mushrooms lengthwise and put them on top of the watercress.

Just before serving, toss the salad with the dressing. Squeeze on a few drops of lemon juice, if needed.

Notes

Store washed endives wrapped in paper towels in an untied plastic bag.

Mushrooms can be washed a few hours in advance and sliced just before serving. They will stay sparkling white.

An equally delicious salad can be made by substituting 1 head of Boston lettuce for the endives and 1 medium-size ripe tomato, peeled and cut into wedges, or 12 cherry tomatoes, peeled, for the mushrooms and watercress.

MUSHROOMS THE GREEK WAY
Champignons à la Grecque

Serves: 6

- 3 tablespoons vegetable oil
- 1 tablespoon olive oil
- 1 lb. mushrooms, preferably small and evenly sized (quarter if larger)
- 2 teaspoons tomato paste (optional)
- ½ cup dry white wine
- 5 sprigs parsley
- ¼ teaspoon dried thyme
- 1 bay leaf
- ½ celery stalk (optional)
- 1 clove garlic, crushed (optional)
- ½ teaspoon coriander seeds, or 6 juniper berries (optional)
  Salt
  Freshly ground black pepper
  Lemon juice to taste
- 1 tablespoon finely chopped parsley

☆Heat the oil slightly in a large saucepan. Stir in the mushrooms, tomato paste, wine, parsley, thyme, bay leaf, celery, garlic, and coriander seeds. Season very lightly with salt and pepper. Cover and simmer over low heat for 10 to 15 minutes, or until crisp and tender.

Uncover and let cool in cooking liquid. Transfer to a serving dish with a slotted spoon. Reduce cooking liquid to 4 tablespoons. Let cool, pour over mushrooms, and season with salt and pepper, if necessary. Add lemon juice to taste and sprinkle with parsley.

Light variation

☆Use only 1 tablespoon vegetable oil and 1 tablespoon olive oil to cook the mushrooms.

Notes

These mushrooms are a good accompaniment for cold meat or fish. They can also be served as an hors d'oeuvre.

Many vegetables can be prepared à la Grecque. The vegetables should be cut evenly for an attractive presentation. Cook each separately and vary the cooking time as necessary, cooking until the vegetables are just crisp but tender. The seasonings can be varied to taste. Experiment with other herbs than those listed in the above recipe. The proportions in the recipe are for 1 lb. of vegetables: green beans, small beets (quarter them if they are large), broccoli, cauliflower, celery hearts, celery roots, leeks, small white onions (blanch these first for 5 minutes), tomatoes (peel, quarter, and cook for just 1 minute after water reaches the simmer), and zucchini (peel off strips so there is a design on the outside of the slices). Cook all vegetables in water to cover, except for mushrooms which render enough of their own liquids. Put the vegetables in separate serving dishes, sprinkle with chopped parsley, and serve as a light first course or a salad course.

MUSHROOM SALAD WITH CREAM SAUCE
Salade de Champignons à la Crème

Serves: 4

   ½ cup heavy cream
   Juice of 1 lemon
 1 small clove garlic, minced
 1 tablespoon finely minced parsley
 1 tablespoon minced chives
   Salt
   Freshly ground black pepper
   ½ lb. mushrooms, whole if very small, halved or quartered if
   larger

☆Mix cream, lemon juice, garlic, parsley, chives, and salt and pepper to taste in a serving bowl. Add the mushrooms and mix well. Let macerate in the refrigerator for at least 2 hours.

Light variation
   ☆In place of the cream, use ½ cup ricotta and 2 tablespoons milk, blended in a food processor.

MOLDED TOMATO MOUSSELINE
Mousseline de Tomates Moulées

Serves: 8

  1 cucumber, peeled, seeded, and cut into 1/16-inch-thick slices
  1 tablespoon lemon juice
  Salt
  2 tablespoons butter
  2½ lbs. ripe tomatoes, peeled, seeded, and roughly chopped, or 2 20-oz. cans Italian plum tomatoes, drained
  2 bay leaves
  ⅛ teaspoon dried thyme
  ½ teaspoon dried or ground rosemary
  ½ stalk celery, cut into medium-size pieces
  Freshly ground black pepper
  2 envelopes unflavored gelatin
  ⅓ cup cold water
  1 tablespoon tomato paste
  1⅓ cups heavy cream
  4 hard-cooked eggs, sliced
  1 tablespoon finely chopped parsley

Special equipment
  7-cup ring mold

Put the cucumber slices into a bowl. Add the lemon juice and a pinch of salt and let macerate for ½ hour.

Use 1 tablespoon butter to butter the ring mold. Line the bottom of the mold with a piece of wax paper, and butter the paper.

Heat the remaining butter in a saucepan and add the tomatoes, bay leaves, thyme, rosemary, celery, and salt and pepper to taste. Cook, stirring occasionally, for 15 to 20 minutes or until the mixture is almost a purée.

Sprinkle the gelatin over the cold water and let soften.

Remove the celery and bay leaves from the purée and discard. Put the purée through the fine disk of a food mill or purée in a food processor. Strain the purée and return it to the saucepan. (There should be about 3 cups.) Stir the tomato paste into the purée and set aside ¼ cup of the purée. Bring the remainder to a boil, stirring. Remove from the heat, add the softened gelatin, and stir for 1 minute, or until the gelatin is completely dissolved. Pour the mixture into a stainless steel bowl and set over a bowl of ice mixed with ½ cup water. Stir once a minute so the mixture chills evenly.

☆Put the heavy cream into a bowl and add a pinch of salt. Put this bowl into a larger bowl of ice mixed with water. Whip the heavy cream until soft peaks form.

When the purée starts to thicken, remove it from the ice. Rapidly fold the cream into the purée, using a whisk, until the cream is completely blended.

Arrange a layer of macerated cucumber slices (reserving a few for garnish) in the bottom of the prepared mold, overlapping them slightly. Fill the middle with overlapping egg slices (reserving a few for garnish). Pour the mousseline mixture into the mold and cover the top with the remaining cucumber and egg slices.

Refrigerate for 2 to 3 hours, or until firm. To unmold, run the tip of a paring knife around the edge of the mold and dip the mold into warm water for about 5 seconds. Tilt the mold so the aspic slides around a bit. (This lets some air in and releases the vacuum.) Put a chilled platter on top of the mold and invert it quickly.

Decorate with a ribbon of reserved purée around the bottom of the mousseline. Sprinkle parsley on top.

Light variation

☆In place of cream use 2 egg whites and 1⅓ cups ricotta, blended in a food processor. Beat the egg whites until stiff (see p. 271). When the purée starts to thicken, remove it from the ice. Fold in the processed ricotta, using a whisk, until it is just blended. Fold in whites rapidly.

Notes

This dish can be made 1 day in advance, unmolded, covered, and refrigerated.

The egg and cucumber slices can be replaced by ½ pound of Poached Shrimp (see p. 112), halved lengthwise, or any other leftover fish or chicken.

9
PASTRIES AND DESSERTS

Surprisingly often people tell us the first French food they can remember tasting was a brown tube closed at the ends and filled with
yellow custard or white cream: a chocolate eclair. No wonder they
grew up well disposed toward French cuisine! Anyway, it's clear
that Americans of all ages dote on French pastries, just as the
French of all ages do.

When it comes to making these confections—some rich and
filling, others light and airy—the same people who most enjoy eating them can become strangely hesitant. One fine cook we know
confidently prepares every course of her celebrated dinners except
the last—and for dessert serves a cake, fruit tarts, cookies, or ladyfingers and the like that she buys in a bakeshop to accompany ice
cream or fruit. And beginning students often confess to us that
since the ignominious collapse of their first attempted soufflé they
haven't quite summoned the nerve to try again.

Such hesitancy isn't so strange after all, for pastry-making is
an exacting discipline, almost a science. Because of the need for
careful measuring to keep the ingredients in balance, and because
of the transformations these ingredients undergo when mixed and
exposed to heat, it is frequently likened to chemistry. But must it
therefore be left to professionals? Chef Jorant, who was already
whipping up all sorts of delicate confections in his teens, thinks not
and says so in emphatic terms. "If pastry-making calls for precision,
dexterity, taste, and close attention, so does cooking in general," he
points out. "Besides," he adds, "pastry-making is easier now than

it's ever been, thanks to modern ovens with accurate temperature gauges, reliable supplies of good-quality flour, and handy gadgets like electric beaters and mixers. Also, more and more kitchens are being designed or revamped these days in ways that simplify a cook's task."

Pastry doughs are wonderfully versatile, and the sheer number of preparations that can be made from them—thousands—is mind-boggling. But again this is no reason for anyone to feel intimidated. On the contrary, once you master four basic doughs—for crêpes, *choux*, *pâte brisée* (pie dough), and puff pastry—plus two simple cakes, *génoise* and *biscuit*, you'll be ready to take on all varieties of haute cuisine desserts.

In French households these imposing treats are normally served once or twice a week, typically after midday Sunday dinner or when company comes. Other meals might conclude with fruit or cheese or both together, a simple custard, or a light pastry. About a third of our recipes are for classic confections, the remainder being for trimmed-down versions of the same and for other desserts, some with light versions. You can eat these light-version desserts every day without fear of putting on weight. We have wherever possible reduced the amounts of eggs, cream, and butter traditionally called for, but in certain pastries, notably puff pastry and *pâte brisée*, this is difficult if not impossible to do without sacrificing taste and/or texture. On the other hand, we have cut down on or eliminated such frills as extra icings, which add a lot to a cook's labor but little to the taste of a preparation and detract from its appearance in some cases.

Apart from the obvious paraphernalia, what you need most to start with are a scale, a hand-held electric mixer, and an oven thermometer—and a knowledge of how to go about assembling the right ingredients.

INGREDIENTS

Flour. Forget what you may have heard about French flour being superior to American; it isn't. The only significant difference between them is that American unbleached all-purpose flour has a little more gluten in it. We recommend unbleached flour because it contains no preservatives—indeed, no additives of any kind—and gives a better texture and taste than processed flours do. In certain cases the blending of two different flours is very valuable. Chef Jorant used to do this in his own bakery to obtain the right amount of gluten in his own flour.

Eggs. The eggs used in our recipes are extra large—that is, 60 to 65 grams, or a little over two ounces. The main requirement of an egg is that it be fresh, so you should only buy those marked U.S. Grade AA or A.

To determine the approximate age of an egg place it in a pan of water. If it lies on the bottom it is fresh, inclining at a slight angle from the bottom it is about a week old, and at a steeper angle about two weeks. If it stands on its ends it is quite elderly and must be broken open to see whether it can still be used. An egg that rises to the surface should be discarded.

Sugar. In the chemistry of pastry-making neither honey nor any synthetic sweetener can take the place of sugar. Granulated, confectioners' sugar, and superfine sugar are the types most frequently employed.

Butter. Salt in butter acts as a preservative, making it difficult to judge the butter's freshness. Its presence also complicates the problem of deciding how much salt to use in making pastry. So unsalted butter is more satisfactory, particularly if it is U.S. Grade A. Butter is 81 percent fat. Occasionally it contains too much water. To rid it of excess water place it, very cold, between tea towels and pound it with a rolling pin.

Cream. Heavy cream is composed of not less than 37.6 percent milkfat. Look for heavy cream that hasn't been ultra-pasteurized; this process boils the cream for two seconds at up to 280° F., killing more bacteria and prolonging its shelf life but also robbing it of much of its flavor and making it harder to whip. By contrast regular pasteurization heats cream at 204° F. or boils it at 212° F. for exceedingly brief periods: one twentieth and one one-hundredth of a second respectively. Cream labeled whipping cream or light whipping cream has a milkfat content of 31.3 percent. Although it can be whipped it has a tendency to break down, and it lacks the rich taste and texture of heavy cream. Half and half, a blend of milk and cream, is only 11.7 percent butterfat.

Ricotta. Whole milk ricotta, which we substitute for cream and butter in certain mousses and Bavarian creams, is a fresh white cheese, a very finely grained cottage cheese. It is unsalted and has a nutty flavor. Four ounces (113 grams), or half a cup, contain just 14 grams of fat. What we call "processed ricotta" is ricotta that's been put through a food processor or blender, with or without liquid, until it is almost liquefied and has a smooth, glossy appearance, resembling lightly beaten heavy cream. Unprocessed, it freezes well.

Oil. We use two oils, corn oil and olive oil, either individually, in combination, or with butter. When they are mixed we like the proportions of two parts corn oil to one part olive oil. These oils are not hydrogenated. Hydrogenation is a solidifying process that eliminates fatty acids necessary to good health. Once opened, oils should be kept refrigerated. Vegetable oils are low in saturated fats and high in polyunsaturated fats. Olive oil is low in polyunsaturated fat, so use it sparingly—in particular, to add flavor.

A GLOSSARY OF TECHNIQUES AND TERMS

Here, alphabetically arranged, are brief descriptions of basic techniques involved in making pastries, custards, and certain other desserts, together with definitions of some relevant terms.

Beating. This is done to mix ingredients in a bowl thoroughly into a uniform mixture. Using a spatula, whisk, or electric beater, you beat the mixture in counterclockwise circles; your implement, tilted toward the middle of the bowl, gathers the ingredients at the center instead of splashing them on the sides.

Breaking up. This term, used chiefly in connection with eggs, describes stirring a mixture gently, with a whisk, a spatula, or a mixer on low speed before adding something else to it in order to facilitate reception of the new element.

Coating. When an English custard is cooked to the right consistency—when it is as thick as it can get without curdling—it will coat a spoon or a spatula. Remove the implement from the mixture and run a finger along the blade; if the mixture holds without running into the strip you have just laid bare the custard is ready.

Custard, temperature test for. Another (and somewhat more reliable) test of a custard is to take its temperature. It is cooked (or, rather, poached, as the cooking is not thorough) at 175° to 180° F. Remove the custard a little before it attains this temperature, as it will continue to cook on its own before it begins to cool and if it gets too hot may scramble. If it is already at 175° to 180°, remove it from the heat and beat it for a minute or two, or set it in a cold *bain-marie* and beat.

Folding. The purpose of this operation is to incorporate one mixture into another delicately. As you fold with your right hand (assuming you are righthanded), turn the bowl counterclockwise with your left.

Suppose you are preparing a cake, cookies, or a *génoise.* Taking a spatula, you cut down through the middle of the mixture leading with the edge of the spatula, then draw the spatula toward you scraping the bottom of the bowl, and finally pull it up along the side of the bowl. The movement, described here in three steps, is actually continuous. You end the fold with the inner side of your wrist up, then you flip your wrist back over to repeat the movement.

Mousses, Bavarian creams, and soufflés are easier to fold with a folding whisk. The movement is the same, except that at the end of each fold you give the whisk a brisk shake to clear it of mixture.

Graining. When egg whites separate into small white particles they are said to grain. Egg whites can grain if you beat them improperly, if you interrupt the beating, if you beat them too much, or if, instead of promptly incorporating them into a mixture, you let them stand.

The Ribbon. While beating eggs or egg yolks and sugar for pastries or custards you are frequently directed to reach the stage called "the ribbon" when, on raising your whisk or beater from the bowl, the mixture adhering to it drops back to the surface as a broad, thick ribbon that floats free for a few seconds before it is reabsorbed. While some cooks cite the ribbon as a sign of a mixture's being well whipped (particularly in the case of a *génoise* which requires a ribbon), in many cases the mixture needn't be that thick. Timing the beating or whipping is the best way to assure you get the consistency you need. After you have completed the operation a few times and seen how the mixture should look when ready you will never again have to time it. Here is what you should do when a recipe calls for the ribbon:

• For *egg yolks and sugar in a custard* 25 vigorous beating motions with a whisk are plenty. The idea is to mix the ingredients so that the yolks are fully protected by the sugar before you add hot milk.

• For *egg yolks and sugar in cakes, omelets, soufflés, and cookies* whip with an electric beater exactly four minutes at high speed. Here the idea is to fluff the mixture up, make it foamy, and lighten it.

• For a *génoise* whip with an electric beater exactly eight minutes at high speed; the mixture will then be thick enough to hold the flour and butter without collapsing. (The timing, here, is for eggs straight from the refrigerator.) The mixture will be fluffy and will have increased in volume, changed in color to white, and become glossy and thick like mayonnaise. Almost no bubbles will show on the surface.

Stirring in figure eights. This technique is employed when cooking a custard in order to reach every point of the inner sides and bottom of the pan so that the mixture will cook evenly without overheating in any one place, or curdling, or lumping. Grasping the handle of the pan in your left hand, lower the spatula vertically into the mixture holding it as you would a pen, then move it continuously through the mixture in figure-eight loops, always keeping its flat "business end" in contact with the bottom of the pan. For an English custard don't do this with a whisk or you will make foam and won't be able to gauge the consistency of your custard by eye. (Note: if you keep a check on the temperature of the custard this isn't so important.)

Frothing a sauce. The hollandaise and all its variations needs a special technique of whisking that we call "frothing." It is a very fast wristy motion in which the whisk is moved quickly to and fro all over the pan. The sauce will froth and double in volume as if it were a mousse. The result is an airy sauce that tastes very light. Butter sauces are easier to make in a *bain-marie*.

Unmolding. To remove a custard or Bavarian cream from its mold run a thin-bladed knife around the mold's inner rim and then dip the mold and its contents in warm water for a few seconds. To free the set mixture from the grip of the vacuum at the bottom, tip the mold gently to let air in, then center an upside-down serving dish on top of the mold and quickly reverse dish and mold.

Whipping. Egg whites, heavy cream, *génoise*, and the like, are whipped to fill them with air, causing them to expand into a foam.

To whip by hand, tilt the bowl to make your task easier and concentrate the mixture. Rotate a balloon whisk around the mixture clockwise in a continuous wide circular lifting motion. Scrape the sides of the bowl repeatedly to make sure none of the mixture is left unbeaten.

If you use an electric mixer, don't tilt the bowl but steer the beater whisks (or blades) counterclockwise around it, moving the beater in small circles. Be sure to bring the beater up against the sides of the bowl so that every bit of the mixture is whipped.

WHIPPING EGG WHITES

Two different methods are used for beating egg whites to a stiff foam, the first with sugar (for cakes, mousses, soufflés, and the like) and the second without sugar (for savory mousses and soufflés). With either method it's important to remember that stiffly beaten egg whites are fragile and unstable; they shouldn't be left to wait before being added into a mixture or they will grain.

Egg whites with sugar. These can be beaten longer and into stiffer peaks than those without. They are particularly useful in cakes for supporting a heavy batter. Being less fragile than the sugarless kind, they can be left standing for a minute or so but no longer; if they begin to grain they can usually be beaten back into shape.

Egg whites without sugar. These should only be beaten to a critical shiny, stiff stage; if beaten further they'll grain and break down. To help stabilize them during the beating and keep them from graining, a pinch of salt and a small amount of lemon juice or vinegar are added. The beaten whites must be combined immediately into the base mixture, for once they grain they can't be revived.

While beating egg whites, whether with a whisk or an electric mixer, be careful to scrape down the sides of the bowl thoroughly so that every part of them is beaten to the same consistency at the same time, otherwise the whites left on the sides may grain and ruin the whole batch. For the same reason you mustn't interrupt the beating. Use a stainless steel or glass mixing bowl the right size for the number of egg whites, and use a balloon whisk or an electric beater, preferably one with whisks. Before beating, both bowl and beater should be clean and free of fat or grease, the presence of which prevents the whites from mounting properly. Even a tiny speck of yolk can ruin a batch of whites, so break each egg into a separate cup. That way, if you get a bad egg or inadvertently leave some yolk in, you'll still have the rest of your whites.

You can use eggs straight from the refrigerator, but their whites will take a bit longer to mount than will whites from eggs at room temperature. A useful fact to remember is that old egg whites are more resistant to graining than fresh ones. Refrigerate them in a jar uncovered; they will keep for as long as a month.

Since our recipes call for both sweet and plain egg whites, we will give the formulas here.

SWEET EGG WHITES (MERINGUE)

Approximate preparation time: 5 minutes by machine, 8 by hand

4 egg whites
  Pinch of salt
  Sugar: use the amount suggested in the pertinent recipe

Place egg whites and salt in a bowl and whip or beat them with the mixer until they just barely hold. Sprinkle in 1 teaspoon sugar and continue whipping until the whites hold a little more. Gradually sprinkle in the remaining sugar while beating and continue to beat until the whites hold in straight, stiff, shiny peaks when the beater is lifted.

PLAIN EGG WHITES

Approximate preparation time: 4 minutes by machine, 6 to 7 by hand.

4 egg whites
¼ teaspoon salt
½ teaspoon lemon juice or vinegar

Place egg whites in a bowl and add salt. Whip or beat with the mixer until they just hold together, then add lemon or vinegar. Continue whipping until the whites just hold in straight, shiny peaks when the whisk or beater is lifted. Fold immediately into the suggested mixture.

TIPS

Below, listed alphabetically, are some pointers you may well find useful in making pastries and certain other desserts.

Baking powder. We use the kind called double-acting, which is two-thirds baking soda and one-third cream of tartar. Don't add too much of it or your cake will rise too high and collapse.

Baking sheets and cookie sheets. When you sprinkle the tops of meringues, cookies, *choux*, puffs, and the like, with sugar or grated cheese you must dispose of the excess that falls between them or it will burn. Raise the sheet and hold it on a slant, then tap its upper corner to dislodge the grains and send them cascading down. Finally, turn the sheet over very fast to make the matter fall off.

The purpose of flouring a baking sheet or cookie sheet is not just to keep batter from sticking but also to prevent it from spreading. For example, Cats' Tongues (page 275) will, if piped onto a greased and floured baking sheet, retain their long, elegant forms. By contrast, Orange Tiles (page 276) are placed on a sheet that has been greased but not floured to insure that they *will* spread.

Buttering. When buttering a pan, use softened butter. You can use melted butter, but turn the pan over to let dry. Butter generously, thoroughly, and evenly. Smearing butter around the inner sides of a pie tin to about half an inch from the rim makes the dough hold to the sides of the pan better during baking.

Cakes. Use a sawing motion with your knife to cut cake into layers. When unmolding a cake, you can prevent it from sticking to the rack by turning it out on a rack and then turning it over onto another rack lined with parchment paper so that its bottom cools flat against the paper. This bottom will be reversed to form the top of the finished cake.

Before frosting a cake, place it on a cardboard dish ¼ inch smaller in diameter so that you can pick it up and frost it in the air. Cement the cake to the cardboard with a touch of frosting.

Chocolate. Of the various brands, types, and forms of chocolate on the market, chocolate chips are, we find, the most satisfactory all around, working well in every kind of preparation.

When heated, chocolate can take the presence of a certain amount of liquid but not just a little: 4½ ounces or 125 grams melted with three tablespoons of liquid will not grain, but the same amount of chocolate with somewhat less liquid will. Also, chocolate can't stand high temperatures. Chopped fine (or in chips) it should be melted covered in a *bain-marie* no hotter than 160° F. Chocolate extends the cooking time of a *génoise* or cake.

Coffee. This is often used to add flavor and color to whipped cream, Bavarian creams, and ice cream. Rather than brewing it, we use instant espresso or freeze-dried coffee.

Combining mixtures. The lighter of two mixtures always goes onto the heavier. If the two are of the same density either can go on the other.

Eggs. They can be beaten either cold or at room temperature, but if they come straight from the refrigerator, they will take a little longer to beat.

Filling a pan. Spread the batter to the sides so that it doesn't rise too much in the middle.

Fruits. As they do in American cooking, fruits—tasty, colorful, and nutritious—loom large in French cuisine. In desserts they are served raw (alone or combined with others, whole or cut up, with cheese, or to garnish or accompany various preparations) or cooked (baked, stewed, poached, or sautéed). They figure in fruit salads, in pastries, they serve as fillings or ingredients in an exceedingly wide range of confections.

Fruits rate very high in nutritional value. Many, including not only the citrus fruits but several others, are especially rich in

Vitamin C, while most red and orange fruits are also good sources of Vitamin A. And fruits are very low in fat and have no cholesterol.

In selecting fresh fruits, apply the same criteria you would to choosing fresh vegetables. Look for unblemished, unwrinkled fruits, firm of flesh and bright in color, free of bruises and signs of decay. Feel and smell them to confirm the evidence of your eyes. Fruit is perishable, so fruits that are not destined for consumption soon should be refrigerated; unripe fruits left standing at room temperature away from sunlight usually ripen in a couple of days. Because fruits stay fresh and tasty longer if they are unwashed, don't wash them until you are ready to serve them or use them in some preparation.

In France, grapes are ubiquitous in cuisine in a fermented state—as wine.

Ice cream. Ordinary ice cubes broken up with an ice pick (or, more expeditiously, with a mallet) will do fine as the crushed ice needed for making ice cream in a machine. Rock salt or kosher salt helps to dissolve ice and drop the temperature of the brine. A good proportion for salt and ice is 5 pounds ice to 1 pound salt.

Never load an ice cream maker while it is running: Water and electricity don't mix, and a short circuit could well ensue. Load and operate your machine in accordance with the manufacturer's instructions.

Preheating an oven. Set the dial at 50 degrees above the desired temperature and set it back to the desired temperature when you start cooking.

Puff pastry. Always keep it refrigerated or frozen at four turns so that when you are ready to bake it you will still have two more turns with which to restore strength to the gluten and get back a smooth dough.

Soufflés. A soufflé often falls not because it is fragile but because it is overcooked, in which case it shrinks. It should be moist inside; if it is cooked to the point that it begins to pull away from the sides of the dish it is overcooked and will promptly fall.

To fill a soufflé dish, grease its inner surfaces well with softened butter, then coat lightly (for sweet soufflés) with very fine crumbled *génoise* or cookie crumbs. For savory soufflés you can dust the mold with very fine bread crumbs to obtain a nice crust all around. Sugar and cheese have a tendency to burn.

Fill the mold to the top and level the mixture with a long spatula. Make a trough with the handle of a spoon around the edge of the dish. The trough keeps the soufflé from toppling over as it rises and saves having to fit a collar around the mold.

Soufflés can wait before baking! Those with a béchamel base can wait an entire day. Refrigerate your soufflé at once, not because cold holds the whites better, but because you don't want to leave it in a warm kitchen.

Soufflés made without béchamel—like the Carrot Soufflé on page 232—are more delicate, since there is nothing but the texture of the purée to hold the ingredients together. But even these are sufficiently sturdy to permit you to wait four hours before baking.

Whisks. A folding whisk has fewer wires than a beating whisk. The models we prefer are a 12-inch folding whisk with eight wires and a 14-inch beating (balloon or whipping) whisk with fifteen or more slightly thinner wires.

Approximate Weights, in Grams, of Pastry-Making Ingredients Per Unit of Volume (measuring tools are scant leveled)

	1 tablespoon (3 teaspoons)	½ cup (8 tablespoons)	1 cup (16 tablespoons)
Confectioners' sugar	7.5	60	120
Superfine sugar	12	100	200
Regular sugar	12	100	200
Cornstarch	10	80	160
All-purpose unbleached flour	9	70	140
Ricotta	12	100	200
Butter	14	115	225
Oil	12	100	200
Water	14	115	225
Rice	11	95	190
Unsweetened cocoa	5	40	80
Salt	17.5	140	280

Amounts of Salt, in Grams, Needed in Pastry-Making

	Per 1 Kilogram of Flour	Per 2 Pounds of Flour
Unsweet dough	20	18 (1 tablespoon)
Sweet dough	10	9 (½ tablespoon)

Weights of Eggs (extra large) and Components

	Grams	Spoons
1 egg	60-65	approximately 3 tablespoons
Yolk of 1 egg	20	approximately 1 tablespoon
White of 1 egg	35	approximately 2 tablespoons
Shell	10	

CATS' TONGUES
Langues de Chats

Yield: 100 small cookies

Butter

Flour

7 tablespoons butter, at room temperature

¾ cup confectioners' sugar

2 eggs, lightly beaten

1 cup less 2 tablespoons all-purpose flour

Special equipment

Pastry bag with a #3 round pastry tip

Preheat oven to 400°. Butter 2 baking sheets and sprinkle them lightly with flour. Shake out any excess flour.

Beat the butter and sugar together vigorously with a wooden spatula for 2 minutes, or until well blended. Add a quarter of the beaten eggs and beat until the mixture cleans the sides of the bowl. Add the remaining eggs in three batches, beating after each addition until the mixture cleans the sides of the bowl. Sift the flour over the dough and mix it in until it is just blended. Do not over-mix.

Fill the pastry bag and pipe the batter onto the prepared sheets in 4-inch diagonal strips 1 inch apart.

Bake for 10 minutes, or until brown around the edges and still pale in the center. Transfer the cookies to a rack to cool.

Notes

The cookies will keep for 10 days in an airtight container.

ORANGE TILES
Tuiles à l'Orange

Yield: 60 to 70 small cookies

   Butter
 2 egg whites
 ¾ cup confectioners' sugar
 ½ cup blanched and flaked almonds
 ¼ cup finely chopped candied orange zest
 ½ teaspoon grated orange or lemon zest
 ⅓ cup all-purpose flour
 2 tablespoons butter, melted but not hot
 3 tablespoons heavy cream

Special equipment
   Foil-covered broomstick or other 1½-inch tube

Preheat oven to 400°. Butter 2 cookie sheets.

   Use a whisk to break up the egg whites and mix in the sugar. Add the almonds, flour, candied and grated orange zest, cream, and butter. Mix until well blended.

   Drop batter by scant teaspoons 2 inches apart onto the prepared cookie sheets. Flatten each cookie with the tines of a fork dipped in cold water. Bake for 10 minutes, or until brown around the edges.

   Remove cookies carefully from the sheets, sliding them off with a long spatula. Immediately shape the cookies around the broomstick to give them the shape of roofing tiles. (Work quickly as they harden fast.)

Notes
   The cookies will keep for 10 days in an airtight container.
   These cookies are so thin and delicious, one can easily eat 30 at a time. If desired, make them larger, or make 10 very big ones, bend up the edges to make bowls, and serve ice cream in them.

CIGARETTES

Yield: 70 small cookies

> 7 tablespoons butter, at room temperature, plus butter for the baking sheets
> 1 cup confectioners' sugar
> 1 teaspoon vanilla extract
> 3 egg whites
> ½ cup all-purpose flour

Special equipment

Pastry bag with ¼-inch round tip; 8-inch wooden dowel, approximately 1 inch in diameter, or a wooden spoon with a long handle

Preheat the oven to 400°. Butter 2 14- by 17-inch baking sheets.

Blend the 7 tablespoons butter and sugar thoroughly, stirring with a whisk for 1 minute. Add the vanilla and the egg whites one at a time, beating well after each addition. (The whites must be thoroughly incorporated each time.)

Sift the flour over the top of the mixture and stir with a whisk until just blended. Do not overmix.

Fill the pastry bag and pipe little dollops of the mixture 2½ inches apart onto the prepared baking sheets. Each dollop should be about 1 inch wide (the size of a quarter) and ½ inch high. As soon as the sheet is filled, raise it to a height of about 5 inches and drop it onto a counter to settle and flatten the cookies. Make sure the sheet is not tilted or askew.

Bake the cookies for 10 minutes, or until light brown around the edges and pale in the center.

Remove the baking sheets from the oven immediately. Put them on top of the stove so they will stay as hot as possible to keep the cookies flexible.

Remove 1 cookie with a long, flexible metal spatula to a scrap of parchment. Lift one edge and begin to roll the cookie around the dowel or wooden spoon handle. Roll up completely without pressure, pressing down gently at the end to seal the cookie. Slide the cookie off the dowel onto a rack to cool. This process will become easier with practice. Repeat with the remaining cookies.

(continued)

Notes

The cookies will take any shape a cook's imagination and dexterity wants to give them. One good shape is little horns that, when cool can be filled with berries or whipped cream to serve with coffee. To form horns, pick up each warm cookie and bring two edges together to form a cone shape. Slide this little cone into a large pastry bag tip and immediately drop a second tip into the first to enclose the cookie. Allow to cool this way for 1 to 2 minutes. Then carefully pull apart and remove pastry tips.

Instead of little cookies, bake big ones by piping larger circles onto the baking sheet. In this case, the dollops should be about 2 inches wide by ¾ inches high or 1 heaping teaspoon. Spread with a spatula into a circle with a diameter of 5 inches. Only 3 large cookies should be baked on 1 sheet. Bake until light brown around the edges and immediately remove and mold over the round bottom of a small bowl, such as a custard cup. Carefully put another bowl over the cookie to shape and cool for 1 to 2 minutes. When cool these can be filled with ice cream, berries, or both.

MERINGUE
Meringue Ordinaire

Yield: 78 small meringue mushrooms, *or*
           40 3- x 1½-inch plain oval meringue cookies, *or*
           40 3- x 1½-inch oval meringue spirals

    Butter
    Flour
  4 egg whites
1¼ cup sugar
1½ ozs. unsweetened cocoa (optional)
    Confectioners' sugar

Special equipment
    Large pastry bag with #5 round tip, #6 round tip, and star tip

Preheat oven to 200°. Lightly butter and flour 2 baking sheets and shake out any excess flour.

Put the egg whites in a stainless steel bowl and beat until they start to hold soft peaks. Add 1½ teaspoons sugar and beat until the whites stand firmer. Gradually beat in half the remaining sugar, beating until the whites are glossy and very stiff. Then fold in the rest of the sugar and the cocoa.

To shape meringue mushrooms

Put the meringue in a pastry bag fitted with a #5 round tip. Pipe little domes, 1 inch in diameter and ½ inch tall, onto 1 baking sheet. Make the stems on the other baking sheet by piping a thick base 1 inch tall and pulling the bag straight up and releasing the pressure at the same time.

To shape meringue cookies

Put meringue in a pastry bag fitted with a #6 round tip. Pipe onto the baking sheets in long ovals 3 inches long and 1½ inches wide by drawing the tube along the pan. Space the ovals 1 inch apart.

To shape meringue spirals

Put the meringue in a pastry bag fitted with a star tip. Pipe spiral corkscrew shapes 3 inches long and 1½ inches wide onto the baking sheets, overlapping the spirals a bit. Space the spirals 1 inch apart.

To bake the meringues

Dampen a finger in cold water. Blot the points of the meringues lightly to flatten them. Sift a light coating of confectioners' sugar over the meringues and bake for 1½ to 2 hours, or until they are crisp and firm. Do not let them color. Transfer the meringues to a rack to cool.

To assemble meringue mushrooms

The moment the mushrooms start to crust and can be held, gently stick each dome on top of a stem and continue to bake.

Notes

Meringue mushrooms, cookies, and spirals will keep for 4 weeks in an airtight container.

LADYFINGERS
Biscuits à la Cuillère

Yield: 50 cookies

Butter
Flour
4 eggs, separated
½ cup sugar
½ teaspoon vanilla extract, or 1 teaspoon grated zest of lemon
   or orange
Salt
⅔ cup plus 1 tablespoon all-purpose flour, sifted
Confectioners' sugar

Special equipment
Pastry bag and large round #9 tip

Preheat oven to 400°. Butter 2 baking sheets and sprinkle them lightly with flour. Shake out any excess flour.

Beat the egg yolks and half the sugar with an electric mixer on high speed for 4 minutes, or until very thick and pale. Beat in the vanilla.

Beat the egg whites with the remaining sugar and a pinch of salt until they hold stiff, shiny peaks when the beaters are lifted.

Sift all of the flour over the yolk mixture. Spoon one quarter of the egg whites on top and fold in roughly. Add the rest of the egg whites and fold in until just blended, about 30 strokes.

Spoon the batter into a pastry bag and pipe it onto the prepared baking sheets in diagonal 5-inch strips 1½ inches apart. Sift a light coating of confectioners' sugar over the top. Just before baking, sift a heavy coating of confectioners' sugar over the tops again. Tap the baking sheets lightly and turn them over so all excess sugar falls off (the cookies will not fall off). Put the cookies in the oven, lower the oven temperature to 375°, and bake for 12 to 14 minutes, or until firm. Transfer to racks to cool.

Notes

If it is necessary to bake the cookies in 2 batches, cut parchment paper to fit the baking sheets and pipe the cookies onto the paper. Remove the first batch of cookies, slide the parchment paper with the second batch of cookies onto the baking sheet, and bake.

Sifting the confectioners' sugar over the ladyfingers gives them a little crust.

For chocolate ladyfingers, substitute 2 tablespoons unsweetened cocoa for 1 tablespoon flour.

Ladyfingers keep for 2 weeks in an airtight container.

PAIN DE GÊNES

Serves: 6 to 8

Butter
Flour
4 tablespoons cornstarch
½ teaspoon double-acting baking powder
5½ ounces blanched almonds
¾ cup sugar
4 eggs
¼ teaspoon almond extract
5½ tablespoons butter, melted and cooled

Special equipment
8-inch round cake pan, 1½ inches deep

Preheat oven to 375°. Butter the pan and line the bottom with parchment paper cut to fit. Butter the paper, dust with flour, and shake out any excess flour.

Sift the cornstarch and baking powder onto a piece of wax paper.

Put the almonds and sugar into the container of a food processor and blend until pastelike.

Separate 1 egg, reserve the yolk, and add the egg white and

the almond extract to the almond-sugar mixture. Blend until the mixture gathers together in a mass. Transfer to a bowl, add the reserved yolk and 1 whole egg and mix thoroughly with a wooden spatula. Add a third egg and beat at high speed with an electric mixer for 1 minute. Add the fourth egg and beat for 7 to 8 minutes, or until the mixture becomes thick and glossy and has doubled in volume.

Sprinkle the cornstarch-baking powder mixture over the dough and fold in roughly 5 times. Pour the melted butter over the surface and fold in 15 to 20 times, or until combined.

Pour the batter into the prepared pan. Move the batter slightly up the sides of the pan with a rubber spatula to prevent swelling in the center of the cake.

Lower the oven temperature to 350° and bake for 35 to 40 minutes, or until a thin blade or skewer inserted in the center of the cake comes out clean.

Unmold onto a rack and invert immediately onto a parchment-lined rack so that the top of the cake will remain flat and even and will not stick to the rack. Let cool.

Notes

It is traditional not to remove the paper until serving the cake, as the paper keeps the cake from drying out.

This cake keeps well for 2 to 4 days if it is wrapped tightly in foil.

ALMOND SPONGE CAKE
Biscuit de Savoie aux Amandes

Serves: 8 to 12

- ¼ lb. butter, at room temperature (if chilled, cut into small pieces first)
- ¾ cup plus 2 tablespoons sugar
- 6 eggs
- 1 egg yolk
- ½ cup all-purpose flour
- ½ cup cornstarch

½ teaspoon double-acting baking powder
Grated zest of 1 orange and 1 lemon
2 tablespoons orange juice
½ teaspoon vanilla extract
½ cup powdered almonds
½ cup slivered almonds
1 tablespoon confectioners' sugar

Special equipment
2 5-cup cake pans or brioche molds

Preheat oven to 375°.

Melt the butter in a small heavy saucepan over low heat. Using a pastry brush, spread melted butter over the inside of the cake pans. Invert and let the butter dry. Reserve the remaining melted butter. Roll 1 tablespoon of sugar around each pan to coat the inside entirely. Shake out any excess sugar.

Separate the eggs and put all of the yolks in the bowl of a mixer and the whites in a separate bowl.

Put the flour, cornstarch, and baking powder into a sieve or sifter on a piece of wax paper.

Mix the egg yolks with an electric mixer. Beat while gradually adding half the sugar. Add the citrus zests, orange juice, vanilla, and powdered almonds and beat until the mixture is a pale yellow, 5 to 6 minutes at high speed (see p. 268).

Beat the egg whites with the remaining sugar until they hold stiff, shiny peaks when the beater is lifted.

Sift the flour mixture over the yolk mixture and fold in, making 5 to 7 strokes. Add one third of the egg whites and fold them in roughly with 3 to 4 strokes. Fold in the remaining egg whites with a few strokes. Dribble the remaining butter on the surface of this mixture and fold just until all ingredients are blended. Do not overblend.

Pour the cake mixture into the prepared pans equally. The pans should be two thirds full. Smooth the top of the cake mixture with a plastic pastry scraper, pushing toward the center to form a slight dome shape. Sprinkle slivered almonds on top and sift confectioners' sugar over the almonds.

Put the cakes in the center of the oven, lower the oven temperature to 350°, and bake for 30 to 35 minutes, or until a skewer inserted in the center comes out clean.

Let the cakes stand for 2 minutes in the pans. Invert the cakes onto racks and put them back into the pans upside down. Let cool and invert to serve.

Notes

This cake is delicious plain, served lukewarm or cold, or served with ice cream, Crème Chantilly (see p. 328), or fruit salad. It will keep refrigerated for 2 to 3 days, wrapped well, or it can be frozen.

GÉNOISE

Serves: 8

Génoise Souple
 Butter
 Flour
3 tablespoons butter
1 cup less 2 tablespoons all-purpose flour
3 eggs
2 egg yolks
⅔ cup sugar
 Vanilla, or the grated zest of 1 orange or 1 lemon (optional)

Chocolate Génoise Souple
 Butter
 Flour
4 tablespoons butter
⅔ cup all-purpose flour
6 tablespoons unsweetened cocoa
½ teaspoon double-acting baking powder
3 eggs
2 egg yolks
¾ cup sugar

Special equipment
 8-inch round cake pan, 1½ inches deep

Preheat oven to 375°. Butter and flour the cake pan and shake out any excess flour.

Melt the butter in a small saucepan and let it cool to a little warmer than room temperature. Sift the flour with the baking powder (and cocoa, if using) onto a piece of wax paper.

Put the eggs, yolks, sugar (and vanilla, if using) in a large bowl. Beat at high speed, circulating the beaters all over the bowl, touching the sides and bottom, for exactly 8 minutes. The mixture will triple in volume and the surface will be glossy and smooth with no trace of bubbles and have a creamy mayonnaise-like consistency. When the beaters are lifted, the last drops will cling to them.

Sift the flour over the surface and fold it in 10 times with a wooden spatula. Pour the butter over the entire surface and fold it in about 20 times, or until combined. Do not overfold or the Génoise will deflate.

Immediately pour the batter into the prepared pan. Smooth the top with a plastic pastry scraper, mounding the batter a little higher around the edge (and away from the center). Bake for 20 minutes, or until a thin skewer inserted in the center comes out clean.

Line a rack with parchment paper. Unmold the cake onto a rack and invert immediately onto the parchment-lined rack so that the top of the cake will remain flat. (The parchment will prevent the cake from sticking to the rack.) Let the cake cool completely.

Notes

Do not let the eggs stand with the sugar in the bowl. The sugar will "burn" the yolks, hardening them and making them impossible to beat properly.

Génoise will keep for 2 to 3 days in the refrigerator if it is well wrapped in foil, or it can be frozen.

QUEEN OF SHEBA
Reine de Saba

Serves: 8 to 12

 Butter
 Flour
 4½ oz. semisweet chocolate, broken into small pieces
   (semisweet morsels are excellent)
 3 tablespoons water
 ⅓ cup all-purpose flour
 ½ teaspoon double-acting baking powder
 ¼ lb. butter, at room temperature
 ⅔ cup sugar
 4 eggs, separated
 1 teaspoon vanilla extract
 4½ oz. ground blanched almonds (about ¾ cup)
   Ganache filling and icing (see p. 330)
   Chocolate curls

Special equipment
 9-inch round cake pan, 1½ inches deep

Preheat oven to 375°.

Butter the cake pan, line the bottom with parchment paper, and butter the paper. Flour the pan and shake out any excess.

Sift flour and baking powder onto a piece of wax paper.

Put the chocolate and water in a small bowl. Set the bowl in a pan of hot water (the water should not be too hot or the chocolate will dry out) and cover. When the chocolate is melted, stir until smooth, remove the bowl from the larger pan, and let the chocolate cool almost completely.

Put the butter and half the sugar into a large bowl and mix thoroughly with an electric mixer. Add 2 egg yolks and mix thoroughly. Add the remaining egg yolks and vanilla and mix thoroughly. Beat on high speed, circulating the beater all over the bowl, for exactly 5 minutes, or until the mixture is fluffy. Fold in the almonds.

Beat the egg whites in a mixing bowl with the remaining

sugar until the whites hold stiff peaks when the beater is lifted (see p. 270).

Add the cooled chocolate to the yolk mixture, sprinkle flour over the surface, and fold in with a spatula. Gently fold in the beaten egg whites until mixed. Do not overmix.

Pour the batter into the prepared pan and spread the batter slightly up the sides of the pan to prevent swelling in the center of the cake. Lower the oven temperature to 350° and bake for 35 to 40 minutes, or until a skewer inserted in the center of the cake comes out clean. Unmold onto a rack and invert immediately onto a parchment-lined rack so the top of the cake remains flat. Let cool.

Prepare the ganache and reserve one third of it in its melted stage for the glaçage. Let cool, but do not refrigerate. Prepare remaining ganache for filling as directed.

Cut a circle of cardboard ¼ inch smaller than the diameter of the cake. Put the cake on it and peel off the paper.

Cut the cake into 3 horizontal layers. Using a long, metal spatula, spread the bottom layer evenly with half the remaining ganache filling. Top with the second layer and spread it with the rest of the ganache; top with third layer.

Chill for at least 30 minutes. Remove from refrigerator and put cake on a rack over a plate.

☆Pour ganache glaçage slowly over the cake, using a long, metal spatula to coat the top and sides with a thin layer. Transfer the cake to a serving platter. □Garnish with chocolate curls and refrigerate. Remove the cake from the refrigerator at least 20 minutes before serving.

Light variation

☆Ice the cake as one layer with half a recipe of ganache.
□Omit the chocolate curls.

Notes

If ganache glaçage hardens before being used, put the glaçage in a larger pan of warm water for a few seconds and stir slightly (overstirred glaçage loses its sheen). Any leftover ganache glaçage may be thinned with 1 to 2 tablespoons heavy cream, water, or Cointreau and served as a sauce with the cake.

CHRISTMAS LOG
Bûche de Noël

Serves: 8 to 10

Génoise Souple
    3½ oz. all-purpose flour (⅔ cup)
    3½ oz. sugar (½ cup)
    2 whole eggs
    2 egg yolks
    2½ tablespoons butter
        Ganache (see p. 330)

Sugar syrup
    ¼ cup confectioners' sugar mixed with ¼ cup water and ¼ cup
        rum, Cognac, or Grand Marnier or Cointreau
        Crème Chantilly (see p. 328)
    2 oz. fresh, unsalted pistachios, skinned and chopped coarsely
    10 to 15 meringue mushrooms (see p. 278)

Special equipment
    6-cup mold or bûche mold 18 inches x 3½ inches x 2 inches

Make the cake, following instructions for *Génoise Souple*. Assemble it on a plastic or wooden board or cookie sheet so it can be easily refrigerated once filled.

Cut 1-inch slices from the ends of the cake. Slice cake horizontally into thirds. With a 1-inch round cutter (such as wide end of pastry tube), make 4 or 5 rounds or "knots" from the end slices.

Divide chocolate filling into 2 parts, ½ for filling and ½ for frosting. Brush cut side of bottom cake slice with sugar syrup and spread with half the reserved filling. Brush a cut side of the second slice with the syrup and place syrup side down on top of the filling. Brush other side with syrup and spread with Crème Chantilly. Brush cut side of the top slice with syrup and put on top of filling. Brush slices one at a time to prevent their getting soggy.

Coat each "knot" with reserved frosting and spread the remaining frosting over the top and sides of the cake with a long metal spatula. Place knots on top and sides. With the back of a spoon, simulate the rough texture of tree bark by making strokes toward the knot.

Sprinkle the top and sides of the cake with the chopped pistachios to give the effect of moss. Refrigerate for 15 minutes. Place cake on a long wooden board or serving dish, using 2 long spatulas and sliding them lengthwise underneath the cake to help move it. Arrange the mushrooms at the sides and on top of the cake either in groups or singly. Chill cake until ready to serve.

Notes

Filled cake will keep for 2 to 3 days wrapped in foil and refrigerated.

CARAVEL WITH CHOCOLATE MOUSSE
Caravelle à la Mousse au Chocolat

Serves: 8 to 12

    Chocolate Génoise Souple (see p. 284)
4½ oz. semisweet chocolate, finely chopped (semisweet morsels are excellent)
  3 eggs, separated
  4 tablespoons butter, at room temperature
  1 tablespoon orange liqueur
  5 tablespoons sugar
4½ oz. semisweet chocolate, cut into ¼-inch pieces

Special equipment

Round 6-cup cake pan, 8 inches x 1½ inches

Have the Chocolate Génoise ready for filling and icing.

Put the chopped chocolate in a small bowl and set it over a larger pan filled with hot water. Cover and let the chocolate melt slowly. As soon as it has melted, remove from the hot water (it shouldn't be warm) and beat in the yolks and butter. Add the orange liqueur and beat the mixture until smooth.

Beat the egg whites with the sugar until they hold stiff, shiny peaks when the beater is lifted (see p. 270). Fold into the chocolate mixture and divide into two parts, half for the filling and half for the frosting.

Cut a circle of cardboard ¼ inch smaller than the diameter of the génoise. Cut the génoise horizontally into three layers. Put a few dabs of mousse on the cardboard circle to act as glue and put the bottom layer on the circle.

Spread the bottom layer of cake with half the chocolate filling using a long, flexible metal spatula. Put the second layer on top and spread with the remainder of the filling. Top with the third layer and spread the top and sides of the cake with the chocolate frosting. Refrigerate the cake briefly to let the frosting stiffen.

Cut a 12-inch circle of wax paper and cut another cardboard circle ¼ inch smaller than the diameter of the cake. ☆Melt the ¼-inch chocolate pieces in a small covered bowl, set in a larger pan of hot water. Using a flexible metal spatula, spread the melted chocolate into a rough circle on the wax paper, keeping an even thickness of $\frac{1}{16}$ inch.

When the chocolate has almost hardened, put the cardboard circle on top and trace the circumference with a sharp paring knife, cutting through the chocolate and paper. Cut the chocolate circle and paper into 8 to 12 equal wedges with a long knife. When they are completely firm (refrigerate the wedges to hasten this), carefully remove the wax paper.

Use the chocolate wedges to form a propeller design on the top of the cake. Do this by pushing one long edge of each chocolate triangle into the top of the cake (the tips should meet in the center). Be careful not to let the surface of the chocolate triangles touch the frosting, but cock the "blades" at a 45-degree angle to the top of the cake, overlapping each other a bit.

Roughly chop any leftover chocolate and press it onto the sides of the cake.

Light variation

☆Omit the chocolate garnish and finish the cake, instead, by arranging five halved almonds to overlap each other in the center of the top of the cake to form the petals of a flower. Refrigerate.

Notes

The cake will keep for 2 to 3 days in the refrigerator.

APRIL FOOL
Poisson d'Avril

Serves: 6 to 8

    Flour
    ⅔ of Puff Pastry recipe made with ½ lb. flour (see p. 337)
    1 egg, lightly beaten with small pinch of salt
    ½ Frangipane recipe (see p. 327)
    1 raisin

Special equipment
    Fish pattern about 15 inches x 5 inches, made from cardboard or heavy paper; plain pastry tube #6

Lightly flour a pastry board, give the puff pastry the last 2 turns, and refrigerate it for 20 minutes. Return the pastry to a lightly floured board and roll it out into a 11- x 16-inch rectangle. (This will give you enough pastry to cut out 2 fish patterns.) Use a wheel cutter to cut the first fish. If it is necessary to use a sharp knife instead of a wheel cutter, cut the pastry with short strokes so the dough does not tear or stretch. Brush a baking sheet lightly with water and transfer the pastry fish to it. Press the ends of the fish lightly with the fingertips so it adheres to the baking sheet and does not shrink. Cut out the second fish in the same manner.

    Mound Frangipane along the center of 1 fish. Paint a 1-inch-wide border of cold water around the edge of the fish, put the second fish on top, and press gently with the fingertips all around the Frangipane mound to seal it well and prevent its spilling out while baking. Then press lightly around the entire border.

    Make slanting shallow slashes with the back tip of a paring knife all around the edge to seal the two fish together, or press with the back of a fork. Refrigerate for 10 to 15 minutes.

    Preheat the oven to 425°. Paint the top of the fish with the egg glaze. Let dry for a few minutes and paint a second layer of glaze. Take extreme care not to let the glaze drip over the edges onto the baking sheet as this would prevent the dough from rising properly. Use the back tip of a paring knife to trace a line 1 inch in from the edge on both sides (back and belly) of the fish. Make slanting streaks on that border to represent the little bones. Do the same on the fish tail. Cut the mouth and outline the eye and head. Press in a raisin for the eye. Make scales using the narrow end of the pastry tube held almost parallel to the pastry, pressing it firmly and cutting through slightly all over the body in half-circles.

Bake the pastry for 20 minutes, lower the oven temperature to 375°, and bake for 15 to 20 minutes, or until puffed and golden brown.

Notes

This pastry is at its best when baked the same day as it is to be served.

STRAWBERRY CHANTILLY FEUILLETÉ
Feuilleté aux Fraises et Chantilly

Serves: 8–10

Puff Pastry made with ½ lb. flour (see p. 337)
Flour
½ recipe Red Currant Jelly Glaze (see p. 326)
1 to 2 pts. strawberries, washed and hulled
Crème Chantilly (see p. 328)
2 tablespoons confectioners' sugar

Special equipment
Pastry bag with medium star tip #5

Lightly flour a pastry board, give the puff pastry the last 2 turns, and refrigerate it for 20 minutes. Return the pastry to a lightly floured board and roll it out into a 14- x 18-inch rectangle, ⅛ inch thick. Use the rolling pin as a straight edge and trim the edges with a dough cutter or sharp knife. (Do not press the rolling pin into the dough.)

Brush a baking sheet lightly with water. Roll the dough gently over the rolling pin and transfer it to the baking sheet. Prick the

APRICOT TART
Tarte aux Abricots

Yield: 1 tart, 6 to 8 servings

½ of Puff Pastry recipe made with ½ lb. flour (see p. 337)
1½ lbs. ripe apricots, washed and halved, or 2 16-ounce cans unpeeled apricots in heavy syrup, drained
Apricot Glaze (see p. 325)
Sugar

Lightly flour pastry board, give the puff pastry the last 2 turns, and refrigerate for 20 minutes. Roll out the dough on a lightly floured board into a 7- x 18-inch rectangle ⅛ inch thick. Use the rolling pin as a straight edge and trim the edges with a dough cutter or sharp knife. Cut two ½-inch strips lengthwise from dough. Brush a baking sheet lightly with water. Roll dough gently over rolling pin and transfer to center of sheet. Brush a ½-inch border down each long side of the pastry with cold water. Put the 2 strips along each edge and press down lightly so they adhere to the pastry base.

Scallop the long sides of the tart using the dull edge of the tip of a paring knife. Prick the bottom of the tart all over with the tines of a fork so it will cook evenly. Refrigerate 20 minutes.

Preheat oven to 425°.

Arrange apricot halves cut side up on the pastry in crosswise rows of 2 or 3, depending on size. Sprinkle fresh apricots lightly with sugar. Overlap the rows a little as fruit will shrink during baking. Bake for 35 minutes in the upper part of the oven. Lower heat to 400° if pastry is browning too quickly. Slide carefully onto a rack using a long, thin metal spatula. Let cool.

Brush with Apricot Glaze just before serving.

Notes

Dampening the baking sheet slightly holds the dough down at the beginning of baking.

The tart is at its best on the day when it is baked.

Tart can also be made with sliced apples. Toss them with a little lemon juice after slicing to prevent discoloration, then sprinkle with a little sugar before baking.

Also you can roll the entire dough in a rectangle about 18 x 14 x ⅛-inches and make two tarts.

dough all over with a fork or a rolling dough pricker. Refrigeı
for 20 minutes, if possible. (The dough will bake more evenly if
allowed to rest, but it is not essential.)

Preheat oven to 425°.

Bake the pastry in the upper part of the oven for 20 t
minutes, or until it is crusty brown. (Lower the oven tempera
to 400° if the pastry is browning too quickly.) Slide pastry oı
rack and let it cool.

Use a sharp paring knife to cut the pastry lengthwise iı
neat, equal strips.

Slice the strawberries lengthwise into 3 pieces. Fill the ı
bag with Crème Chantilly.

Brush the center of the first pastry slice lightly with
leaving a ¾-inch border. Arrange half the sliced strawberı
overlapping rows in the center of the pastry. Brush the strawl
lightly with glaze and pipe a swirl of cream around the bord
not pipe too close to the edge of the pastry or the creaı
squeeze out while the Feuilleté is constructed.

Top with the second pastry strip, smooth side up. Pres
lightly. Repeat with glaze, strawberries, and cream. Top w
third strip, smooth side up, and sift confectioners' sugar o
top.

Slip 2 long spatulas underneath the Feuilleté and c
transfer it to a platter.

Notes

It is best to bake the pastry the same day it is to be seı
keep it in a dry spot. Fill it no more than 2 hours before se
that it does not get soggy.

To prepare a Mille-feuille with Pastry Cream, prepare
try, bake, and cut into strips as directed. Have ready 1
Pastry Cream (see p. 329). Spread half the Pastry Cream ı
the pastry strips. Do not spread too close to the edge or
will squeeze out when the other strips are pressed on top.
a second strip, smooth side up, spread remaining Pastry
that, and top with the third strip. Sift confectioners' sugз
top.

BANANA TART
Tarte aux Bananes

Yield: 1 tart, 6 to 8 servings

½ of Puff Pastry recipe made with ½ lb. flour (see p. 337)
Pastry Cream (see p. 329)
4 or 5 medium ripe bananas
Juice of 1 lemon
Apricot Glaze (see p. 325)

Lightly flour a pastry board, give the puff pastry the last 2 turns, and refrigerate for 20 minutes. Roll out the dough on a lightly floured board into a 18- x 7-inch rectangle ⅛ inch thick. Use the rolling pin as a straight edge and trim the edges with a dough cutter or sharp knife. Cut 2 ½-inch-wide strips lengthwise from the dough. Brush a baking sheet lightly with water. Roll dough over rolling pin and transfer to center of sheet. Brush a ½-inch border down each long side of the pastry with cold water. Put the 2 strips along each edge and press down lightly so they adhere to the pastry base.

Scallop the long sides of the tart using the dull edge of the tip of a paring knife. Prick the bottom of the tart all over with the tines of a fork so it will cook evenly. Refrigerate for at least 20 minutes.

Preheat oven to 425°.

Bake the shell in the upper part of the oven for 20 to 25 minutes. Lower heat to 400° if pastry is browning too quickly. Transfer shell carefully with a long thin metal spatula to a rack. Let cool completely.

Cut bananas into ⅜-inch slices and toss them with the lemon juice to prevent discoloration.

Spread the baked shell with a ⅜-inch layer of Pastry Cream and arrange bananas in neat rows on top. Brush with Apricot Glaze just before serving.

Notes

This tart is simply an assembly job. Use strawberries, raspberries, blueberries, or poached fruits such as pears or peaches (see p. 322) instead of bananas.

(continued)

Pastry Cream can be made 1 day in advance.

It is best if shell is baked the day tart is assembled and served. Assemble and glaze the tart as close to serving time as possible.

For a lighter tart, omit Pastry Cream. Glaze pastry shell, arrange the fruit, and glaze.

Also you can roll the entire dough in a rectangle about 18 x 14 x ⅛-inches and make two tarts.

UPSIDE-DOWN APPLE TART
Tarte Tatin

Serves: 6

 5 or 6 Golden Delicious apples
 ¼ lb. butter
 1 cup sugar
 2 tablespoons rum
 1 teaspoon vanilla extract
   Unsweetened Short Pastry (No. 1) (see p. 335)
   Whipped Cream, see p. 328 (optional)

Special equipment

8-inch round copper or enameled cast iron saucepan, 3 to 3½ inches high

Core, peel, and slice the apples into ⅜-inch-thick rings. Spread the butter over the bottom of the saucepan. Sprinkle the sugar over the butter and arrange the apple slices, standing on edge, in a circle around the sides of the saucepan. Keep them very close together. Put the ends of the apples in the middle of the apple circle.

Pour the rum and vanilla over the apples and cook over very low heat until the butter and sugar have melted. Bring to a boil over medium heat and boil slowly for 35 to 50 minutes, or until the syrup starts to caramelize lightly around the edge of the pan. Remove from heat and let cool for 5 minutes.

Preheat oven to 425°.

Lightly flour a pastry board and roll the pastry into a 10-inch circle ⅛ inch thick. Prick the pastry several times with a fork. Place the dough over the apples and crimp the edges into a 1-inch-high collar around the edge of the pan.

Bake the tart in the upper part of the oven for 20 to 25 minutes, or until the crust is golden brown. Invert the tart onto a serving dish and serve warm or cold with whipped cream, if desired.

Notes

The tart can be made 1 to 2 days in advance. Reheat lightly in a 325° oven, or eat cold.

LEMON TART WITH ALMONDS
Tarte au Citron aux Amandes

Serves: 6 to 8

Flour
Sweet Short Pastry (No. 2), made with 1 egg (see p. 335)
Dry rice or beans

Filling
3 eggs
Grated zest of 2 lemons
Juice of 2 lemons, strained (½ cup)
¾ cup sugar
¼ lb. butter, at room temperature
¾ cup blanched ground almonds
Poached Lemon Slices (see p. 324), optional

Special equipment
8- or 9-inch pie pan or quiche pan with removable bottom

Preheat oven to 400°.

Lightly flour a pastry board and roll the dough into a 13-inch circle ⅛ inch thick. Roll the pastry carefully over the rolling pin and transfer it to the pie pan. Put the dough into the pan by pressing it lightly with the fingers so it conforms to the shape of the pan. Press a ¼-inch collar of dough around the inside of the rim of the pan. Roll the rolling pin around the edges of the pan to cut off any excess dough. Push the dough collar above the edge of the pan and press a decorative edge with the fingers around the rim. Prick the dough with a fork, holding the fork at an angle, not straight up, so that the holes are on the diagonal. (If the holes go straight down through the dough, the filling could leak out.)

Line the shell with foil and fill it with rice or beans to hold the dough against the pan during baking. Bake for 10 minutes. Remove foil and weights and bake for 5 to 7 minutes. Leave shell in the pan if finishing the tart immediately. Unmold onto a rack if using the shell later. Replace the shell in the pan when ready to continue.

Lower oven temperature to 375°.

To make the filling, put the eggs in a saucepan and beat them with a whisk until they are foamy. Add the lemon zest, lemon juice, and sugar, and mix well.

Put the saucepan with the custard in a larger pan, pour 1 inch of water into the larger pan, and bring the water to just below a simmer over moderate heat, frothing the custard vigorously with a whisk. Reach all over the sides and bottom of the pan. Cook, whisking, until the custard has the consistency of mayonnaise and the foam disappears. Do not let the water in the larger pan boil, or the eggs will overheat and scramble. Remove from the heat, but leave the smaller saucepan in the larger pan. Beat in the butter, one tablespoon at a time, being sure that each piece is thoroughly incorporated before adding the next. Stir in the almonds.

Pour the custard into the pastry shell and bake for 20 minutes, or until the custard puffs a little and a skin has formed over the custard. Unmold onto a rack and cool. Decorate the top with Poached Lemon Slices (see p. 324), if desired.

Notes

The partially cooked pastry shell will keep for 1 to 2 days on a shelf in a dry spot. Cover with foil or paper before storing.

The tart can be completed several hours to 1 day in advance. The tart will keep in the refrigerator for 1 to 2 days.

PLUM, BLUEBERRY, OR CHERRY TART
Tarte aux Prunes, Myrtilles, ou Cerises

Serves: 6 to 8

  1¼ lbs. Italian plums, halved lengthwise and pitted, or 1½ pts. blueberries, or 1¼ lbs. sweet cherries, pitted
      Flour
      Sweet (No. 2) or Unsweet (No. 2) Short Pastry (see p. 335)
    ½ cup ground blanched almonds
    2 drops almond extract
      Red Currant Jelly Glaze (see p. 326), or Apricot Glaze (see p. 325)
      Confectioners' sugar (for blueberry tart only)
      Crème Chantilly (see p. 328), optional

Special equipment

9-inch pie pan with fluted sides and removable bottom, preferably black steel

Pick over fruits and wash and dry them.

Preheat oven to 400°.

Lightly flour a pastry board and roll the dough into a 13-inch circle ⅛ inch thick. Roll the dough carefully over the rolling pin and transfer it to the pie pan. Put the dough into the pan by pressing it lightly with the fingers to make it conform to the shape of the pan. Press a ¼-inch-wide collar of dough around the inside of the rim. Roll the rolling pin over the edges of the pan to cut off any excess dough. Push the dough collar above the edge of the pan and press a decorative edge with the fingers around the rim. Hold a fork at an angle and prick the dough all over.

Line the shell with foil and fill it with rice or beans to hold the dough against the pan during baking. Bake for 10 minutes if using the sweet dough or for 15 minutes if using the unsweet. Remove foil and weights.

While the shell is baking, gather the leftover scraps of dough and roll them into a circle ⅛ inch thick, or a square. Roll the dough over the rolling pin and transfer it to a baking sheet. Bake for 10 to 15 minutes, or until golden brown.

(continued)

Leave shell in the pan if finishing the tart immediately. Unmold onto a rack if using it later. Replace the shell in the pan when ready to continue.

Use a blender or food processor to grind the pastry circle or square into a powder. Measure ½ cup of the pastry powder and combine it in a bowl with the ground almonds. Add the almond extract and mix well. Sprinkle a ⅛-inch-thick layer of the mixture in the bottom of the baked shell and arrange the fruit on top. Make circles of the plums, skin side down, overlapping each half a little and working from the outer edge to the center. Reserve 1 cup of the blueberries and put the rest, in an even layer, into the shell. Place the cherries as close together as possible in the shell.

Bake the tart in the middle of the oven for 15 minutes, or until just before the fruits release their juice. Remove from the oven, unmold onto a rack, and let cool.

When ready to serve the blueberry tart, brush top with glaze, top with reserved blueberries, and sprinkle confectioners' sugar on top.

Brush plum or cherry tart with glaze just before serving. Serve with dollops of Crème Chantilly, if desired, or pipe a swirl of it around the edge of the tart with a pastry bag.

Notes

The almond pastry mixture absorbs the juices from the fruits and prevents the crust from becoming soggy. There is enough for three 9-inch tarts. Leftovers keep for 1 to 2 months in a sealed jar in the refrigerator.

Partially cooked pastry shell will keep for 1 to 2 days in a dry spot covered with foil or paper.

The tart should be served the day it is prepared to avoid sogginess.

CRÊPES

Yield: 20 5-inch crêpes

Plain crêpes
- 1 cup all-purpose flour
- ½ teaspoon salt
- 2 eggs
- 1 egg yolk
- About 1⅓ cups milk
- 2 tablespoons butter, melted and cooled to room temperature

Sweet crêpes
- 1 cup all-purpose flour
- ⅛ teaspoon salt
- 1 teaspoon sugar
- 2 eggs
- 1 egg yolk
- 1⅓ cups milk
- ½ teaspoon vanilla extract
- 2 tablespoons butter, melted and cooled to room temperature

Special equipment
- 5-inch crêpe pan

Put flour, salt, and sugar (if using it) in a bowl and mix roughly. Make a well in the center and add the eggs and yolk. Use a whisk to break the eggs up a little. Gradually pour 1 cup of the milk on top of the eggs, whisking as you pour. Whisk to incorporate the flour from the inside edges of the well, a little at a time, until all the flour is incorporated and the batter is very smooth. (Crêpe batter should have the consistency of heavy cream. Add more milk to thin the batter to the correct consistency.) Strain through a fine sieve, if necessary, and stir in the vanilla (if using it) and the melted butter.

"Bandage" a fork for buttering the pan by rolling a quadruple thickness of paper towel around a fork and tying it with thread.

Slowly heat the crêpe pan over moderate heat. When hot, dip the prepared fork in melted butter and run it lightly over the pan. Remove the pan from the heat and quickly ladle 2 tablespoons of batter into the pan. Tilt and swirl the pan so the batter flows and covers the bottom in an even layer. Put the pan over moderate heat and cook briefly, until the crêpe sets and has browned lightly. Flip the crêpe over or turn it with a spatula and cook briefly on the other side. Turn the crêpe out onto a plate. Continue in this manner until all the batter is used, stacking the crêpes on the plate as they are cooked. Butter the pan as necessary to prevent sticking. (Note: If you have 2 5-inch crêpe pans, you can use both pans and make the crêpes in much less time.)

Notes

If making crêpes in advance, interlayer with parchment paper, wrap in foil, and refrigerate. Crêpes freeze well, too, wrapped in this manner. Use the number specified in a recipe and then freeze the remainder.

If the crêpes are too thin, add 1 lightly beaten egg to the batter.

Good fillings for plain crêpes are Scallops and Vegetables in Cream Sauce (see p. 109), or Stuffed Mussels Sailor-style (see p. 104), or Sole Fillets with Seafood (see p. 86). Put a spoonful down the center of each crêpe, roll up, and arrange, seam side down, in a gratin dish. Sprinkle with grated Swiss cheese, if desired, drizzle with a little melted butter, and bake in a 325° oven for 15 minutes, or until heated through.

Sweet crêpes are delicious with a squeeze of lemon and a sprinkling of sugar, then rolled up and served on a hot platter. Sautéed Apples (see p. 322) or sliced pineapple are also good fillings.

CRÊPES WITH ORANGE SYRUP
Crêpes Suzette

Serves: 4 to 6

3 tablespoons sugar
3 tablespoons butter
Zest of ½ orange, cut into julienne strips
Juice of 2 oranges

Juice of ½ lemon
3 tablespoons Grand Marnier
12 sweet crêpes, 5 inches in diameter (see p. 301)
3 tablespoons Cognac

Special equipment
Chafing dish or large skillet, 10 to 11 inches in diameter

Spread the sugar in the chafing dish and cook over low heat until it starts to color lightly. Add the butter and stir rapidly with a wooden spoon, reaching all over the bottom of the pan. Stir until the sugar and butter are well blended and melted. Add the zests and juices, bring to a boil, and add the Grand Marnier.

Add a crêpe to the syrup in the pan. Turn the crêpe over with a spoon and fork, fold it in half, and in half again to form a wedge. Move it to the side of the pan and repeat the procedure with the remaining crêpes. Arrange the crêpes close to the center of the dish and reduce the liquid for 1 to 2 minutes, or until it is syrupy. Add the Cognac and ignite it. Be careful to keep your face and hair away from the flames. Spoon the syrup over the crêpes until the flames subside. Serve immediately.

THREE CHOCOLATE MOUSSES
Trois Mousses au Chocolats

Serves: 6 to 12

½ lb. semisweet chocolate, cut into small pieces (semisweet morsels are excellent)
5 eggs, separated
2 tablespoons orange liqueur
1 cup heavy cream
3 tablespoons sugar
Whipped Cream, see p. 328 (optional)
Grated chocolate (optional)

Place chocolate in a large bowl and set in a larger pan filled with hot water. Cover and let chocolate melt. Chocolate dries out and gets grainy if it is overheated. As soon as it has melted, remove from larger pan.

☆Beat in egg yolks and stir in liqueur. □Beat heavy cream over ice and water until thick enough to cling to the whisk. Fold into the chocolate mixture.

Beat egg whites with the sugar until they hold shiny, stiff peaks (see p. 270). Spoon whites over chocolate mixture and fold in gently. Beaten egg whites do not wait and will turn grainy if not incorporated into the mixture immediately.

Ladle mousse into individual serving dishes and chill for at least 1 hour. Garnish each dish with Whipped Cream or grated chocolate, if desired.

Light variation
  □Omit cream

Lighter variation
  ☆Omit 5 egg yolks as well as cup heavy cream. Fold beaten egg whites into melted cooled chocolate. (Chocolate should be melted with 5½ tablespoons water or 3½ tablespoons water and 2 tablespoons orange liqueur.)

Notes
  Light variation is already light since it relies on the chocolate for flavor and is made without adding cream. The lighter variation is an almost dietetic chocolate mousse. It is a very good way to use up leftover egg whites. Total calories (without whipped cream garnish) are about 158 calories per serving.

  The mousse may be prepared well in advance and kept refrigerated for 2 to 3 days in a covered dish.

SOUFFLÉED OMELET
Omelette Soufflé

Serves: 2 or 3

    Butter
3 eggs, separated
⅓ cup sugar
    Confectioners' sugar
½ pt. berries, such as blueberries, raspberries, or strawberries (optional)
3 tablespoons brandy (optional)

Special equipment
    Pastry bag with #6 star tip

Preheat oven to 400°. Butter an 8-inch baking dish.

Beat the egg yolks with half the sugar on high speed for 4 minutes, rotating the beater all over the bowl. Beat the egg whites in another bowl with the remaining sugar until stiff peaks form when the beaters are lifted (see p. 270). Beat the yolk mixture into the egg whites, using medium speed.

Fill the pastry bag with the mixture and pipe it into the dish in layers of overlapping shells. Leave an open space in the center if using the fruit. Sift confectioners' sugar lightly over the top and bake for 7 to 8 minutes. If not well colored, put the omelet under the broiler, 4 to 5 inches from the flame, for 1 minute.

If using blueberries (which are very good baked), fill the center with the berries and cook with the omelet. Or, fill the baked omelet with fruit.

Heat the brandy in a small saucepan, ignite it, and pour it over the omelet. (Be careful to keep your face and hair away from the flames.) Serve the omelet immediately.

To make the omelet in an ovenproof skillet, heat the skillet slowly, add 1½ teaspoons butter, and melt the butter. Add the omelet mixture and cook over moderate heat for 2 minutes. The mixture will begin to puff. Sprinkle the top with the blueberries, if desired, but do not add so many that the soufflé is weighted down. Bake in the oven for 3 to 4 minutes and put under the broiler, if necessary. Flame with the brandy immediately and unmold onto a plate, if desired.

Notes

The omelet must be baked immediately after mixing and served without delay. One minute of overbaking will make it dry and tough.

Other fruits, such as bananas, pears, apples, peaches, and apricots are delicious fillings. Slice them thinly and macerate them in 3 tablespoons Cointreau or Grand Marnier and 1 tablespoon sugar if the fruit is not very sweet. Allow about ⅓ pound of fruit.

STRAWBERRY BAVARIAN CREAM
Bavarois aux Fraises

Serves: 6

> 1½ envelopes unflavored gelatin
> ⅓ cup cold water
> 2½ pts. strawberries to make 2 cups purée
> ⅔ cup superfine sugar
> 3 tablespoons lemon juice
> 1 cup heavy cream, chilled
> Crème Chantilly (see p. 328), optional

Special equipment

> 6-cup round mold or cake pan, 1½ inches deep

Sprinkle the gelatin over the water in a small saucepan and let it soften.

Wash and hull the strawberries. Reserve 1 large berry and 5 to 6 small ones. Put the remaining strawberries through the fine disk of a food mill or purée them in a blender or food processor, and strain through a fine-mesh sieve into a bowl. ☆Add the sugar and lemon juice and stir until the sugar dissolves completely.

Put the gelatin over very low heat until it dissolves completely. Whisk the melted gelatin into the strawberry purée and set the mixture over a pan filled with a tray of ice cubes and ½ cup water. Stir about once a minute, reaching the bottom and sides of the bowl, so the mixture chills evenly and the sides do not set before the center. When the purée starts to thicken lightly, remove it from the ice.

□Beat the cream over ice and water until it clings to the whisk in soft peaks when lifted. Fold the cream rapidly into the purée with a whisk until it is completely blended. Work fast as the mixture sets quickly.

Rinse the mold with cold water and pour in the mixture. Refrigerate for 2 to 3 hours, or until firmly set.

To unmold, run the tip of a paring knife around the edge of the mold and dip the mold into warm water for 5 seconds. Tilt the mold so the cream slides around a bit. This lets some air in and releases the vacuum. Put a chilled platter on top of the mold and invert quickly. ✧Ice the top and sides of the Bavarian Cream evenly with Crème Chantilly. Arrange the reserved berries like a bouquet in the center.

Light variation

☆Stir only ⅓ cup sugar into the purée.

□In place of the heavy cream, use 3 egg whites and 1 cup ricotta, blended in a food processor. Beat the egg whites with the remaining ⅓ cup sugar until they are very stiff (see p. 270). Fold the processed ricotta rapidly into the purée. Scoop the beaten egg whites on top of the purée and fold them in rapidly and completely. Work fast as the mixture sets quickly.

✧Omit the Crème Chantilly and garnish the Bavarois with additional fresh strawberries.

Notes

The Bavarois can be made 1 day in advance, unmolded when set, covered, and refrigerated. Garnish no more than 1 to 2 hours before serving. The Bavarois should be unmolded before being refrigerated because if it is in a metal mold, the acid in the fruit can react with the metal and cause a metallic taste.

If the purée sets too much over the ice, hold the bowl over a heat source, such as the steam of a kettle or on top of a warm stove for a few seconds, beating to break up any lumps.

COFFEE BAVARIAN CREAM
Bavarois au Café

Serves: 6

1 envelope unflavored gelatin less a pinch
¼ cup water
3 egg yolks
⅓ cup sugar
1 cup milk
1 vanilla bean, or ½ teaspoon vanilla extract
1 cup heavy cream
1 tablespoon freeze-dried coffee dissolved in 1 tablespoon boiling water
Whole coffee beans (optional)
½ cup Crème Chantilly (see p. 328), optional

Special equipment
4-cup mold

☆Sprinkle gelatin over the water in a small saucepan and let soften.

▫Beat egg yolks in a bowl with a whisk and gradually beat in sugar until mixture is well combined, about 20 to 25 strokes.

Meanwhile, bring the milk to a boil with the vanilla bean, if using it. Remove, rinse, dry and save bean for another use. Beat ⅓ of the hot milk into the yolks in a thin, steady stream, then add all the rest at once. Return mixture immediately to the warm saucepan. Set over medium-low heat and stir constantly with a wooden spatula, making figure 8's and reaching all over the sides and bottom of the pan. Cook and stir until custard thickens. To tell if it is done: foam will have disappeared, custard will lightly coat a spoon, and it will register 175° F. on a candy thermometer. Do not cook beyond that point or custard will curdle. Remove from heat and immediately strain into a bowl.

✦Beat heavy cream over ice and water until cream clings to the whisk when lifted. Put the gelatin over very low heat until it dissolves completely. Whisk into egg yolk mixture, add coffee and vanilla extract (if using), and set over a pan filled with a tray of ice and ½ cup water. Stir until mixture starts to thicken. Remove from ice and rapidly fold in whipped cream with a folding whisk. Work fast as it sets quickly.

Rinse mold with cold water and pour in mixture. Chill for at least 2 to 3 hours or until firmly set. Run the tip of a paring knife around the edge of the mold and dip mold into warm water for 5 seconds. Tilt mold so cream slides around a bit. This lets some air in and releases the vacuum. Put a chilled platter on top of the mold and invert quickly. Garnish with coffee beans and pipe rosettes of ○Crème Chantilly over mold, if desired.

Light variation

☆Use 1 full envelope unflavored gelatin.

□Stir only ½ of sugar into yolks.

✦In place of cream, use 3 egg whites. Beat egg whites with remaining sugar until they hold stiff peaks (see p. 270). When custard starts to thicken, remove it from ice and rapidly fold in the egg whites with a folding whisk. Work fast as it gels quickly.

○Omit Crème Chantilly.

Notes

If custard curdles, froth custard violently. If custard sets too much over the ice, hold bowl over a heat source such as the steam of a kettle or top of warm range for a few seconds, beating to break up lumps.

Do not beat the whites too soon but synchronize it with the cooling of the custard. Neither of them can wait.

The Bavarian Cream can be made 1 day ahead, unmolded, and kept covered in the refrigerator. Garnish 2 to 3 hours before serving.

RICE BAVARIAN CREAM WITH STRAWBERRIES
Bavarois au Riz aux Fraises

Serves: 6

    Butter
    Superfine sugar
1 qt. water
⅓ cup plus 1 tablespoon long-grain rice
2 cups milk
1 vanilla bean, or 1 teaspoon vanilla extract
1 envelope unflavored gelatin
¼ cup cold water
⅔ cup sugar
3 egg yolks
1 cup heavy cream, chilled
1 pt. strawberries
    Strawberry and Raspberry Sauce (see p. 324)
    Crème Chantilly (see p. 328), optional

Special equipment
    4- to 5-cup ring mold or charlotte mold

Butter the mold lightly and sprinkle the inside of the mold with the superfine sugar, rolling the sugar around so that the bottom and sides of the mold are coated. Shake out and discard any excess sugar.

Bring the water to a boil, sprinkle in the rice, stir, and boil for 7 minutes. Drain.

Bring the milk to a boil with the vanilla bean in a heavy saucepan. Stir in the drained rice and bring back to a boil over moderate heat, stirring occasionally. Cover, lower the heat, and simmer for 35 minutes on top of the stove or in a 325° preheated oven. Remove vanilla bean, rinse, dry, and save for another use.

☆Sprinkle gelatin over ¼ cup cold water and let soften.

□Add sugar to the rice mixture, bring back to a boil over moderate heat, and simmer until the sugar is completely dissolved. Remove from the heat.

✧Mix egg yolks in a small bowl. Gradually stir one third cup of the rice mixture into the egg yolks. Then stir this mixture into the hot rice mixture. Bring back to a simmer, stirring, and remove from the heat. Add the gelatin and stir for 2 minutes, or until the gelatin has completely dissolved. (Stir in the vanilla extract now if using it.)

Transfer the rice mixture to a bowl and set it over ice and water to cool. Stir about once a minute, reaching the bottom and sides of the bowl so the custard cools evenly and the sides do not set before the center of the custard cools.

○Beat the cream over ice and water until the cream clings to the whisk with soft peaks. Remove slightly set custard from the ice and rapidly fold in the whipped cream with a whisk. Work fast as it sets quickly.

Pour the mixture into the prepared mold and chill for at least 2 hours, or until firmly set.

Run the tip of a paring knife around the edge of the mold and dip the mold into warm water for 5 seconds. Tilt the mold so the cream slides around a bit. This lets some air in and releases the vacuum. Put a chilled platter on top of the mold and invert quickly.

Garnish with the berries. Spoon some of the sauce over the berries and the remainder over the custard. Pipe swirls of Crème Chantilly onto the custard, if desired.

Light variation

☆Use 1½ envelopes of unflavored gelatin.

□Add half the sugar to the rice mixture, bring back to a boil over moderate heat, and simmer until the sugar is completely dissolved. Remove from the heat.

✦Omit egg yolk step. Add the gelatin to the rice and stir for 2 minutes, or until the gelatin has completely dissolved. (Stir in the vanilla extract now if using it.) Transfer the rice mixture to a bowl and set it over ice and water to cool. Stir about once a minute, reaching the bottom and sides of the bowl so the custard cools evenly and the sides do not set before the center of the custard cools.

○In place of the heavy cream, beat 3 egg whites with the remaining sugar until they hold stiff peaks. Spoon the beaten egg whites on top of the slightly set rice mixture and fold them in rapidly and completely. Work fast as it sets quickly. Continue according to the above recipe.

(continued)

Notes

The custard can be made 1 day in advance, unmolded, covered, and refrigerated.

The rice tends to harden in the refrigerator, so remove the dessert from the refrigerator 20 minutes before serving.

If the custard sets too much over the ice, hold the bowl over a heat source, such as the steam from a kettle or the top of a warm stove for a few seconds, beating to break up any lumps.

Rice Bavarian Cream can be garnished with many fruits, such as raspberries, sliced bananas, fresh ripe apricots, orange segments, blueberries, poached fruits, or a mixture of fruits.

PINEAPPLE ICE CREAM
Glace à l'Ananas

Serves: 8

The custard
>   2 egg yolks
>   ⅓ cup sugar
>   1 cup milk

The purée
>   1 4- to 5-lb. pineapple (enough to make 2 cups purée)
>   ½ cup superfine sugar

The cream
>   1 cup heavy cream
>   2 tablespoons confectioners' sugar
>   1 tray ice
>   ½ cup cold water

Beat the egg yolks in a bowl, gradually whisk in half the sugar, and beat until well combined, 20 to 25 strokes.

Bring the milk and remaining sugar to a boil and pour one quarter of the hot milk in a thin stream over the egg yolks, whisking vigorously. Pour the remaining milk into the eggs all at once and return the mixture to the warm saucepan. Cook over moderate heat until the custard thickens, stirring constantly with a wooden spoon, making figure eights and being sure the spoon touches all over the sides and bottom of the saucepan. (When the custard is done, the foam will have disappeared, the custard will lightly coat a spoon, and it will register 175° F. on a candy thermometer. Do not cook beyond this point or the custard will curdle.) Strain the custard into a mixing bowl to stop the cooking. Let cool and refrigerate.

If using the pineapple shell for a mold, cut a 1-inch-thick slice off the top of the pineapple, keeping on the leaves. Put the top in the freezer. Empty the pineapple of pulp, leaving a ½-inch-thick shell. Use a pineapple corer or a serrated knife and try not to cut through the bottom. Put the pulp and juice in a bowl and freeze the shell.

Put the pulp and juice in a blender or food processor and blend until smooth. Strain the purée through a fine sieve into a bowl, pressing with the back of a ladle to extract all juice. Add sugar and combine, stirring until the sugar is completely dissolved. Refrigerate, stirring occasionally.

Beat the cream and confectioners' sugar over ice and water until the cream clings to the beater when it is lifted. Combine the custard and cooled pineapple purée and fold in the whipped cream. Pour the mixture into the container of an ice-cream maker and freeze according to manufacturer's instructions (see p. 273). Pack into an ice-cream mold if using one.

When ready to serve, dip the mold into warm water and unmold onto a chilled platter. Or spoon the ice cream into the frozen pineapple shell, replace the top, and serve in a serving bowl full of ice.

Notes

If using an ice-cream maker which requires ice and salt, it is not necessary to use finely crushed ice and rock salt. Regular ice cubes chopped with an ice pick and kosher salt do a good job. A good proportion for salt and ice is 5 lbs. ice to 1 lb. salt.

STRAWBERRY ICE CREAM
Glace aux Fraises

Serves: 6

2 pts. strawberries to make 2 cups purée
¾ cup superfine sugar
2 tablespoons lemon juice
½ cup heavy cream
1 tray ice cubes
½ cup cold water

Put the strawberries in a metal salad basket or strainer. Dip the basket into very hot water for 3 seconds and remove immediately. Hull the berries and purée through the finest disk of a food mill or in a food processor. (Strain the purée through a fine sieve if using a food processor.) Add sugar to purée and stir occasionally until sugar is completely dissolved. Stir in lemon juice.

Pour cream into a small bowl and set the bowl into a larger bowl of ice and water. Tilt the smaller bowl so the cream gathers in one spot. Beat the cream with a whisk until it just begins to thicken and cling to the whisk. Fold the cream into the purée thoroughly.

Pour the mixture into the container of an ice-cream maker and freeze according to the manufacturer's instructions. When frozen, serve immediately or pack into a chilled mold or freezer container. When ready to serve, unmold, if necessary, and decorate with fresh berries and mint leaves.

Notes

Dipping the berries into hot water makes them shiny and dries them quickly.

LEMON SHERBET
Sorbet au Citron

Serves: 12

  2 cups sugar
3½ cups water
    Zest of 1 lemon
1⅓ cups lemon juice, strained
  1 or 2 egg whites, beaten until foamy
    Lemon shells (optional)
    Mint leaves (optional)

Combine sugar, water, and lemon zest in a saucepan and bring to a boil. Simmer for 3 minutes, strain, and let cool. Mix in lemon juice and egg whites, pour into the container of an ice-cream mixer, and freeze according to manufacturer's instructions. When frozen, pack into a chilled mold or freezer container.

For formal presentation, serve the sherbet in lemon cups. There are two ways to make these: 1. Cut the lemons in half, juice them without damaging the skin, and scoop out the pith with a spoon. Take a little slice off bottom so that they will stand up. Store the shells in the freezer. Or, 2. Cut a thin slice off one side of the lemons so they will not roll. Cut "hats" from the opposite side. Use a paring knife and then a spoon to remove all the pith. Store the shells and hats in the freezer. (Put the pith through a food mill to juice it.)

When ready to serve, mound the sherbet in the shells, replace the hats, if desired, and garnish with a mint leaf.

Notes

Serve sherbet as soon as it is frozen for maximum flavor. Homemade sherbet and ice cream will keep at least 1 week, but they lose their texture quickly.

COFFEE ICE CREAM BOMBE
Bombe au Café

Serves: 6 to 8

¾ cup sugar
¼ cup water
6 egg yolks
1½ tablespoons instant espresso coffee dissolved in
    1½ tablespoons boiling water, cooled
1 cup heavy cream
   Whole coffee beans (optional)

Special equipment
   4-cup mold

Bring sugar and water to a boil, stirring once or twice to make sure the sugar dissolves. Boil just to the softball stage, 238° on a candy thermometer. Be very careful it does not go beyond this stage; it would be better to stop at 236°.

Put the egg yolks in a large bowl and use the beater on low speed to break them up a little. Slowly pour in the hot syrup in a thin, steady stream, while beating on high speed. Make sure that the syrup goes into the eggs and not all over the edges of the bowl. Beat for 10 to 15 minutes, or until the mixture is completely cool, moving the beater all over the sides and bottom of the bowl. (The mixture will be light like a mousse and doubled in volume.) Add the espresso to taste. (The flavor should be strong since the cream has to be added and the flavor will be less intense when cold.)

Whip the cream to soft peaks over ice and water and fold into the yolk mixture. Pour into a 4-cup mold and freeze for 3 to 4 hours, or until hard. Unmold onto a chilled platter and decorate with coffee beans, if desired.

Notes

The bombe will keep several days in the freezer.

A delicious variation can be made by adding 4½ oz. of sweet chocolate, chopped and melted with 3 tablespoons of milk in a bowl over a pan of hot water. Cool just to lukewarm and add to the egg and sugar syrup just before mixture cools completely.

CHOCOLATE SOUFFLÉ
Soufflé au Chocolat

Serves: 6

1 tablespoon butter, at room temperature
1 cup heavy cream
5 oz. semisweet chocolate, finely chopped (semisweet chocolate morsels are an excellent substitute)
1 tablespoon unsweetened cocoa powder
2 tablespoons rum or orange-flavored liqueur
4 egg yolks
6 egg whites
5 tablespoons sugar
Crème Chantilly (see p. 328)

Special equipment

6-cup soufflé dish (with sides not higher than 3 inches), or 6 individual soufflé dishes

Preheat oven to 425°. Butter the bottom and sides of the soufflé dish.

☆Put the cream in a heavy saucepan and bring to a boil slowly. Remove the cream from the heat and add the chocolate, whisking the mixture until it is smooth. Then add the cocoa, stirring until the mixture is smooth. Add the rum and the egg yolks and mix well. Let the mixture cool to lukewarm.

Beat the egg whites with the sugar until they hold stiff, shiny peaks when the beater is lifted (see p. 270). Gently fold the chocolate mixture into the egg whites. Pour into the prepared dish and level the top of the mixture with a long metal spatula. Run your thumb or the end of a spoon handle around the edge of the dish to make a trough. Lower oven temperature to 400°.

Bake the soufflé in the middle of the oven for 20 minutes for the large dish and 10 minutes for the individual dishes. Serve at once with Crème Chantilly.

Light Variation

☆In place of cream, use 1 cup of milk and 1 tablespoon of cornstarch. Combine the cornstarch with 2 tablespoons milk in a saucepan. Add remaining milk and bring slowly to a boil, stirring. Remove from heat and add chocolate; then continue with the recipe.

Notes

The unbaked soufflé can wait for 1½ to 2 hours, covered, in the refrigerator.

MOCHA SOUFFLÉ
Soufflé au Moka

Serves: 6

   4 tablespoons butter, at room temperature
3½ oz. semisweet chocolate, chopped into ¼-inch pieces
   3 tablespoons strong coffee, or 1½ teaspoons instant coffee powder dissolved in 3 tablespoons boiling water
   1 cup milk
   3 tablespoons flour
   4 egg yolks
   ½ teaspoon vanilla extract
   5 egg whites
   ⅓ cup sugar
     Crème Chantilly (see p. 328)

Special equipment

6-cup soufflé dish or 6 individual soufflé dishes

Preheat oven to 425°. Spread 1 tablespoon of butter over the bottom and sides of the soufflé dish.

Put the chocolate in a small stainless steel bowl, add the coffee, and set the bowl over a larger pan filled with hot water. Cover and let the chocolate melt. As soon as it has melted, stir until smooth. Leave the chocolate over the hot water and continue with the recipe.

Put the milk in a saucepan and bring it to a boil over moderate heat.

Melt the remaining 3 tablespoons of butter in another saucepan over low heat. Whisk the flour into the melted butter and cook slowly, stirring, for 2 minutes, or until the butter and flour froth and bubble. The mixture should not brown. Remove from the heat and add the milk all at once, whisking vigorously. Bring to a boil over moderate heat, stirring, for 1 to 2 minutes. Remove from the heat and beat in the chocolate mixture until well blended. Beat in the egg yolks and vanilla, cover, and keep warm.

Beat the egg whites with the sugar until they hold stiff, shiny peaks (see p. 270). Transfer the chocolate mixture to a large bowl, spoon the egg whites on top, and gently fold the egg whites into the chocolate mixture. Scoop the mixture into the soufflé dish and level the top with a long metal spatula. Run your thumb or the end of a spoon handle around the edge of the dish to make a trough. Lower the oven temperature to 400°. Put the soufflé in the middle of the oven and bake for 25 minutes for the large dish and 10 minutes for the individual dishes. Serve at once with Crème Chantilly.

Notes

The soufflé can wait 1 day, covered, in the refrigerator.

CARAMEL CUSTARD
Crème Renversée au Caramel

Serves: 8 to 12

Caramel Coating (see p. 326)
1 qt. milk
⅔ cup sugar
1 vanilla bean, or 1½ teaspoons vanilla extract
6 whole eggs
4 egg yolks
Caramel Syrup (see p. 326), optional

Special equipment

6-cup charlotte mold or soufflé dish

Preheat oven to 325°. ☆Pour hot caramel into mold, tipping the mold in all directions to coat the sides and bottom evenly, until caramel stops running and has hardened.

(continued)

Bring the milk, half the sugar, and the vanilla bean to a boil in a saucepan, stirring occasionally. Remove the bean, rinse, dry, and save for another use.

▫Put the eggs and yolks into a bowl with the remaining sugar and beat for 2 minutes, or until well combined. Pour 1 cup of boiling milk in a thin stream into the eggs, stirring constantly. Add the remaining milk all at once. (Add the vanilla extract now if using it.)

Pour the custard into the prepared mold, put the mold into a larger pan, and pour 1 inch of boiling water around the mold. Bake for 1¼ hours, or until a thin skewer inserted in the center of the custard comes out clean. Do not let the water boil or the custard will not be smooth. Remove the mold from the oven and the water bath and let cool. Cover and refrigerate for at least 6 hours.

Run the tip of a paring knife around the edge of the mold. Tilt the mold so the custard slides around a bit. This lets some air in and releases the vacuum. Put a cold platter on top of the mold and invert quickly. ✧Serve with Caramel Syrup, if desired.

Light variation

☆Omit the Caramel Coating.

▫Omit the egg yolks, but be sure that the 6 eggs used are extra-large eggs.

✧Omit caramel syrup.

Notes

The custard will keep in the refrigerator for 2 to 3 days.

The custard can be baked without coating the mold with caramel, which makes the dessert much easier to prepare. Just before serving, pour a thin layer of Caramel Syrup on top of the custard and serve the rest in a sauceboat.

PEARS IN RED WINE
Poires au Vin Rouge

Serves: 9

3 cups dry red wine
1½ cups sugar
　Juice of 1 lemon or 1 orange
　Zest of ½ lemon or ½ orange
1 cinnamon stick
½ teaspoon ground ginger
4 whole cloves
⅛ teaspoon grated nutmeg
9 large, unblemished, and slightly underripe pears, peeled
　About 2 cups boiling water
⅓ cup Cognac

Put the wine, sugar, lemon juice, lemon zest, cinnamon, ginger, cloves, and nutmeg in an enameled saucepan large enough to hold the pears. Bring to a boil, stirring once or twice.

Drop the pears into the boiling syrup and add boiling water to barely cover the pears. (The pears float, so press down on them with a wooden spoon while adding the water so as not to add too much water.) Bring to a slow boil and cook slowly, uncovered, over low heat for 25 to 40 minutes, or until tender, depending on the ripeness of the pears. Turn the pears occasionally during the cooking. Remove the pears and strain the liquid. Remove and discard all solids.

Boil the liquid until it is reduced to a light syrup. Add the Cognac, cook for 1 minute, and add the pears. Let cool and refrigerate for 1 to 2 days to let the pears take on color.

Notes

Whole poached fruits are spectacular served in a pastry Timbale (see p. 342). Brush the pastry with Apricot Glaze (see p. 325) and spread with a layer of Crème Pâtissière (see p. 329), if desired.

SAUTÉED APPLES
Pommes au Beurre

Serves: 6

> 3 tablespoons butter
> 4-5 apples (such as Golden Delicious, or any firm apple), peeled, and cut into eighths
> 3 tablespoons sugar
> 3 tablespoons Calvados or apple jack (optional)

Melt the butter in a large, heavy skillet. Add the apples and cook over moderate heat for 4 to 5 minutes, turning the apples gently so they cook evenly and remain firm. ☆Sprinkle the sugar over the apples and cook for 5 to 6 minutes, tossing the apples gently until they turn a light golden. Pour the Calvados over the apples and ignite it. (Be careful to keep your face and hair away from the flames.)

Light variation

> ☆Use only 1 tablespoon of sugar to sprinkle over the apples.

Notes

> The apples are at their best when they are served warm and are especially good when served with pork.

> Using the Calvados changes the name of the recipe to Pommes à la Normande.

POACHED PEACHES
Pêches Pochées

Serves: 10

> 2 cups sugar
> 6 cups water
> 1 vanilla bean, or 1 tablespoon vanilla extract
> 20 firm, ripe, unpeeled peaches, about 2½ inches in diameter, or 10 large peaches
> ⅓ cup sugar
> 1 cup water

Wash and hull the fresh strawberries. Pick over the fresh raspberries and put them in a sieve. Sprinkle some cold running water over them to wash them. Drain on paper towels.

Force the strawberries and raspberries through the fine disk of a food mill or purée in a blender or food processor and strain through a fine-meshed sieve into a bowl. Add sugar or reserved syrup, liqueur, and lemon juice. Stir occasionally until sugar is dissolved.

Notes

Sauce will keep for 2 days in a covered jar in the refrigerator.

APRICOT GLAZE
Glaçage à l'Abricot

Yield: Enough for 2 9-inch tarts

    10 tablespoons (5 oz.) apricot jam
     1 to 2 tablespoons kirsch (optional)

Press the jam through a fine-meshed sieve with the back of a ladle. Stir in the kirsch and blend well.

Notes

This uncooked glaze is delicious but will liquefy rapidly when brushed on pastry or fruit too far in advance. Brush it over fruits just before serving.

RED CURRANT JELLY GLAZE
Glaçage à la Gelée de Groseilles Rouges

Yield:　Enough for 2 9-inch tarts

> 10 tablespoons (5 oz.) red currant jelly, at room temperature
> 2 tablespoons kirsch (optional)

Combine the jelly and kirsch in a small bowl. Mix with a whisk until smooth.

Notes

This uncooked glaze is delicious but will liquefy rapidly when brushed on pastry or fruit too far in advance. Brush it over fruits just before serving.

CARAMEL COATING AND CARAMEL SYRUP

Yield:　⅔ cup coating, or ¾ cup syrup

For the coating
> 3½ oz. sugar cubes
> 4 tablespoons cold water

For the syrup
> Caramel Coating, above
> 4 tablespoons water

To make the coating

Heat the sugar and water in a heavy saucepan over moderate heat, stirring once or twice without splashing the sugar on the sides of the pan. Stop stirring when the sugar has melted and the syrup starts to boil and turns clear. Boil undisturbed until the syrup turns a dark gold. Do not let it darken more or it will taste bitter. (To test the color, dip a teaspoon into the syrup. The small amount in the spoon will look dark amber, while the syrup in the pan will look much darker.)

Remove from the heat and add 1 teaspoon cold water (to make the caramel easier to swirl in the mold). Pour syrup into the mold immediately, or hold for caramel syrup.

To make syrup

Add water to caramel coating off the heat (it will splash and make a lot of noise). Boil and stir until caramel has dissolved.

Notes

Let syrup cool and refrigerate in a covered jar. Syrup will keep indefinitely.

ALMOND CREAM
Frangipane

Yield: 1⅓ cups

- 3 oz. blanched almonds
- 5½ tablespoons butter, at room temperature (if preparing by hand)
- 6 tablespoons sugar
- 1 egg
- 1 tablespoon all-purpose flour

Grind the almonds in a blender or food processor until they are a very fine powder. (Do not overgrind or the almonds will release their oil and become sticky.)

To make by hand, combine the butter and sugar, blending thoroughly with a whisk for 2 minutes. Add the almond powder and mix well. Add the egg, mix well, and blend in the flour thoroughly.

To prepare by machine, leave the powdered almonds in the blender or food processor. Cut the butter into ½-inch pieces and add to the almonds with the sugar. Blend for 3 to 4 seconds. Add the egg and flour and blend just until the mixture gathers into a ball.

(continued)

Notes

Frangipane freezes beautifully and will keep for 2 to 3 days in the refrigerator.

The Frangipane can be used in an apple or pear tart. Spread a thin layer of Frangipane over the puff pastry or short pastry in a tart mold. Top with 3 to 4 apples or pears which have been peeled, halved lengthwise, and cut into thin slices. (If the fruit is a little hard or not too ripe, steam the halves in butter, covered, for 5 minutes before slicing. If very hard, poach the halves in sugar syrup until tender (see p. 322), then drain, slice, and arrange in tart). Bake the tart in a 400° oven for 20 to 25 minutes.

WHIPPED CREAM
Crème Chantilly

Yield: 1½ cups

   1 tray ice cubes
   ½ cup cold water
   1 cup heavy cream, chilled
   2 tablespoons confectioners' sugar
   ¼ teaspoon vanilla extract

Combine the ice and water in a large bowl or pan. Pour the cream into a bowl which will fit into the bowl with the ice and water. Add the sugar and vanilla to the cream.

Tilt the top bowl so the cream gathers in one spot and whip only until the cream holds its shape enough to cling to the whisk in soft peaks when it is lifted.

Notes

If the cream is whipped over ice and water it will always whip properly.

Use 1 teaspoon powdered instant espresso coffee to make Coffee Whipped Cream. Or flavor the cream with 1 teaspoon sifted cocoa, 1 teaspoon (or to taste) Grand Marnier, or anisette, with or without vanilla, according to taste.

To prevent cream from separating when standing, beat in ½ teaspoon unflavored gelatin softened in 2 teaspoons water and melted in a hot *bain-marie*. It will keep the cream smooth and fluffy for 2 to 3 days refrigerated and covered.

PASTRY CREAM
Crème Pâtissière

Yield: 3½ cups

    3 tablespoons all-purpose flour
    3 tablespoons cornstarch
    ½ cup sugar
    2 cups milk
    3 egg yolks
    1 vanilla bean, or ½ teaspoon vanilla extract
       Confectioners' sugar or butter
    4 tablespoons butter, room temperature

Combine the flour, cornstarch, and sugar in a bowl. Add ⅓ cup milk and whisk until very smooth. ☆Whisk in the egg yolks.

Rinse a saucepan with cold water to prevent sticking and pour in the remaining milk. Add the vanilla bean and bring to a boil over moderate heat. Remove the vanilla bean, rinse, dry, and save for another use.

Add ⅓ cup hot milk in a thin stream to the yolk mixture, whisking constantly. Add the remaining hot milk all at once, while whisking. (Stir in the vanilla extract now if using it.)

Pour the custard into the saucepan and bring it to a boil over moderate heat, stirring constantly. As the cream approaches the boiling point, remove from the heat occasionally and whisk vigorously to break up any lumps that may form. Boil for 2 minutes, stirring, making sure the whisk touches all over the sides and bottom of the pan.

Remove the pan from the heat and transfer the cream to a bowl. To prevent a skin from forming, cover the entire surface of the cream with a light sifting of confectioners' sugar, or rub the surface with a piece of chilled butter held on the tip of a knife. Let cool to room temperature.

□Vigorously beat the butter into the pastry cream, one tablespoon at a time, until it is smoothly incorporated. Serve in dessert cups or use as suggested in other recipes.

Light variation

☆Use only 2 egg yolks to make the basic custard mixture.

□Use 2 tablespoons of heavy cream instead of the 4 tablespoons of softened butter.

Notes

The Pastry Cream can be stored in the refrigerator in a covered container for 2 to 3 days.

CHOCOLATE FILLING
Ganache

Yield: 2½ cups, or enough to fill and ice a 6-cup sponge cake

> 1 cup heavy cream
> 10½ oz. semisweet chocolate, cut into small pieces (semisweet morsels are excellent)
> 2 tablespoons Cognac, rum, or Cointreau

Bring the cream to a boil in a saucepan over moderate heat and boil for 1 to 2 minutes. Remove from heat.

Add the chocolate and stir with a wire whisk until the chocolate has melted and the mixture is smooth. Transfer the mixture to a stainless steel mixing bowl and let it cool. The mixture should remain liquid and fresh. Do not refrigerate or the chocolate will lose its sheen.

When the mixture is cool, beat it with an electric mixer, adding the Cognac after a few seconds. Beat for 7 to 10 minutes, or until the mixture has doubled in volume, changed color, and holds its shape when the beater is stopped and lifted.

To speed up the process, set the mixture in a bowl of ice

mixed with ½ cup cold water three to four times for 10 seconds each time. This step is necessary during hot weather.

Notes

Use the ganache as soon as it is ready.
The recipe can be doubled easily.

PUFF SHELLS
Pâte à Choux

Puff shells are the only kind of pastry made on the top of the stove. There are many methods for making them, but the cook who follows our recipe with care can be sure they will come out just right.

Yield: 20 puffs, 2 inches in diameter

1 cup water
6 tablespoons butter
½ teaspoon salt
1 cup all-purpose flour, sifted
4 eggs
1 egg, lightly beaten with a pinch of salt

Special equipment
Pastry bag fitted with a #6 round tip

Preheat oven to 400°. Butter and flour 1 baking sheet.
Bring the water to a boil in a saucepan with the butter and salt. Butter should be completely melted before water begins to steam and evaporate. If butter is chilled, cut it in pieces.
Remove from heat and add the flour all at once, beating rapidly with a whisk or spatula. Put pan back on medium high heat and beat with a wooden spoon for 5 to 7 seconds to dry the dough.
Beat 2 eggs together lightly and add to dough, beating with a wooden spoon or whisk until well incorporated and dough comes back to a smooth consistency. Beat the third egg lightly and add to

dough, beating until totally incorporated. Beat the fourth egg lightly and add half of it. Check consistency. When dough is lifted on spatula, it should fall off 4 or 5 seconds later. If it does not, add remaining egg.

Use a pastry scraper to transfer dough to the pastry bag. Pipe little mounds 1½ inches in diameter and ¾ inch high 1 inch apart onto the sheet. Brush tops lightly with egg glaze. Draw fork tines through glaze twice to make a cross.

Bake the puffs for 25 to 30 minutes or until golden. Turn off oven, leave the door slightly ajar, and let puffs dry in the oven for 5 minutes. Cool on a rack and fill them as desired.

Notes

Filled puffs will keep for several hours refrigerated. Puffs also freeze well, but freeze them empty.

The dough can also be piped into an eclair shape, 3½ x ¾ inches.

Occasionally an extra ½ egg or 1 teaspoon water is needed to get the correct consistency. It depends on how carefully flour is measured.

Puff shells are delicious filled with a vegetable purée such as carrot, broccoli, or spinach (see pp. 229, 231, 247) and used to garnish a roast meat or chicken. Or filled with the filling for Stuffed Green Crêpes (see p. 67), or with cold fish or shrimp combined with mayonnaise for a light lunch or first course.

For dessert puff, sprinkle a few slivered almonds on top of egg glaze before baking if desired. They can be filled with Crème Patissière (see p. 329), Coffee Whipped Cream (see p. 328), or fresh berries with Crème Chantilly.

SHORT PASTRY
Pâte Brisée

In making short pastry the crucial rule to remember is that the amount of butter or other fat must always be at least half the weight of the flour; otherwise the result will be too chewy. The ingredients are all mixed together at once, and the job can be done by hand, following our method, almost as fast as with a food processor.

It is essential to note a few rules before preparing pastry.

1. Always respect the proportions very carefully. Use a scale if available.

2. All ingredients should be very cold but not frozen. (Keep flour in the refrigerator.)

3. Work in the coolest area possible and on a cool surface. A piece of marble or plastic board that can be refrigerated is ideal but a cool counter of any type will suffice.

4. Using the whole egg makes a stronger dough. The dough with only egg yolks produces a finer, more fragile dough.

Unsweetened short pastry for timbales

Dough No. 1 is the finer of the two, and more fragile.

Yield: 1½ lbs. short pastry, enough for a 9-inch-in-diameter timbale with a cone-shaped lid.

No. 1
    7 to 8 tablespoons cold water
    ¾ teaspoon salt
    1 stick and 6 tablespoons unsalted butter, chilled
    2 egg yolks
    1¾ cups all-purpose flour
    ¾ cup plain cake flour

(continued)

No. 2

    5 to 6 tablespoons cold water
    ¾ teaspoon salt
    1 stick and 6 tablespoons unsalted butter, chilled
    1 whole egg, plus 1 egg yolk
    1¾ cups all-purpose flour
    ¾ cup plain cake flour

Sweetened short pastry for timbale

Yield: 1½ lbs. short pastry, enough for a 9-inch-in-diameter
          timbale with a cone-shaped lid.

    5 to 6 tablespoons cold water
    ⅛ teaspoon salt
    1 stick and 6 tablespoons butter, chilled
    2 egg yolks
    ½ cup confectioners' sugar
    1¾ cups all-purpose flour
    ¾ cup plain cake flour

Short pastry with sugar (Pâte brisée sucrée)

Dough No. 1 is a *pâte sablée*, similar in texture to a cookie dough,
very sandy. It is usually baked empty to contain fillings that don't
require baking. Dough No. 2, with its whole egg, is a sturdier
dough and better suited for moist fillings as it will not become
soggy.

Yield: 1 lb. short pastry, enough for a 9- to 10-inch quiche or pie
          pan or 15 tartlets, 3 inches in diameter.

No. 1

    3 to 4 tablespoons water
    Pinch of salt
    6 tablespoons confectioners' sugar
    ½ teaspoon vanilla exract, optional
    1 stick butter, chilled
    1 egg yolk

1 cup all-purpose flour
⅓ cup plain cake flour

No. 2

2 to 3 tablespoons water
Pinch of salt
6 tablespoons confectioners' sugar
½ teaspoon vanilla extract, optional
1 stick butter, chilled
1 whole egg
1 cup all-purpose flour
⅓ cup plain cake flour

Short pastry with whole egg and no sugar

Dough No. 1 is especially good for quiche because it can hold liquid without getting soggy, due to the use of hardy, all-purpose flour. Dough No. 2, partially made with cake flour, is finer and more fragile—better suited for tarts and less liquidy preparations.

Yield: 1 lb. short pastry, enough for a 9- to 10-inch quicke or pie pan or 15 tartlets, 3 inches in diameter.

No. 1

3 to 4 tablespoons cold water
½ teaspoon salt
1 stick butter, chilled
1 egg
1⅓ cups all-purpose flour

No. 2

3 to 4 tablespoons cold water
½ teaspoon salt
1 stick butter, chilled
1 egg
1 cup all-purpose flour
⅓ cup plain cake flour

Dough by hand

Put smaller amount of water in a bowl with the salt, sugar (if using it), butter, and egg or egg yolk. The butter must be cold but softened and malleable, cut in pieces to ease mixing. Make a fist and mix ingredients together roughly with the knuckles to bind all the ingredients. Add the flour and gather the dough together by making circles as a machine would do, with fingertips open and straight. If too dry, add remaining water by drops.

Complete the blending of ingredients by smearing the dough ball out and away from you on a lightly floured board, pushing bits of dough with the heel of your hand or, preferably, with a pastry scraper until all the dough has been worked. Gather dough up with the pastry scraper and repeat the process if necessary. There should be no trace of butter. Using a scraper keeps the pastry cooler than doing it by hand.

Dough by machine

Put butter, cut into 1-inch pieces, into beaker of a food processor. Blend with quick on/off turns 2 or 3 times until butter is softened, smooth, and malleable. Stop machine, add salt, sugar (if using it), smaller amount of water, and egg or egg yolk. Blend with on/off turns twice more. Stop machine and add flour. Blend until dough gathers on the blade. If too dry, add remaining water by drops, and blend with one or two on/off turns.

Gather the dough into a ball, wrap it in plastic wrap, and chill for ½ hour or overnight.

For timbale

Form the dough into 2 tight balls. Dough should weigh about 14 oz. for the bottom crust, the remainder for the lid.

PUFF PASTRY
Pâte Feuilletée

Yield: This recipe with 1½ cups or ½ lb. flour gives 1 lb. puff
pastry, enough for
2 17- by 7-inch tarts, or
1 April Fool's Cake (Poisson d'Avril), or
1 three-layered Mille-feuilles

Puff pastry, that most amazing and fascinating dough, with
its hundreds of layers of dough and butter, has such texture, such
saveur, an indescribable feel and taste in the mouth as it crumbles
and melts. It can be mastered if the time is taken to understand it.
Puff pastry is basically a preliminary pie dough that is then
wrapped around butter. The many layers are created by rolling and
folding the dough. A food processor speeds up the making of the
preliminary dough.

Before you begin
   It is essential to note a few rules before preparing the pastry:
   1. Always respect the proportions carefully. Use a scale if
available.
   2. All ingredients should be very cold, but not frozen. (Keep
flour in the refrigerator.)
   3. Work in the coolest area possible and on a cool surface. A
piece of marble or plastic board that can be refrigerated is ideal but
a cool counter of any type will suffice.
   4. When starting to work, the preliminary dough (détrempe)
and the butter pat should have the same temperature and consistency.
   5. There will be 6 "turns," done 2 at a time between 20-min-
ute refrigerated rests.
   6. If dough is to be refrigerated for a day or two or frozen, do
so after 4 turns. Wrap it airtight. Defrost in refrigerator for at least 7
hours. Dough may be too hard to roll straight from the refrigerator.
If it is too cold, it will crack so remove it 10 to 15 minutes before
rolling. It must be supple enough to roll easily and smoothly but
still cold. Do remaining 2 turns and let rest 20 minutes in refrigerator before shaping it.

7. Never allow the egg glaze that is brushed on top of pastry before baking to run over the edge and down the sides of the dough. This would seal the layers and prevent them from rising.

Puff pastry consists of equal parts flour and butter, about ½ part plus 10 percent of weight of flour of water, and 1 teaspoon salt per ½ lb. of flour.

Note

In this recipe 10 percent of the butter will be mixed with the détrempe. Doing this ensures a flakier feuilletage and less elasticity in détrempe. The détrempe will be rolled out into a circle and the butter worked into a square "pat."

Flour	Butter	Water	Salt
½ lb. (1½ cups) 225 grams	½ lb. (2 sticks) 225 grams 10% = 1½ tablespoons (22½ grams)	½ cup + 1½ tablespoons plus a few drops if necessary 130 grams	¾ teaspoon 4 grams
1 lb. flour (3¼ cups) 450 grams	1 lb. butter (4 sticks) 450 grams 10%=3 tablespoons	1 cup + 3 tablespoons + a few drops if necessary 260 grams	1½ teaspoons 8 grams

The détrempe by hand

Take 10 percent of the butter and soften it by using a quick pressing down and twisting motion with a rolling pin or the knuckles. Put the butter, in small pieces, the salt, and the water (reserving 2 tablespoons) in a bowl. Add the flour and work into a dough using the fingers open and stiff and making a circular motion. If dough is too dry, sprinkle remaining water on, a bit at a time, just until the dough holds together in a mass and the dough cleans the sides of the bowl.

Make sure butter is well incorporated. A good trick for doing this is to use a pastry scraper and cut it straight down into the dough, quickly making crisscrosses. Lightly flour a board and form dough into a ball. Wrap in plastic wrap and chill for 10 minutes.

The détrempe in a food processor

Take 10 percent of the butter from the refrigerator, cut it into 2 or 3 pieces, and put it in the bowl. Blend with the steel blade with 2 or 3 quick on/off turns to soften it a little. Add water, salt, and flour and blend until mixture forms a ball. Gather it up, flour the ball lightly, wrap in plastic wrap, and refrigerate.

Dimensions of détrempe and butter pat for first turn

For one pound of puff paste, roll détrempe into a circle 9 inches in diameter and shape the butter into a 4½-inch square. For two pounds of puff paste, roll détrempe into a circle 11 inches in diameter and shape butter into a 6- to 6½-inch square.

The butter pat by hand

Flour remaining butter lightly, put on a lightly floured board, and soften by pressing down and quickly twisting with a rolling pin. Do this until butter is malleable but still cold. Sprinkle with more flour if it sticks.

Shape into a square. Refrigerate for 10 minutes. If the butter has been worked immediately after refrigerating the détrempe, then the détrempe and butter will be of correct temperature and consistency at the same time.

The butter pat in a food processor

Cut remaining butter into 1-inch pieces and blend with the steel blade with quick on/off turns until softened but still cold and firm. Do not overblend. Shape into a square. Wrap in plastic wrap and chill for 10 minutes.

Rolling and folding the pastry

Roll the dough into a circle. Put the butter pat in the center. Fold in both sets of opposite sides so that they overlap slightly in the center and press down to seal. Press each seam a bit with the knuckles to seal edges and enclose butter in the détrempe.

Do the first turn: Turn the pastry seam side down on a floured board. It rolls more evenly on the smooth side. Roll out firmly, smoothly, and quickly into a rectangle whose length is 2½ times its width. Turn the pastry over and fold in thirds like a piece of writing paper.

Seal (collar) the dough: Turn pastry around so long open flap edge is toward you. Press down lightly with the rolling pin and roll away from you so that the layers stick together.

If dough sticks at any time when rolling, flour board, dough, and rolling pin lightly and evenly.

The second turn: Turn dough seam side down and narrow end toward you. Roll into a rectangle as in the first turn. Turn pastry over again, fold in thirds, and seal as before.

To remember the number of turns completed, press 2 finger-tips lightly into center of dough to make 2 indentations or 4 or 6 depending on number of turns completed. Wrap dough in plastic wrap and refrigerate for 20 minutes.

Turns 3-4, 5-6: Repeat exactly the steps for first and second turns. After turn 6, chill dough for 20 minutes.

CASES MADE WITH PUFF PASTRY SHAPES

Yield: 8 or 9 bouchées and 8 to 9 amuse-gueules, *or*
12 diamond-shaped cases

Puff Pastry made with ½ lb. flour, all 6 turns completed (see p. 337)
1 egg, lightly beaten with a pinch of salt
Grated Parmesan cheese (optional)

Special equipment
2 fluted round cookie cutters, one 2½ inches in diameter and one 1½ inches in diameter

Bouchées
Preheat oven to 425°. Brush a baking sheet lightly with water.
Lightly flour a pastry board and roll dough into a 17- x 10-inch rectangle a good ⅛ inch thick. Cut 16 2½-inch rounds and transfer 8 of them to baking sheet. Press small cutter in the middle

of remaining 8 rounds. Brush the rounds on baking sheet lightly with egg glaze. Be extremely careful not to let glaze run down over side. Put the 8 cut rings on top of rounds on baking sheet. Brush top ring and middle with glaze. Bake for 18 to 20 minutes or until puffed and browned. Let cool on a rack. Carefully cut and lift out center to use as a hat when shell is filled.

The leftover centers can be brushed with egg and sprinkled with grated cheese, if desired. Bake them with the bouchées. They are delicious amuse-gueules.

Diamond-shaped cases

Preheat oven to 425°. Brush baking sheet lightly with water.

Lightly flour a pastry board and roll dough into a 15- by 12-inch rectangle a good ⅛ inch thick. Trim all around. Cut rectangle lengthwise into 4 strips about 2½ inches wide. Cut diamond shapes about 4 inches long. (Transfer to baking sheet.) Flute sides with the dull side of the tip of a paring knife. Brush lightly with glaze all over. Let dry a minute, and brush on a second coat. Trace a line ⅜ inch in from edge with tip of paring knife, cutting just halfway through pastry. Make decorative shallow lines in a design in the center. Bake for 18 to 20 minutes or until puffed and browned. Let cool on a rack. Carefully cut and lift out inner diamond to make a hat when case is filled or halve cases horizontally to make a bottom and a top.

Notes

Pastry cases are at their best when eaten the day they are baked. They will keep for 1 to 2 days covered in a dry spot. Recrisp in 400° oven for 5 minutes.

They can be filled with any sauced dish such as Seafood with Sauce Suprême (see p. 51), Scallops and Vegetables in Cream Sauce (see p. 109), boiled asparagus tips, topped with poached egg and Lemony Hollandaise (see p. 42), Boned Chicken Breast with Mushroom Sauce (see p. 179; cut breasts into bite-size pieces or in thin strips).

TIMBALE

Serves: 6 to 8

> Short pastry for timbale, sweet or unsweetened (see
> p. 333), divided as directed
> 1 egg yolk, lightly beaten

Preheat oven to 425° for unsweetened pastry, 400° for sweet pastry.

Lightly flour a pastry board and roll the bottom crust dough into a round ⅛ inch thick, roll it carefully over the rolling pin, and transfer to the bottom of a timbale mold. Put dough into mold by pressing lightly with the fingers to conform to the shape of the mold. Press a ¼-inch collar of dough around the inside of the rim. Roll the rolling pin over the edges of the pan to cut off excess dough. Push the dough collar above the edge of the mold and flute a decorative edge around the rim.

Prick the bottom of the pastry shell with a fork, line the shell with foil, and fill it with rice to hold dough against the mold during baking. Bake for 10 to 15 minutes, remove foil and rice, and bake until inside of crust is lightly brown.

Roll the dough for the lid into a round ⅛-inch thick, roll it carefully over the rolling pin, and transfer it to the lid mold. Pat lightly all over to make dough lie flat against outside of mold. Cut off excess dough all around with a knife. Make a decorative edge with the tip of the dull side of a knife by pulling pastry edge into tiny scallops. Paint the entire lid with egg glaze. Use scraps of the leftover dough to make decorative cutouts and place on top. Shape a small ball of dough to make a knob. Draw S's between the cutouts with the tip of a dull side of a knife held tightly at a 30° angle to pastry so as not to cut through it. Paint cutouts with glaze. Bake for 15 minutes. Let cool for 1 to 2 minutes. Carefully unmold onto a rack. Keep it warm if using immediately in a recipe.

Notes

Baked timbale will keep several days on a shelf in a dry spot. Reheat in 350° oven for 5 to 10 minutes.

Fillings

Sole Fillets with Seafood (see p. 86) are a perfect filling. Add mushroom, scallops, and shrimp to the sauce suprême. Spoon in as much of the creamed seafood mixture as will fill the base almost up to the edge. Keep the remainder warm to refill for more servings. Rest the folded fillets of sole on top in a circle, points to the center and wide sides hanging over the edge by about 1 inch. Sprinkle with the parsley. Place lid on top.

Other fillings

Savory: Pâtés cut into bite-size pieces with parsley sprigs for garnish, Chicken Salad, Veal Blanquette, Scallops and Vegetables in Cream Sauce, Salmon Mousse, Chicken Breasts with Mushroom Sauce, Salmon Terrine, Fish Salad, Vegetable Purées, Scrambled Eggs.

Sweet: Poached peaches or pears or assorted berries. Spread bottom crust with a layer of Crème Pâtissière. Rest berries or fruits on top. Glaze with Apricot Glaze. Decorate with Crème Chantilly if desired. Top with lid. Fruit should be apparent. Other fillings include Chocolate Mousse, Bavarian Cream, and ice cream combinations.

SAMPLE MENUS

MENUS FOR COMPANY

Salmon Terrine
Boned Fresh Ham Stuffed with Spinach   Mashed Potatoes
Caravel with Chocolate Mousse

Tomato Soup
Beef Tenderloin Stuffed with Mushrooms   Sautéed Potatoes
Millefeuilles

Artichokes Vinaigrette
Sole Fillets and Seafood Timbale
Strawberry Ice Cream

Tomatoes Stuffed with Shrimp
Roast Duck with Orange Sauce   French Fried Potatoes
Chocolate Soufflé

Mussel Soup
Roast Butterflied Leg of Lamb   Potatoes Lyonnaise
Cream Puffs

Country Terrine
Veal Chops with Mushroom and Garlic   Sand Potatoes
Crêpes Suzette

Crab Quiche
Chicken Legs Stuffed with Leek and Spinach   Buttered Rice
Banana or Apricot Tart

CHRISTMAS MENU

Poached Whole Fish   Green Mayonnaise
Cucumber Salad   Grated Carrot Salad
Truffled Roast Turkey with Mushroom Sauce
Braised Chestnuts   French Fried Potatoes
Bûche de Noël

MENUS FOR EVERY DAY
In an hour or less

Broiled Striped Bass with Champagne   Parsleyed Potatoes
Red Fan

Hamburgers with Herbs and Shallots   Salad
Omelet Soufflé

Grated Carrot Salad
Sautéed Chicken Breasts with Green Peppercorns
Buttered Noodles or Spaghetti
Cheeses

Poached Eggs
Country Style Vegetables   Creole Rice
Fruits

Mushroom Salad with Cream Sauce
Grilled Duck   Cubed Sautéed Potatoes

Spaghetti with Mussels   Creamed Cucumbers
Light Chocolate Mousse

Boned Chicken Breasts with Mushroom Sauce   Creole Rice
Poached Peaches

Veal Strips in Lemon Sauce   Buttered Noodles or Spaghetti
Salad

Asparagus the Flemish Way
Strawberries with Chantilly

INDEX

Italic numbers indicate that the dish appears in the Sample Menus.